Adobe®
InDesign® CS5
Digital
Classroom

Adobe®
InDesign® CS5
Digital Classroom

Christopher Smith and AGI Creative Team

Wiley Publishing, Inc.

Adobe® InDesign® CS5 Digital Classroom

Published by
Wiley Publishing, Inc.
10475 Crosspoint Boulevard
Indianapolis, IN 46256

Copyright © 2010 by Wiley Publishing, Inc., Indianapolis, Indiana
Published by Wiley Publishing, Inc., Indianapolis, Indiana
Published simultaneously in Canada
ISBN: **978-0-470-60781-7**
Manufactured in the United States of America
10 9 8 7 6 5 4 3 2 1

For general information on our other products and services or to obtain technical support, please contact our Customer Care Department within the U.S. at (800) 762-2974, outside the U.S. at (317) 572-3993 or fax (317) 572-4002.

Please report any errors by sending a message to errata@agitraining.com

Library of Congress Control Number: 2010924559

About the Authors

Christopher Smith is the president of American Graphics Institute (AGI). He provides business strategy and technology related consulting services to creative, marketing, and publishing organizations. Educated as a journalist, he works extensively with marketing and corporate communications departments, advertising agencies, along with magazine and newspaper clients who are migrating to InDesign and InCopy. Christopher regularly speaks at events and conferences around the world, and has delivered InDesign seminars, lectures, and classes in Europe, North America, Australia, and New Zealand. He helped develop the Adobe Certified Expert and Adobe Certified Instructor exams for InDesign and was hired by Adobe to help promote InDesign prior to the launch of the first version of the product, and has been working with the software ever since. He is also the co-author of the Adobe Creative Suite for Dummies, also published by Wiley.

Outside of AGI, he has served as an elected member of the school board in his hometown in suburban Boston, Massachusetts and has served as a board member for a private K-8 Montessori school. Prior to founding AGI, Christopher worked for Quark, Inc.

Chad Chelius is an instructor with AGI Training. His formal education is in publishing technology, but it is his trial-by-fire production experience working with the Mac OS and many creative software programs that makes him such a valuable contributor to every project on which he works. He has served as the lead consultant for major publishing technology migrations at leading book and magazine publishers. In his work with AGI Training, he has assisted such clients such as Rodale Press (publishers of Prevention Magazine, Runner's World, and multiple other magazine titles), and the publishing group of the National Geographic Society. Chad holds professional certifications from both Adobe and Apple.

The AGI Creative Team is comprised of Adobe Certified Experts and Adobe Certified Instructors from American Graphics Institute (AGI). The AGI Creative Team has authored many of Adobe's official training guides, and works with many of the world's most prominent companies, helping them to use creative software to communicate more effectively and creatively. They work with marketing, creative and communications teams around the world, and teach regularly scheduled classes at AGI's locations, and are available for private and customized training seminars and speaking engagements. More information at agitraining.com.

Acknowledgments

Thanks to our many friends at Adobe Systems, Inc. who made this book possible and assisted with questions and feedback during the writing process. To the many clients of AGI who have helped us better understand how they use InDesign and provided us with many of the tips and suggestions found in this book. A special thanks to the instructional team at AGI for their input and assistance in the review process and for making this book such a team effort.

Credits

Additional Writing
Chad Chelius

President, American Graphics Institute and Digital Classroom Series Publisher
Christopher Smith

Executive Editor
Jody Lefevere

Technical Editors
Cathy Auclair, Barbara Holbrook, Haziel Olivera

Editor
Marylouise Wiack

Editorial Director
Robyn Siesky

Business Manager
Amy Knies

Senior Marketing Manager
Sandy Smith

Vice President and Executive Group Publisher
Richard Swadley

Vice President and Executive Publisher
Barry Pruett

Senior Project Coordinator
Lynsey Stanford

Graphics and Production Specialist
Lauren Mickol

Media Development Project Supervisor
Chris Leavey

Proofreading
Nick Simione

Indexing
Michael Ferreira

Contents

Starting Up

Lesson 1: InDesign CS5 Essential Skills

Lesson 2: Building Documents with Master Pages

Lesson 3: Working with Text and Type

Lesson 4: Working with Styles

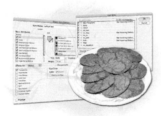

Lesson 5: Working with Graphics

Lesson 6: Creating and Using Tables

Lesson 7: Using Color in Your Documents

Lesson 8: Using Effects

Lesson 9: Advanced Document Features

Lesson 10 Document Delivery: Printing, PDFs, and XHTML

Lesson 11: Using XML with InDesign

Lesson 12: Creating Interactive Documents

Lesson 13: What's New in Adobe InDesign CS5?

Starting up

About InDesign Digital Classroom

Adobe® InDesign® CS5 lets you create print layouts for brochures, magazines, flyers, marketing and sales sheets, and now with InDesign CS5 you can convert these to interactive documents and projects. InDesign CS5 also provides tight integration with other Adobe products such as Photoshop® CS5, Illustrator® CS5, and Dreamweaver® CS5. You can even export your InDesign documents to Adobe® Flash®, as both an animation and as an editable file. The *Adobe InDesign CS5 Digital Classroom* helps you to understand these capabilities and to get the most out of your software so that you can get up and running right away. You can work through all the lessons in this book, or complete only specific lessons. Each lesson includes detailed, step-by-step instructions, along with lesson files, useful background information, and video tutorials.

Adobe InDesign CS5 Digital Classroom is like having your own expert instructor guiding you through each lesson while you work at your own pace. This book includes 13 self-paced lessons that let you discover essential skills, explore new ones, and pick up tips that will save you time. You'll be productive right away, with real-world exercises and simple explanations. Each lesson includes step-by-step instructions, lesson files, and video tutorials, all of which are available on the included DVD. The *Adobe InDesign CS5 Digital Classroom* lessons are developed by the same team of Adobe Certified Instructors and InDesign experts who have created many of the official training titles for Adobe Systems, so you can be confident that you will discover useful skills quickly and easily.

Prerequisites

Before you start the *Adobe InDesign CS5 Digital Classroom* lessons, you should have a working knowledge of your computer and its operating system. You should know how to use the directory system of your computer so that you can navigate through folders. You also need to understand how to locate, save, and open files, and you should also know how to use your mouse to access menus and commands.

Before starting the lessons files in the *Adobe InDesign CS5 Digital Classroom*, make sure that you have installed Adobe InDesign CS5. The software is sold separately, and not included with this book. You may use the free 30-day trial version of Adobe InDesign CS5 available at the *adobe.com* web site, subject to the terms of its license agreement.

System requirements

Before starting the lessons in the *Adobe InDesign CS5 Digital Classroom*, make sure that your computer is equipped for running Adobe InDesign CS5, which you must purchase separately. The minimum system requirements for your computer to effectively use the software are listed on the following page.

System requirements for Adobe InDesign CS5

These are the minimum system requirements for using the InDesign CS5 software:

Windows OS

- Intel® Pentium® 4 or AMD Athlon® 64 processor
- Microsoft® Windows® XP with Service Pack 2 (Service Pack 3 recommended); Windows Vista® Home Premium, Business, Ultimate, or Enterprise with Service Pack 1; or Windows 7
- 1GB of RAM (2GB recommended)
- 1.6GB of available hard-disk space for installation; additional free space required during installation (cannot install on removable flash-based storage devices)
- 1024x768 display (1280x800 recommended) with 16-bit video card
- DVD-ROM drive
- Adobe® Flash® Player 10 software required to export SWF files
- Broadband Internet connection required for online services

Macintosh OS

- Multicore Intel processor
- Mac OS X v10.5.7 or v10.6
- 1GB of RAM (2GB recommended)
- 2.6GB of available hard-disk space for installation; additional free space required during installation (cannot install on a volume that uses a case-sensitive file system or on removable flash-based storage devices)
- 1024x768 display (1280x800 recommended) with 16-bit video card
- DVD-ROM drive
- Adobe Flash Player 10 software required to export SWF files
- Broadband Internet connection required for online services

Menus and commands are identified throughout the book by using the greater-than symbol (>). For example, the command to print a document appears as File > Print. This indicates that you should click the File menu at the top of your screen and choose Print from the resulting menu.

Starting Adobe InDesign CS5

As with most software, Adobe InDesign CS5 is launched by locating the application in your Programs folder (Windows) or Applications folder (Mac OS). If you are not familiar with starting the program, follow these steps to start the Adobe InDesign CS5 application:

Windows

1   Choose Start > All Programs > Adobe InDesign CS5.

2   Close the Welcome Screen when it appears. You are now ready to use Adobe InDesign CS5.

Mac OS

1   Open the Applications folder, and then open the Adobe InDesign CS5 folder.

2   Double-click on the Adobe InDesign CS5 application icon.

3   Close the Welcome Screen when it appears. You are now ready to use Adobe InDesign CS5.

Fonts used in this book

Adobe InDesign CS5 Digital Classroom includes lessons that refer to fonts that were installed with your copy of Adobe InDesign CS5. If you did not install the fonts, or have removed them from your computer, you may substitute different fonts for the exercises or re-install the software to access the fonts.

If you receive a Missing Font warning, replace the font with one available on your computer and proceed with the lesson.

Resetting the InDesign workspace and preferences

To make certain that your panels and working environment are consistent, you should reset your workspace at the start of each lesson. To reset your workspace, choose Window > Workspace > Typography. The selected workspace determines which menu items display, which panels display, and which options display within the panels. If menu items that are identified in the book are not displaying, choose Show All Menu Items from the menu in which you are working to locate them, or choose Window > Workspace > Advanced to show all panel options.

You can reset the settings for InDesign at the start of each lesson to make certain you match the instructions used in this book. To reset the InDesign preferences, start Adobe InDesign, and immediately press Shift+Alt+Ctrl (Windows) or Shift+Option+Command+Control (Mac OS). In the dialog box that appears, press OK to reset the preferences.

Loading lesson files

The *InDesign CS5 Digital Classroom* DVD includes files that accompany the exercises for each of the lessons. You may copy the entire lessons folder from the supplied DVD to your hard drive, or copy only the lesson folders for the individual lessons you wish to complete.

For each lesson in the book, the files are referenced by the name of each file. The exact location of each file on your computer is not used, as you may have placed the files in a unique location on your hard drive. We suggest placing the lesson files in the My Documents folder (Windows) or at the top level of your hard drive (Mac OS).

Copying the lesson files to your hard drive:

1   Insert the *InDesign CS5 Digital Classroom* DVD supplied with this book.

2   On your computer desktop, navigate to the DVD and locate the folder named idlessons.

3   You can install all the files, or just specific lesson files. Do one of the following:

 •   Install all lesson files by dragging the idlessons folder to your hard drive.

 •   Install only some of the files by creating a new folder on your hard drive named idlessons. Open the idlessons folder on the supplied DVD, select the lesson(s) you wish to complete, and drag the folder(s) to the idlessons folder you created on your hard drive.

Unlocking Mac OS files

Macintosh users may need to unlock the files after they are copied from the accompanying disc. This only applies to Mac OS computers and is because the Mac OS may view files that are copied from a DVD or CD as being locked for writing.

If you are a Mac OS user and have difficulty saving over the existing files in this book, you can use these instructions so that you can update the lesson files as you work on them and also add new files to the lessons folder

Note that you only need to follow these instructions if you are unable to save over the existing lesson files, or if you are unable to save files into the lesson folder.

1   After copying the files to your computer, click once to select the idlessons folder, then choose File > Get Info from within the Finder (not InDesign).

2   In the idlessons info window, click the triangle to the left of Sharing and Permissions to reveal the details of this section.

3   In the Sharing and Permissions section, click the lock icon, if necessary, in the lower right corner so that you can make changes to the permissions.

4   Click to select a specific user or select everyone, then change the Privileges section to Read & Write.

5   Click the lock icon to prevent further changes, and then close the window.

Working with the video tutorials

Your *InDesign CS5 Digital Classroom* DVD comes with video tutorials developed by the authors to help you understand the concepts explored in each lesson. Each tutorial is approximately five minutes long and demonstrates and explains the concepts and features covered in the lesson.

The videos are designed to supplement your understanding of the material in the chapter. We have selected exercises and examples that we feel will be most useful to you. You may want to view the entire video for a lesson before you begin. The DVD icon, with appropriate lesson number, indicates that an overview of the exercise being described can be found in the accompanying video.

DVD video icon.

Setting up for viewing the video tutorials

The DVD included with this book includes video tutorials for each lesson. Although you can view the lessons on your computer directly from the DVD, we recommend copying the folder labeled *Videos* from the *InDesign CS5 Digital Classroom* DVD to your hard drive.

Copying the video tutorials to your hard drive:

1   Insert the *InDesign CS5 Digital Classroom* DVD supplied with this book.

2   On your computer desktop, navigate to the DVD and locate the folder named Videos.

3   Drag the Videos folder to a location on your hard drive.

Viewing the video tutorials with the Adobe Flash Player

To view the video tutorials on the DVD, you need the Adobe Flash Player 8 or later. Earlier versions of the Flash Player will not play the videos correctly. If you're not sure that you have the latest version of the Flash Player, you can download it for free from the Adobe web site: *http://www.adobe.com/support/flashplayer/downloads.html*

Playing the video tutorials

1   On your computer, navigate to the Videos folder you copied to your hard drive from the DVD. Playing the videos directly from the DVD may result in poor quality playback.

2   Open the Videos folder and double-click the IDvideos_PC.exe (Windows) or IDvideos_Mac.app (Mac OS) to view the video tutorial.

3 Press the Play button to view the videos.

The Flash Player has a simple user interface that allows you to control the viewing experience, including stopping, pausing, playing, and restarting the video. You can also rewind or fast-forward, and adjust the playback volume.

The file extension of .exe or .app may not display, based upon your system preferences.

A. Go to beginning. B. Play/Pause. C. Fast-forward/rewind. D. Stop. E. Sound Off/On. F. Volume control.

Playback volume is also affected by the settings in your operating system. Be certain to adjust the sound volume for your computer, in addition to the sound controls in the Player window.

Additional resources

The Digital Classroom series goes beyond the training books. You can continue your learning online with training videos, or at seminars, conferences, and in-person training events.

Book series

Expand your knowledge of creative software applications with the Digital Classroom training series which includes books on Photoshop, Flash, Dreamweaver, Illustrator, and more. Learn more at *digitalclassroombooks.com*.

Training & Professional Development

The authors of the Digital Classroom seminar series frequently conduct in-person seminars and are available for in-person training and professional development for your organization, company, school, or university. Learn more at *agitraining.com*.

Resources for educators

Visit *digitalclassroombooks.com* to access resources for educators, including instructors' guides for incorporating Digital Classroom into your curriculum.

What you'll learn in this lesson:

- Understanding the InDesign workspace
- Working with panels and tools
- Navigating through InDesign documents
- Flowing text
- Using Styles to format text and objects

InDesign CS5 Essential Skills

This lesson helps to get you started with InDesign right away, covering the essential skills necessary for creating, editing, and working efficiently with InDesign documents. You'll start by understanding how to navigate within an InDesign document; you'll then place graphics and add formatting to text, creating a finished newsletter.

Starting up

Before starting, make sure that your tools and panels are consistent by resetting your preferences. See "Resetting the InDesign workspace and preferences" on page 3.

You will work with several files from the id01lessons folder in this lesson. Make sure that you have copied the id01lessons folder onto your hard drive from the Digital Classroom DVD. See "Loading lesson files" on page 4. If you are new to InDesign, it may be easier to follow the lesson if the id01lessons folder is placed on your desktop.

See Lesson 1 in action!

Use the accompanying video to gain a better understanding of how to use some of the features shown in this lesson. The video tutorial for this lesson can be found on the included DVD.

InDesign tools

InDesign uses tools for creating or modifying everything that appears in your document. You'll also use tools for navigating around the document. All tools are found in the Tools panel, located along the left side of your screen.

Many tools have related tools available for selection by clicking and holding on the tool that is displayed. You can identify the tools that offer additional functionality by the small arrow in the lower-right corner of these tools. You can also right-click (Windows) or Ctrl-click (Mac OS) to access hidden tools instead of clicking and holding on the tool and waiting for the hidden options to display.

If you place your cursor over any tool in the Tools panel without clicking, a tooltip appears, displaying the tool's name and keyboard shortcut. You can use the keyboard shortcut to access a tool instead of clicking it.

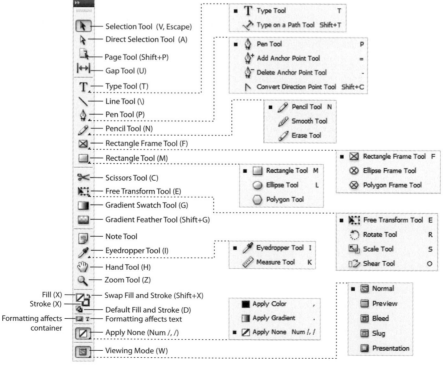

The Tools panel.

The InDesign workspace

InDesign documents are displayed in the center of the work area, while panels that let you control objects or perform specific tasks are displayed along the right side of the workspace in the panel docking area. InDesign has many panels that are critical to the editing and design work you perform. InDesign includes various workspaces that provide easy access to the panels and tools you'll use for specific tasks. Let's take a closer look at the InDesign workspace, including the document window and panels.

The document window

InDesign pages are displayed within a black border. Anything positioned within this area appears when the page is finished. The area outside of the black border is referred to as the pasteboard. Anything that is placed completely outside this black border on the pasteboard is generally not visible when the final document is distributed.

You can use the pasteboard to temporarily hold elements while designing your project. You can move design elements such as images from the pasteboard to the page, trying different layout variations. The pasteboard can also be useful for placing notes to colleagues—or even yourself—regarding the project. To get a better understanding of the InDesign workspace, you'll open up the completed project, reset the workspace, and look at the work area.

1 Choose File > Open. In the Open dialog box, navigate to the id01lessons folder and select the id01_done.indd file. Click Open.

2 Choose Window > Workspace > Typography. Panels containing controls that help you work with type are now displayed.

You can also use the dedicated Workspace switcher, located in the Application bar above the Control panel. The Workspace switcher displays the name of the current workspace and can also be used to change between workspaces or to reset the current workspace. The selected workspace determines which panels display and which menu items are available. The number of available panels and menu choices is based upon the selected workspace.

3 Choose Window > Workspace > Reset Typography to reset the InDesign panels to their default positions for the Typography workspace. This ensures that your panels are in position, making them easier to locate during this lesson.

A. The document window. B. The page border (black lines). C. Bleed guides. D. Margin guides. E. Column guides. F. The pasteboard.

Using guides

Non-printing guides help you align content on your page and create an organized layout. Margin guides define the space around the edge of your document—a space you generally want to keep free from objects. White space around the edge of your document creates good design, and also eliminates the risk of content being cut off if your document is printed and trimmed to a specific size at a printing plant. Margin guides are displayed in magenta by default, immediately inside the page border. By default, they display one-half inch inside of the page edge, but you can adjust them, as you will learn in Lesson 2, "Building Documents with Master Pages."

You can also add individual page guides manually by dragging them from the rulers onto the page. Both page guides and margin guides are useful, but they can also be distracting when you want to see the elements of your page design. In this case, you can hide the guides.

1 Choose View > Grids & Guides > Hide Guides, or use the keyboard shortcut Ctrl+;
(Windows) or Command+; (Mac OS), to hide all the guides in the open document.

2 Choose View > Grids & Guides > Show Guides, or use the keyboard shortcut Ctrl+;
(Windows) or Command+; (Mac OS), to show all the guides in the open document.

3 You can show or hide guides by toggling back and forth using these commands.

Viewing modes

You can also use viewing modes to hide guides and other items that will not display when the
final document is printed or distributed.

Just as you can hide guides, you can also have InDesign hide content that is positioned on the
pasteboard. The viewing modes option lets you choose whether all content and guides display,
or whether InDesign displays only content that is positioned on the page and will print. Next,
you'll explore the various viewing modes.

1 At the bottom of the Tools panel, click and hold the Mode button (▣), and choose
Preview from the available modes. Notice that the entire pasteboard appears gray and all
elements located on the pasteboard are hidden.

2. Click and hold the Mode button again and choose Bleed from the menu. This shows
the allowable bleed area that was specified when the document was created. Bleed is an
area outside of the page that is intentionally used by designers so that any inaccuracies in
the cutting, trimming, and binding process do not create a visible white space along the
edge of an object that is intended to print all the way to the edge of a document. This
mode is useful when you need to make sure that all the elements on your page extend to
a specific bleed value. In this document, the bleed is set to 1/8 inch, which is a standard
bleed value in the printing industry.

3. Click and hold the Mode button again and choose Presentation from the menu. This
new mode in InDesign CS5 presents your document on a black background with no
distracting interface elements. This is great for viewing your document or showing it
to a client. When in this mode, you can navigate through the pages of your document
by using the up and down or left and right arrow keys on your keyboard. To exit
Presentation mode, simply press the Escape key on your keyboard.

4. Click and hold the Mode button again and choose Normal.

You can also use the shortcut key W to toggle between Preview and Normal modes, and Shift+W
to activate Presentation mode, or you can use the Screen Mode button in the Application bar.
Keep in mind that keyboard shortcuts do not work if you are using the Type tool and working
with text inside a text frame. You can simply press the Escape key in this instance to make the
Selection tool active, and then use the W or Shift+W keyboard shortcut to toggle between the
various viewing modes.

Working with panels

Now that you understand the different parts of the workspace, you can begin working with the interface to learn more about the different panels. You can access panels by clicking on their name in the panel docking area, or choose the panel you want to access from the Window menu.

The Tools panel

The Tools panel is located on the left side of your screen and contains all the tools necessary to draw, add, or edit type, and edit items in your document. The Tools panel appears as a single column attached to the left side of your screen. You can modify the appearance and location of the Tools panel to accommodate your needs.

1   Click on the double-arrow icon at the top of the Tools panel. The Tools panel changes from a single column to a double column. If the Tools panel is not docked, you have a third option when you click the double-arrow; it changes to a horizontal layout, then to a single column, and then a double column each time you click. Go to step 2 to learn how to dock and undock panels in InDesign.

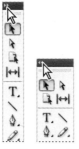

Clicking on the double arrow icon at the top of the Tools panel changes its appearance.

2   Click the gray bar at the top of the Tools panel, and while holding down the mouse button, drag the panel to the right, into the document area. Release the mouse button when over the document area. The Tools panel is repositioned as a free-floating panel at the location where you released the mouse button. You can position the panel anywhere on your display, or return it to the docking area on the side of the workspace.

3   Click the gray bar at the top of the Tools panel and drag the panel to the right so that it is positioned just to the left of the panels. A blue, vertical bar appears. Release the mouse button, and the Tools panel is docked to the right of your screen. If you have trouble moving the panel by clicking on the gray bar, click on the dotted area just below the gray bar at the top of the Tools panel to reposition and dock the panel.

Managing panels

InDesign contains panels that help you create the layout and design you desire. The various workspaces include several panels that are docked at the right side of the document window. The available panels change based upon the selected workspace. When the panels display only their name, they are in collapsed mode. Collapsed mode saves screen space by allowing you quick access to many panels, and only displaying the full panel options when you need them.

1 Click the double-arrow icon (⑭) at the top-right corner of all the docked panels along the right side of the document window. Notice how all the docked panels expand to reveal their options.

2 Click the double-arrow icon again to collapse the dock and return the panels to their previous state.

3 Click the Pages button in the dock. This reveals the entire contents of the Pages panel. When you click a panel button, only the individual panel expands.

4 Click the Pages button again, and the panel closes and is displayed only as a button.

5 Click and drag the Pages button, moving it to the far-left side of the document window. When a vertical bar appears, release the mouse button. The Pages panel is docked to the left side of the document window.

You can place panels anywhere on your workspace, including over the document or on either side of the work area. You may customize panels in any way that makes it easier for you to work. Don't worry if you make a mess, as you can always return to the default layout of the panels by choosing Window > Workspace > Reset.

Working with the Control panel

The Control panel appears across the top of the workspace. The panel is contextual, so the content of the panel changes depending on what tool you are using and what object you have selected.

1 Choose the Selection tool (⬉) in the Tools panel. The Control panel changes based upon the tool being used and the items selected in the layout.

2 Using the Selection tool, click the headline, *Fending off the winter blues*, positioned at the top of the page. The Control panel now displays information about this text frame.

3 Double-click the same headline. When you double-click the text frame, the Selection tool switches to the Text tool. The Control panel now displays information relating to the text.

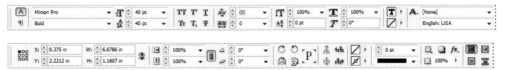

The Control panel displays information about objects in your layout. The information displayed changes based upon the tool used for selection and the object selected. The icons displayed in the Control panel on your computer may differ slightly based on the resolution of your computer's display.

Saving your workspace

Once you have selected the panels that you need, and positioned them in the locations that let you work most efficiently, you can save the location of the panels being used as a workspace.

Once you have saved a workspace, you can quickly access the exact panels displayed and their location by returning to the default setup of that workspace.

1 From the Workspace drop-down menu, located in the Application bar to the left of the Help search text field, choose New Workspace.

2 In the New Workspace window, type **My Workspace** in the Name text field, and then click OK, leaving all of the settings at their defaults.

Saving your workspace allows you to easily restore the panel positions.

You've now saved the locations of your panels.

3 From the Workspace switcher drop-down menu, choose Typography. Then click on the Workspace switcher drop-down menu again and choose Reset Typography. Note how the panels revert to their default locations.

4 From the Workspace switcher drop-down menu, choose My Workspace. Alternatively, choose Window > Workspace > My Workspace. All the panels are restored to the workspace that you saved earlier in this project.

InDesign allows you to create and save multiple workspaces. Workspaces are not document-specific, and so you can use them in any document. Before proceeding to the next section, reset your workspace to the default Typography workspace using the Workspace switcher drop-down menu. This allows the panels to match the descriptions used in the remainder of this lesson. If necessary, you can also choose Reset from the Workspace switcher drop-down menu to reset the workspace to its default appearance.

Navigating through an InDesign document

In this exercise, you'll continue working with the id01_done.indd file, which is the completed newsletter that you opened at the beginning of the lesson. You'll explore the tools used to navigate to different pages in an InDesign document, and how to change the document's magnification to see more or fewer details in the document layout.

Using the Pages panel

The Pages panel provides a quick overview of the contents of each page in an InDesign document. You can use it to navigate between document pages, rearrange pages, and also add or remove pages.

1 Press the Pages button (⊞) in the dock at the right of the workspace to display the Pages panel. The bottom-left corner of the Pages panel indicates that there are four pages displayed in three spreads within this document.

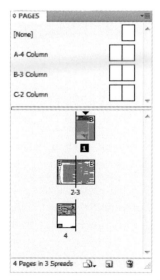

You can use the Pages panel to add and delete pages as well as navigate between pages within your InDesign documents.

2 Double-click page 2 in the Pages panel to display page 2 of the document. The left page of the inside spread, which is page 2, appears in the document window.

3 Double-click page 4 in the Pages panel to display page 4 of your document.

If you are unable to see all the pages displayed in the Pages panel, you can make the panel larger by clicking and dragging on the bottom-right corner of the panel to enlarge it. Additionally, InDesign allows you to scroll through the pages in the Pages panel by using the scroll bar in the document window or the scroll wheel on your mouse, or you can click and hold on the side of the page thumbnails and drag up or down to navigate through the pages.

With page 4 selected, click on the panel menu (-≡), located in the upper-right corner of the Pages panel, and from the Color Label submenu, choose a color to apply to your page thumbnail. This new feature in InDesign CS5 is a great way to mark the status of pages, such as complete or incomplete.

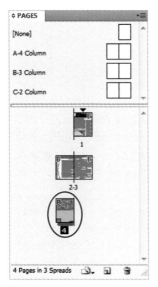

Color Labels in InDesign CS5 provide a convenient way to mark the status of pages in your document.

Changing the magnification of your document

So far, you've been viewing this document at the magnification level that was used when the document was last saved. You may find it necessary to get a closer look at parts of your document to check it for alignment, spacing of type, or position of objects. Here you'll find that InDesign provides tools that make it easy to change the magnification and inspect components of the document.

1   In the Pages panel, double-click on the page 1 icon to display the first page of
    the document.

2   Select the Zoom tool (⌕). Using the Zoom tool, click and hold in the upper-left corner
    of the Spinnews logo at the top of the page, and then drag down to the lower-right
    corner of the logo. Release the mouse once you have reached the lower-right corner of
    the logo. The area you have selected with the Zoom tool is magnified.

Click and drag to increase the magnification of a specific area.

3   You may find that you enlarged the document either too much or not enough. To
    fine-tune the magnification, click with the Zoom tool to increase the magnification
    incrementally. Or, if you zoomed in too close, decrease the magnification by pressing and
    holding the Alt (Windows) or Option (Mac OS) key while clicking with the Zoom tool.

*You can quickly increase or decrease the magnification of the document by using the keyboard
shortcut Ctrl+plus sign (Windows) or Command+plus sign (Mac OS) to zoom in on a
document, or Ctrl+minus sign (Windows) or Command+minus sign (Mac OS) to zoom out. If
you have an object selected or your cursor is inserted within a text frame, the page will center on
the selected object or cursor when changing the magnification.*

4   Select the Hand tool (✋) from the Tools panel, and then click and hold down on your
    page. Notice that the page magnification changes and a red frame appears, indicating
    which portion of the document will be visible when you have finished scrolling.

5   Arrange the page so that the logo is in the center of your display. Use the Hand tool to
    move the page within the document window, allowing you to focus on specific areas of
    the layout.

6   Reposition the red frame so that the entire border of the image is visible, and then
    release the mouse. The zoom returns to its original level, focused on the portion of the
    page you identified.

You can also access the Hand tool without selecting it from the Tools panel. Press and hold the space bar on your keyboard, and your cursor changes to the Hand tool. If you have the Type tool selected, press the Alt (Windows) or Option (Mac OS) key to access the Hand tool.

7 To make your page fit the document window, choose View > Fit Page in Window or press Ctrl+0 (Windows) or Command+0 (Mac OS). The currently selected page is displayed inside the document window.

8 Choose File > Close to close the document. If asked to save, choose No (Windows) or Don't Save (Mac OS).

Working with type

Now that you've had an overview of the InDesign workspace, you'll move into some of the tools that are used for working with type. InDesign provides complete control over the formatting and placement of type on a page and allows you to save formatting attributes so that you can work efficiently and your documents can maintain a consistent appearance. In this section, you'll add the finishing touches to a document, completing the layout by applying formatting to text.

Entering and formatting type

Most text used in an InDesign layout is positioned inside a frame. Frames are containers that hold text or graphics within a layout. InDesign has three types of frames: text, graphic, and unassigned. In this exercise, you'll be working with text frames.

1 Choose File > Open. In the Open dialog box, navigate to the id01lessons folder and select the id01.indd file. Click Open. You will use this project file for the remainder of the lesson.

2 Choose File > Save As. In the Save As dialog box, navigate to the id01lessons folder, or use another folder if you prefer. In the Name text field, type **id01_work.indd**, and then press Save. This allows you to work without altering the original file.

3 If necessary, press the Pages button (⊞) in the docking area along the right side of the workspace. The Pages panel opens. In the Pages panel, double-click on page 1 to center the page in the workspace.

4 In the Tools panel, select the Type tool (T). You will use the Type tool to create a new text frame. Position your cursor along the left side of the page, where the left margin guide and the first horizontal guide meet. Click and hold down, then drag down and to the right, to the location where the right margin and the second horizontal guide meet. Release the mouse button. A new text frame is created, and a cursor blinks in the top-left corner of the new frame you have created.

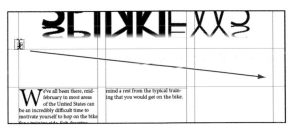

Use the Type tool to create a new text frame. Most text needs to be placed within a frame.

5 Type **Fending off the winter blues with cross training**. The text appears in the default font and size. Keep the cursor within this text frame, and keep the Type tool selected.

6 In the panel docking area along the right side of the workspace, click the Paragraph Styles button (¶) to open the Paragraph Styles panel. Click to select the Heading style from the list of available styles in the Paragraph Styles panel. The Heading style is applied to the paragraph, which includes all the text within this frame.

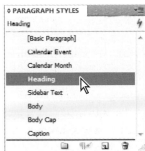

Apply the paragraph style to the text.

7 The top line of the sentence is much longer than the bottom line. To balance the lines, click the panel menu button (⁃≣) in the top-right corner of the Control panel and choose Balance Ragged Lines from the submenu. InDesign automatically balances the lines within the frame.

Apply the Balance Ragged Lines command to the headline.

You can also press the Enter (Windows) or Return (Mac OS) key while holding the Shift key to create a line break after the word blues that does not cause a new paragraph to be created. This is referred to as a soft return. However, the Balance Ragged Lines command is a much more elegant way to achieve this effect.

Placing and formatting type

You can add text to an InDesign document by typing text onto the InDesign page, or by importing the text from an external file, such as a Microsoft Word document or an Excel spreadsheet. InDesign also lets you import ASCII, Rich Text, InDesign Tagged Text, and many other files.

1 If necessary, press the Pages button (⊞) in the panel dock to open the Pages panel. Double-click on page 2 in the Pages panel. If the Pages panel is covering your work area, click the double arrows in the upper-right corner of the panel to reduce it to a button, or you may keep it open if your monitor is large enough to display the panel and the page together.

2 Continuing to use the Type tool (T), click inside the empty text frame that covers the center and right columns, under the headline *Caring for Those Wheels*. The cursor is inserted in this frame, where you will import the text for the body of the story, which was created using word processing software such as Microsoft Word.

3 Choose File > Place. The Place dialog box opens. In the Place dialog box, make certain that Show Import Options is not selected and that Replace Selected Items is selected. These options are explained in more detail later in the book.

Locate and open the Links folder within the id01lessons folder and choose the file Wheels.txt; then click Open. The text from this file is placed inside the frame where the cursor is located and the text is formatted using InDesign's Basic Paragraph style.

4   Place the cursor at the start of the story. Click the Paragraph Styles button to display the Paragraph Styles panel. You will apply a paragraph style to format the text you imported. Click the paragraph style Body, and the first paragraph is formatted using the Body style. Paragraph styles apply formatting to the paragraph where the cursor is located. You will now apply formatting to multiple paragraphs by selecting them and repeating this process.

5   Use the keyboard shortcut Ctrl+A (Windows) or Command+A (Mac OS) to select all the type within the current frame. From the Paragraph Styles panel, choose Body. All the selected paragraphs are now formatted using the Body style.

6   Choose Edit > Deselect All to deselect the type.

Flowing type

Stories often continue from one page or column to another. You will set up links between text frames to allow a story to flow into multiple columns.

1   In the lower-left corner of the document area, click the page number drop-down menu and select page 3 to navigate to this page. You can also use this menu to navigate to different pages in your document.

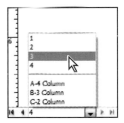

Use the page drop-down menu
to navigate between pages.

2   Using the Type tool (T), click inside the first frame on the left side of the page underneath the headline Race Calendar.

3   Choose File > Place. In the Place dialog box, navigate to the Links folder within the id01lessons folder. Select the file Calendar.txt and click Open to place the text from the file into your InDesign layout.

4 Activate the Selection tool (⬈) from the Tools panel, and then, if necessary, click to select the text frame where you imported the text. You can tell the frame is selected by the small, square handles that appear on each corner of the frame, and also in the middle of each side of the frame.

In the upper-left corner of the text frame, slightly below the corner handle, is a small square. This is the In Port, and it is used to indicate whether this frame is the continuation of a text flow from another frame. Simply put, does the text start somewhere else, or does it start in this frame? Because the In Port is empty, you can tell that the text starts in this frame. If the In Port contained an arrow, then you would know that the text continued from another location.

The lower-right corner of the frame contains an Out Port. This port currently displays a red plus sign, indicating that there is more text in the story than fits within the frame. You can address overset text in a number of ways:

- Delete text

- Reduce the size of the text

- Make the frame larger

- Link the text to another frame

In this case, you will link the text to another frame.

The newly placed text on the page is overset.

5 Using the Selection tool, click once on the red plus sign in the lower-right corner of the text frame. The cursor changes to the Place Gun to indicate that you are about to link the text to a new location, and displays some of the text that will be linked. The next area you click will be the continuation of the story, so be careful to only click where you want the text to continue.

6 Move your cursor to the center of the middle column. Notice that the cursor changes to show a linked chain. Click to link the first and second frames together. Now you will link the second frame to the third frame.

Linking text from one frame to another.

7 Click the red plus sign on the lower-right corner of the second frame, and then click inside the frame located along the right side of the page. The frames in the second and third columns are now linked together.

8 Choose File > Save to save your work.

Using styles

Earlier you worked with paragraph styles to format type. As you saw, these provided a method of applying consistent formatting to the text. Similarly, styles let you easily and repetitively format smaller groups of text along with entire frames and even tables. You'll review the process of applying paragraph styles, and then move into other types of styles that you can apply. Later, in Lesson 4, "Working with Styles," you will work with styles in more detail.

Applying paragraph styles

As you've seen, paragraph styles apply formatting to an entire paragraph of text, and you are not able to apply paragraph styles to an individual word within a paragraph—unless it is the only word in the paragraph, as in this example.

1 Select the Type tool (T) from the Tools panel and click anywhere inside the word *January* located in the first line of the frame on the left side of page 3.

2 In the Paragraph Styles panel, choose Calendar Month to apply the correct formatting to the word *January*. Repeat the process to format the word *February*, and then format *March* by applying the Calendar Month Paragraph Style.

3   Using the Type tool, click and drag to select the text located between the *January* and *February* headings, and then click the Calendar Event style in the Paragraph Styles panel. Repeat this process to select all the text between *February* and *March*, and also all the March events.

Format the text using the Calendar Event style from the Paragraph Styles panel.

Notice that the Calendar Event style applies several attributes to the events in a single click, styling the date bold, the name red, and the Web address in italic. The Calendar Event style includes several styles that are grouped together into a nested style. A nested style automatically applies several formatting attributes to text within a paragraph. You will learn more about nested styles in Lesson 4, "Working with Styles."

Applying character styles

You can apply character styles to individual words or characters. They are useful when you apply common formatting attributes such as bold and italic. Character styles are the foundation for the nested styles that you applied to the event listings in the previous section. Here you will apply a character style to individual words.

1   Double-click on page 2 in the Pages panel to display page 2 within the workspace.

2   Using the Zoom tool (🔍), increase the magnification so you can easily see the first paragraph, which starts with the text *Your wheels*.

3   Select the Type tool (T) from the Tools panel and select the word wheels at the top of the first paragraph. You can select the text by either clicking and dragging or double-clicking on it.

Double-clicking on a word selects the word, triple-clicking selects the line, and quadruple-clicking (that's four clicks) selects the paragraph.

4   Click the Character Styles button (A) in the dock on the right side of the workspace to open the Character Styles panel. Choose Italic from the Character Styles panel to apply the Italic style to the selected word.

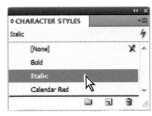 

The Character style applies to a word rather than a whole paragraph.

Apply styles using Find/Change

Character Styles make it easy to automate the process of formatting text. In the current story, you want every instance of the word *wheels* to be italicized. Finding each of them individually would be very time-consuming, so let's speed up the process a bit using the Find/Change capabilities and character styles.

1   Using the Type tool (T), right-click (Windows) or Ctrl+click (Mac OS) anywhere within the text frame on page 2. Choose Find/Change from the contextual menu that appears. The Find/Change window opens.

Contextual menus offer a quick way to access commands that apply to the part of the document in which you are working. The available commands change based upon the location of the cursor, the tool you are using, and the object selected.

2   In the Find/Change window, working in the Text tab, type **wheels** in the Find what text field and choose Story from the Search drop-down menu. This forces InDesign to search all of the text within the current story.

3 In the Change Format section at the bottom of the window, click the Specify Attributes to Change button (✐). The Change Format Settings window opens.

Be careful to not select the Specify Attributes to Find button, which is an identical button located above the Specify Attributes to Change button.

Click the Specify attributes to change button.

4 In the Change Format Settings dialog box, choose Italic from the Character Style menu and click OK. This changes the format of all text that is found, applying the Italic style to the found text.

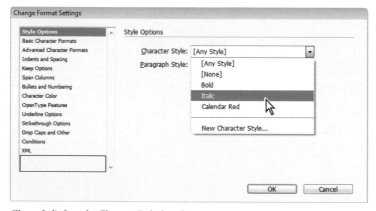

Choose Italic from the Character Style drop-down menu.

5 Click the Change All button. A window appears indicating that five instances of wheels have been formatted with the specified style. Press OK, then Press Done to close the Find/Change dialog box.

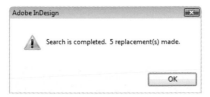

InDesign will notify you of how many replacements are made when using the Find/Change option.

Applying object styles

Object styles let you apply formatting to entire objects such as text frames, picture frames, or lines. You can use object styles to quickly and consistently apply color to the fill or stroke (border) of an object, or to apply effects such as a drop shadow.

In this next section, you'll place some text into a text frame and then apply an object style to the frame so that the entire frame is formatted.

1 Double-click on page 1 in the Pages panel. You may need to zoom out a bit to see the full page. You can quickly change the page magnification by choosing a percentage from the magnification drop-down menu located in the top of the workspace.

2 Choose the Hand tool (✋) from the Tools panel, and then drag from the right to the left until you are able to see the text frame in the pasteboard, located to the right of the page.

3 Select the Type tool (T) from the Tools panel, and click to insert the cursor inside the text frame on the pasteboard.

4 Choose File > Place. In the Place dialog box, navigate to the Links folder within the id01lessons folder and select the file Sidebar.txt. Press Open.

5 Choose the Selection tool (▸) from the Tools panel and confirm that the text frame is selected. If necessary, click the frame to select it. You can accomplish all of this in one step by simply pressing the Escape key on your keyboard.

6 Choose Window > Styles > Object Styles to open the Object Styles panel. In the Object Styles panel, choose Sidebar from the list. The entire frame, including the text, is formatted.

Object styles allow you to apply background colors, effects, and nested styles to a frame in a single click. This makes it possible to quickly apply repetitive formatting, and keep your document design consistent.

Object styles format entire objects, including text within objects.

7 Using the Selection tool, click in the middle of the frame and drag it to the column on the right side of the first page, aligning the right and bottom edge of the frame with the right and bottom margin guides.

Working with graphics

Graphics are an integral part of page design, and InDesign puts you in control of cropping, sizing, borders, and effects that control the appearance of images you place into your layout. You can place a wide variety of graphic types into your layouts, including PDF, TIFF, JPEG, and EPS. You can also place native Creative Suite files such as Photoshop (.psd), Illustrator (.ai), and InDesign (.indd) into your InDesign layout.

Placing graphics

Graphics are placed inside of a frame when you import them into your layout. As you discovered when you imported text, you can create the frame first, and then import the text. Alternatively, you can define the frame at the same time you import the image, letting InDesign create a frame for you.

1   Double-click on page 4 in the Pages panel to display page 4 of the document, and then choose Edit > Deselect All so that no other objects are selected in the layout. If Deselect All is not available, then no objects are selected.

2   Click on the Layers button to display the Layers panel, and click on the Graphics layer to make it active. This puts any graphics that you add to your document on the Graphics layer. Layers are a great way to organize content in your InDesign document.

Layers are a great way to organize content within your InDesign document.

3   Choose File > Place. In the Place dialog box, navigate to the Links folder within the id01lessons folder and select the file cyclist.psd; then click Open. Because no frame has been selected, InDesign displays a Place Gun, indicating that the image is ready to be placed in the document.

4   Click once in the upper-left corner of the workspace where the red bleed guides intersect, outside of the page area. This places the image at its full size.

5   If the upper-left corner of the image is not correctly positioned at the intersection of the bleed guides, use the Selection tool (➤) to click and drag the image to the correct position. Next you will resize the image to cover the top half of the layout and extend (bleed) off the edges.

6 Press and hold Shift+Ctrl (Windows) or Shift+Command (Mac OS), and then click and hold the lower-right handle of the frame. After pausing for a brief moment, continue to hold the keyboard keys and drag down and to the right until the image extends off the page and the right edge aligns with the bleed line. You have scaled the frame and image proportionately.

Generally you should limit scaling to within 20 percent of the original size of an image so that it remains clear when printed or distributed. Increasing the scaling too much will cause many images to become pixelated or bitmapped, and they will appear to be unclear and of poor quality when printed or converted to PDF.

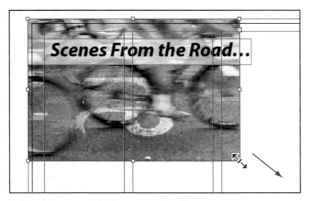

Scaling the image and the frame proportionately.

7 Continuing to use the Selection tool, click and drag upwards on the middle handle located along the bottom of the frame. Drag up until the bottom edge of the frame snaps to the guide located in the middle of the page.

Moving the handles of a frame using the Selection tool changes the size of the frame and adjusts how much of the image is displayed. Using the Shift+Ctrl (Windows) or Shift+Command (Mac OS) modifier keys allows you to scale the image and the frame together.

Positioning graphics within a frame

You may need to crop or scale images that are placed in your layout. Here you will explore some visual tools that help with the positioning and scaling of graphics.

1 Navigate to page 1 by using the page drop-down menu or the Pages panel.

2 To simplify your document, it may help to hide the Text layer so you can focus on the graphics. Do this by clicking on the Layers button to open the Layers panel, and then clicking the visibility icon (👁) to hide the contents of the text layer.

3 Choose the Selection tool (⬉), and then click to select the graphic frame at the bottom-left corner of page 1. The frame spans the left and center columns. InDesign displays empty graphic frames with an X inside the frame.

4 Choose File > Place. In the Place dialog box, navigate to the Links folder within the id01lessons folder and select the snowshoe.psd image. Click Open. The image is placed inside the selected frame at 100 percent, and is larger than the frame. Next you will determine the size of the image and adjust it to fit within the frame.

5 Hover your cursor over the center of the snowshoe image. You should see a transparent circle in the center of the photo called the Content Indicator. Click on the Content Indicator to select the photo within the frame. The edges of the image are displayed with a light-blue border, showing the actual size of the graphic within the frame. The color of the border will vary when you are using multiple layers in InDesign.

The Content Indicator is a new feature in InDesign CS5 that saves you a lot of time when working with graphics. Traditionally you'd have to switch to the Direct Selection tool to make adjustments to a graphic within a frame, and you can still do so with the Direct Selection tool (⬈). The Content Indicator alleviates the need to switch tools, allowing you to make adjustments to a graphic on the fly.

The Content Indicator makes it easy to adjust a graphic within a frame without having to choose a different tool to do so.

6 Hold down the spacebar on your keyboard to temporarily access the Hand tool (✋). Click and hold on the document. As you noticed earlier in this lesson, the page magnification changes and a red frame appears when using the Hand tool.

7 Reposition the red frame so that the entire border of the image is visible, and then release the mouse. The zoom returns to its original level, focused on the portion of the page you identified. Release the space bar. You may need to zoom out slightly in order to see the entire bounds of the graphic.

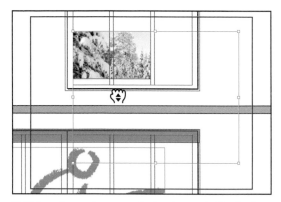

Hold down the space bar on your keyboard to use the Hand tool to reposition the document so the entire area of the snowshoe image is visible.

8 With the content of the frame (the snowshoe image) still active, press and hold Shift on your keyboard. Click the handle in the bottom-right corner of the image and drag the handle up and to the left, reducing the size of the image. Holding the Shift key maintains the proportions of the image while it is scaled. Reduce the size of the image until its width is slightly larger than the width of the frame, and then release the mouse button.

9 Position the cursor in the middle of the frame and notice that the cursor changes to a hand. Click and drag to reposition the graphic within the frame until it is positioned where you want it.

When you click on the Content Indicator, the graphic is selected and a hand icon appears so that you can reposition the graphic. While the icon is identical to the Hand tool, it does not have the same functionality and the two tools are used to perform different tasks.

The cropped image.

10 To stop editing the content and change focus to the frame, double-click anywhere on the graphic, and the frame becomes selected again.

11 Use the keyboard shortcut Ctrl+0 (Windows) or Command+0 (Mac OS) to fit page 1 within the document window.

12 Open the Layers panel by clicking on the Layers button, and turn the visibility of the Text layer back on by clicking on the box to the far left of the text layer. This displays all of the text in your document.

13 Choose File > Save to save your work.

Applying text wrap

You can control the position of text relative to graphics and other objects. In some cases, you may want text to be placed on top of an image, while in other cases, you may want text to wrap around the shape of an image or object. You'll continue to work on the first page of the brochure by applying text wrap to an image.

1   Using the Selection tool (⃗), select the snowshoe image at the bottom of the page. If you have trouble selecting the image, hold down the Ctrl (Windows) or Command (Mac OS) key and click again on the image to select it. This image is currently below the text along the bottom part of the first column. You'll enable text wrap on the image to force the text away from the image.

2   Choose Window > Text Wrap to open the Text Wrap panel.

3   Click the Wrap Around Bounding Box button (▣) at the top of the Text Wrap panel to apply the text wrap to the selected image. The text wrap forces the text to flow into the second column, making all the text visible.

The Wrap Around Bounding Box button in the Text Wrap panel wraps the text around the bounding box of the frame or shape of an object.

4   To get a better understanding of how the text wrap is being applied to the text surrounding the graphic frame, use the Selection tool to move the snowshoe image up and down on page 1. As you move the image, you can see how the text moves around the frame. When you're finished, move the image back to its original location.

5   Click the two arrows in the upper-right corner of the Text Wrap panel to close it.

Understanding layers

Layers help you organize the images and text in your layout. Layers are like transparent sheets of cellophane lying on top of each other. If you put an object on a layer that is below another layer, you can see the object as long as there aren't any objects directly above it, regardless of how many layers are on top of it. Layers can also be used to create different versions of projects, or different variations of projects, such as those versions being sent to different audiences or created in different languages.

Layers also allow you to place text and graphics on separate layers, making it easy to proofread text without looking at graphics. Here you'll see how layers can be used in this manner:

1   Navigate to page 2 using the Pages panel, and then choose View > Fit Spread in Window to display the entire spread in the workspace. This command displays pages 2 and 3 together.

2   Click the Layers button (◉) in the panel docking area to open the Layers panel.

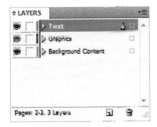

The Layers panel.

If you have closed a panel instead of placing it in the docking area, you can access it from the Window menu. For example, you can choose Window > Pages. The list of available panels is also determined by the current workspace. To access all panels, choose the Advanced workspace.

3   In the Layers panel there are three layers: Text, Graphics, and Background Content. Click the visibility icon (◉) next to the Text layer. The content becomes hidden when you disable its visibility, and all the text is temporarily hidden because the text has been placed on this layer. Click the visibility icon again to show the contents of the Text layer.

4   Turn the visibility of the Graphics and Background Content layers on and off to see the items that are on each of these layers.

InDesign layers are document-wide. When you create a layer, it is available on every page in the document, including the master pages. When you hide or show a layer, you are making an adjustment that impacts all pages in the document.

5   In the Pages panel, double-click page 1.

6 Using the Selection tool (⬥), select the snowshoe image at the bottom of the page. If you have trouble selecting it, hold down the Ctrl (Windows) or Command (Mac OS) key to drill down in the stacking order until it is selected. In the Layers panel, notice the red square (■) located to the right of the Graphics layer. This indicates that the currently selected object is located on the Graphics layer.

7 In the Layers panel, click and drag the red square to the Text layer. The object is moved to this layer, and the edge of the frame containing the snowshoe graphic is now blue, the color of the Text layer.

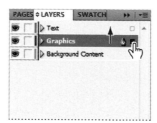

Move the image from the Graphics layer to the Text layer.

8 You actually want to keep the snowshoe image on the Graphics layer, so click on the blue square and move it back down to the Graphics layer, returning it to its original position.

9 Click the visibility icon (👁) of the Graphics layer to hide the contents of the layer, confirming that the snowshoe image is on this layer. Click the visibility icon again to make the layer visible.

10 Click the square immediately to the left of the Graphics layer to lock this layer. Locking the layer prevents you or others from modifying any contents on a layer.

Locking a layer prevents any changes to objects on the layer.

11 Choose the Selection tool and click on the Spinnews logo at the top of page 1. You cannot currently select it because the layer is locked.

12 Unlock the layer by clicking on the padlock icon (🔒) immediately to the left of the Graphics layer, and then select the Spinnews logo using the Selection tool. Now that the layer is unlocked, you can select it and move it. If you accidentally select the wrong object, choose Edit > Deselect All, or if you accidentally move an object, choose Edit > Undo to return it to the original location.

Locking a layer prevents all items on that layer from being selected. You can use this to organize your layout as you construct your documents. For example, you can create a layer that contains all the guides for your document. This provides another method of hiding and showing your guides quickly.

Applying effects

You can use InDesign to apply special effects to images or objects in your layout. These effects can save you time, as you do not need to use another program, like Photoshop, to achieve some common effects. Effects allow you to alter the appearance and transparency of objects and images without destroying the original. You can remove or alter effects after they have been applied, and the original object or image is not modified. Some of the common effects you can apply using InDesign include Drop Shadow, Bevel and Emboss, and Feathering. Next you will apply an effect to an object in this newsletter.

1 Navigate to page 2 by using either the page drop-down menu in the lower-left corner of the workspace or the Pages panel.

2 Using the Selection tool (⤢), select the blue border in the upper-left corner of the page. The border spans pages 2 and 3. As you discovered earlier, if the object were placed on a locked layer, you would first need to unlock the layer before being able to select and edit the object. This object should not be on a locked layer, so you should be able to select it without difficulty.

3 Click the Effects button (*fx*) in the panel docking area or choose Windows > Effects to open the Effects panel. Remember, if you've changed workspaces, some of the panel buttons may not be available. You may need to choose the Advanced workspace to see all the panels, such as the Effects panel.

4 Confirm that Object is highlighted in the Effects panel. Click the Add an Object Effect to the Selected Target button (*fx*) at the bottom of the panel. Choose Bevel and Emboss from the menu. If you want to see what this effect will do to the selected object, click the Preview check box to enable a preview of the effect.

You can apply an effect independently to an entire object or only to the stroke or fill of the selected object.

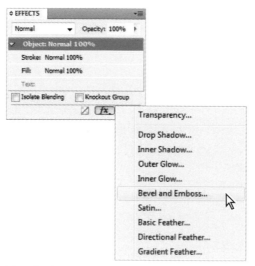

The Effects button at the bottom of the Effects panel allows you to choose which effects to apply to selected objects.

5 In the Effects dialog box, leave the settings at the defaults and press OK.

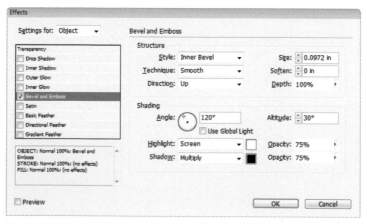

Use the default Bevel and Emboss settings in the Effects dialog box.

6 Switch to the Preview viewing mode using the viewing mode button in the Application bar at the top of the workspace. You can also press the keyboard shortcut W to switch the viewing mode, or access the same viewing mode controls at the bottom of the tools palette. All three options let you switch to the Preview viewing mode, which provides you with a preview of the final project without displaying any of the non-printing elements.

7 Choose File > Save, and then choose File > Close to close the file.

Congratulations! You have completed the lesson.

Resources for additional help

In-product help

InDesign includes help documentation directly within the application. Choose Help > InDesign Help, and InDesign launches the Adobe Help Viewer, which allows you to search by topic. You can also access help quickly by typing a search query in the help search field, indicated by a (𝒪) in the application bar at the top of your screen.

Online help

Adobe makes the documentation for InDesign available on the Web. The online help tends to be more current, as it is updated regularly. The documentation that shipped with the software was written months before the software was in its final format, so it may not be as complete or current as the online help. In addition, it provides you with the ability to add comments to topics that you view, and even receive an e-mail when someone else adds a comment to the topic. You can also download many of the help files in PDF format for printing or future reference. Find the online help at *adobe.com*.

Forums

Adobe on-line forums are an excellent resource for finding solutions to questions you have about InDesign or how InDesign integrates with other applications. Adobe forums are contributed to by a community of beginning, intermediate, and advanced users who may be looking for the same answer as you, or who have already discovered solutions and answers to questions and are willing to share their solutions with other users. You can access the InDesign Forums page at *http://forums.adobe.com/community/indesign*.

Conferences, seminars, and training

The authors of this book regularly speak at conferences and seminars, and deliver instructor-led training sessions. You can learn more at *www.agitraining.com*.

Self study

Place some of your own graphics into the newsletter that you just created, and then practice cropping and repositioning the graphics within their frames. Move objects to other layers and create your own layer to further refine the organization of the file.

This lesson has given you an overview of the essential capabilities available in the latest version of InDesign. For more in-depth instructions on how to perform many of these tasks in detail, read and work through the other lessons in this book.

Review

Questions

1   What does a red plus sign in the lower-right corner of a text frame indicate?

2   What tool is used to reposition an image inside of a frame?

3   How can you ensure that if you reposition the panels in InDesign to your liking, you can always bring them back to that state?

4   If you cannot see panels that you need to use, how can you display these panels?

Answers

1   There is more text in the frame than can be displayed within the current frame. This is called overset text. You can fix this by linking the text to another frame, editing the text so that it fits within the existing frame, or enlarging the size of the frame.

2   The Direct Selection tool is the most common tool used for manipulating images within a frame.

3   Save a custom workspace by choosing Window > Workspace > New Workspace.

4   When the workspace is changed, the list of available panels also changes. Use the Advanced workspace to view all the panels. All panels can also be found under the Window menu. Simply choose the panel you want to use from the list, and it displays.

What you'll learn in this lesson:

- Creating and saving custom page sizes
- Creating guides
- Adding sections and page numbering
- Applying master pages to document pages
- Copying and linking master pages between documents

Building Documents with Master Pages

Master pages serve as the foundation for most InDesign documents. You can use master pages to maintain consistency throughout your document and work more efficiently.

Starting up

Before starting, make sure that your tools and panels are consistent by resetting your preferences. See "Resetting the InDesign workspace and preferences" on page 3.

You will work with several files from the id02lessons folder in this lesson. Make sure that you have copied the id02lessons folder onto your hard drive from the Digital Classroom DVD. See "Loading lesson files" on page 4. This lesson may be easier to follow if the id02lessons folder is on your desktop.

See Lesson 2 in action!

Use the accompanying video to gain a better understanding of how to use some of the features shown in this lesson. The video tutorial for this lesson can be found on the included DVD.

The project

In this lesson, you will create a magazine. You will use master pages to create layout templates for each section in the magazine, including running headers, which run across the top of the page, and running footers, which run across the bottom of the page. Master pages give the publication a consistent look and feel.

Planning your document

Before you start creating a document using InDesign, you need some important information: the final size of the document after it is finished, also known as the *trim size*; how the pages will be held together, also known as the *binding*; and whether the document has images or graphics that extend to the edge of the document—this is known as *bleed*. Once you have this information, you can create the templates for your document pages.

Creating custom page sizes

For this lesson, you will create a custom-sized magazine with colors that extend to the edge of the page. You'll start by creating a new document, and saving the custom size as a preset, which you can use to create subsequent issues of the magazine.

Creating a new custom-sized document

This document will be measured using inches, so you'll start by setting your units of measurement to inches, and then you'll create the custom document size.

1   Choose Edit > Preferences > Units & Increments (Windows), or InDesign > Preferences > Units & Increments (Mac OS). When the Preferences dialog box appears, choose Inches from the Vertical and Horizontal drop-down menus in the Ruler Units section. Press OK.

    Changing the unit of measurement when no documents are open causes InDesign to use these settings for all new documents you create.

When working in a document, you can switch the unit of measurement by right-clicking (Windows) or Ctrl+clicking (Mac OS) on the vertical or horizontal ruler.

2   Choose File > New > Document, or press Ctrl+N (Windows) or Command+N (Mac OS), to create a new document.

3   In the New Document dialog box, confirm that the Facing Pages checkbox is selected and that Print is chosen from the Intent drop-down menu. In the Page Size section, type **8.125** for the Width and **10.625** for the Height.

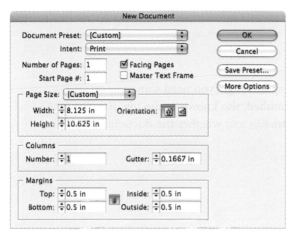

Setting the size of the new document.

4   In the Margins section, make sure that the Make all settings the same button (◉) is not selected. Type **.5** in the Top, Inside, and Outside margin text fields, and **.75** in the Bottom text field.

5   If the Bleed and Slug section is not visible, click the More Options button on the upper-right side of the dialog box. In the Bleed and Slug section, make sure that the Make all settings the same button is not selected, and then type **.125** in the Bleed Top, Bottom, and Outside margin text fields and **0** for the inside value. Because this is a magazine, it won't bleed into the spine of the page, where the pages are bound together.

6   Click the Save Presets button in the upper-right corner of the New Document dialog box. This allows you to save the custom settings you have just entered.

Type **Newsletter** in the Save Preset As text field, then press OK. In the New Document dialog box, the Newsletter preset is listed in the preset drop-down menu. This preset is available the next time you need to create a document with similar specifications.

Press OK to leave the New Document dialog box and create your new document. A new, untitled document is created with the dimensions you entered.

7   Choose File > Save As. In the Save As dialog box, navigate to the id02lessons folder and type **id02_work.indd** in the File name text field. Press Save.

InDesign does include an automatic recovery feature that can help you recover your document if there is a computer or software problem that causes the program to close unexpectedly, but it is still a good idea to save your work often.

You formatted some items with styles in Lesson 1. Here you will import the styles from another InDesign document, so you will not need to create them from scratch. In Lesson 4, "Working with Styles," you will discover how to create and define new styles.

8 Choose Window > Workspace > [Advanced] or choose Advanced from the Workspace drop-down menu in the Application bar at the top of the InDesign interface. You may need to choose Reset Advanced from the Workspace menu to reset the Advanced workspace so that all of the panels for that workspace are displayed. Click the Paragraph Styles button (¶) in the panel docking area in the right side of the workspace to open the Paragraph Styles panel. From the Paragraph Styles panel menu (-≡) in the upper-right corner, choose Load All Text Styles. The Open a File dialog box appears.

9 In the Open a File dialog box, navigate to the id02lessons folder and select the file named id02styles.indd. Click Open. The Load Styles dialog box appears.

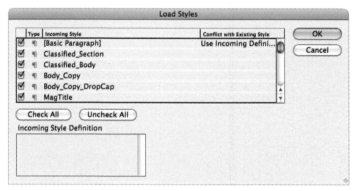

Loading styles lets you import and use styles created in another document.

10 In the Load Styles dialog box, click the Check All button, located in the bottom-left corner, and then click OK. All the paragraph and character styles from this publication are imported into your document.

11 Choose File > Save to save your work. Keep this file open for the next part of the lesson.

Creating and formatting master pages

Master pages serve as a template upon which all document pages are created. They provide the framework for the design of pages. Different master pages may be created for various sections of a magazine or a catalog, ensuring that all pages of these sections maintain a consistent appearance.

The document you are creating currently contains only one document page and one master page. You will add more document pages to complete the magazine, and more master pages to create consistent style and formatting. You will add a master page for the various sections of your magazine. Each of these sections has a different layout, with a different number of columns, margins, and headers. By creating the master pages before working on the document, you will be able to quickly create pages with a consistent design for the magazine.

1   Press the Pages button (⊞) in the panel docking area, or press the keyboard shortcut F12 (Windows) or Command+F12 (Mac OS), to open the Pages panel. Double-click the A-Master label in the top portion of the Pages panel.

The A-Master page is displayed and centered within your workspace. Keep the A-Master page selected in the Pages panel.

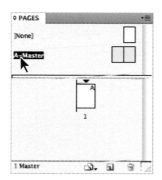

Double-clicking a page label in the Pages panel centers the page in the workspace.

2   In the Pages panel, press the panel menu button (•≡) and select Master Options for A-Master. Alternatively, you can hold down the Alt (Windows) or Option (Mac OS) key and click once on the A-Master text icon (not the page icon) in the Pages panel. The Master Options dialog box appears, allowing you to rename your master page.

3   In the Name text field of the Master Options dialog box, type **Footer**. Leave all other settings unchanged, and press OK. This changes the name from A-Master to A-Footer. You will now add a footer that runs across the bottom of this master page, and then apply it to document pages.

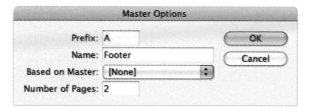

Change the name of a master page using the Master Options dialog box.

Formatting master pages

For this publication, the A-Footer page will also serve as the foundation for the other master pages. Although master pages can be used independent of one another, for this publication you will define that all items appearing on A-Footer will appear on all other master pages. This allows you to create a consistent footer across every page. The other master pages will have unique header information, which is different for each section of the magazine.

Adding automatic page numbering

You can have InDesign automatically apply a page number to pages within a document. If you reposition pages, they are renumbered, and you control the style and appearance of the page numbers.

1 In the Pages panel, double-click the left page icon for the A-Footer master page. This fits the left side of your A-Footer master page in the window. To keep the page numbers a consistent distance from the bottom edge of your page, you will create a guide.

2 Move your Selection tool (▸) onto the horizontal ruler running across the top of the page. Ctrl+click (Windows) or Command+click (Mac OS) and drag down from the ruler to create a horizontal ruler guide. Continue dragging until the ruler guide is positioned at 10.25 inches. You can determine the location of the guide in the Control panel, and by using the live transformation values that appear as you drag the guide. The position updates as you drag the guide.

Pressing and holding the Ctrl or Command key while dragging causes the guide to go across the entire spread, rather than only one page.

If the page rulers aren't visible, choose View > Show Rulers or press Ctrl+R (Windows) or Command+R (Mac OS).

3 Select the Type tool (T) from the Tools panel. Position the Type tool so the intersecting horizontal and vertical lines near the bottom of the tool are positioned at the bottom-left corner of the margin guides, where the left margin guide and the bottom margin guide intersect. Click and drag down and to the right, creating a text frame that extends from the bottom margin guide down to the guide you created in the previous step and to the right to the 1 inch position. You can see the position of the frame being created in the Control panel and in the horizontal ruler located at the top of the page.

*Creating a frame on the master page
for the automatic page number.*

4 Choose Type > Insert Special Character > Markers > Current Page Number to automatically have InDesign enter the page number on all pages to which this master page is applied. If you prefer to use keyboard commands, you can press Shift+Alt+Ctrl+N (Windows) or Shift+Option+Command+N (Mac OS) to have an automatic page number inserted. The letter A is inserted into the text frame. This letter serves as a placeholder for the actual page numbers, and displays as an A because the prefix for the current master page is A.

The Special Characters menu can also be accessed by right-clicking (Windows) or Ctrl+clicking (Mac OS) anywhere in the workspace. If you are working with type, the Special Characters option is available from the contextual menu.

5 Using the Type tool, select the letter A that you inserted into the text frame. From the Character Formatting Controls in the Control panel, choose Myriad Pro Bold from the font drop-down menu, and choose 12pt from the font size drop-down menu. Click the Paragraph Formatting Controls button in the Control panel, and then click the Align away from Spine button (≣). This aligns the text to the opposite edge of the binding of the publication.

6 Choose Object > Text Frame Options or press Ctrl+B (Windows) or Command+B (Mac OS). The Text Frame Options dialog box appears. In the General tab, locate the Vertical Justification section and choose Bottom from the Align drop-down menu. Click OK. The baseline of the text aligns to the bottom of the text frame.

Now you will place a copy of the automatic page number on the opposite page.

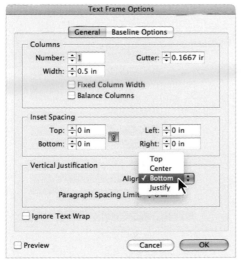
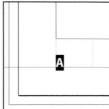

Using the Text Frame Options dialog box to vertically justify text.

7   Choose the Selection tool (↖) and make certain the text frame containing the footer is selected. Choose Edit > Copy to copy the frame.

8   Double-click on the right-hand page of the A-Footer master in the Pages panel. Choose Edit > Paste to place the copied text frame into the right-hand page.

9   Use the Selection tool to reposition the text frame so that the top of the frame is aligned to the bottom margin, and the right edge of the frame aligns to the right margin.

Notice that the page number automatically changes to align to the right side of the text frame because you selected the Align away from Spine option.

Using text variables

You use text variables to insert dynamic text that changes contextually. InDesign includes several pre-defined text variables including Chapter Number, File Name, Output Date, and Running Header. You can also edit any of these variables, or create new variables.

Defining new text variables

You will create variable text for your magazine title and page footers.

1   Choose Type > Text Variables > Define. The Text Variables dialog box appears.

2   Select Running Header from the Text Variables section of the dialog box and click the New button on the right side of the dialog box. The New Text Variable dialog box appears.

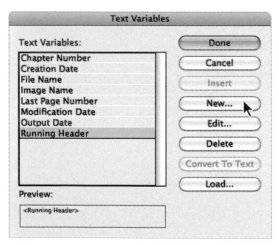

Defining the settings for text variables.

3   In the New Text Variable dialog box, type **Magazine Title** in the Name text field. Leave the Type text field as Running Header (Paragraph Style). From the Style drop-down menu, choose the MagTitle paragraph style. In the Options section, select the Change Case checkbox, then select the Title Case radio button below it. Press OK.

A new Magazine Title variable appears in the Text Variables dialog box.

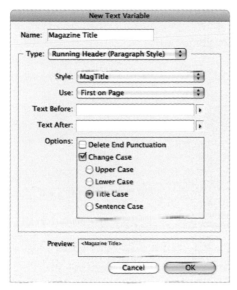

Defining the settings for text variables.

4   Repeat steps 1 and 2 to create another Running Header text variable. Name this text variable **Magazine Issue** and select the MagIssue paragraph style from the Style drop-down menu. All the other settings should match the settings used in step 3. The variables for Magazine Title and Magazine Issue are now available in the Text Variables dialog box. Press Done to save these new variables.

Creating page footers

In the previous steps, you created a Running Header text variable. Even though it is called a Running Header variable, it can be used anywhere on the page, including the footer. Now you will use the variables you have created to build the footers. Later, you'll discover how InDesign can automatically populate these variables.

1   In the Pages panel, double-click the left page icon of the A-Footer master page.

2   Select the Type tool (T) from the Tools panel. Position the cursor at the bottom-right corner of the page, where the bottom and right margin guides meet. Click and drag down and to the left until the bottom of the frame reaches the bottom ruler guide and the left edge of the frame is approximately at the center of the page. A guide appears once the cursor has reached the center of the page.

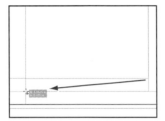

Creating a text frame for the magazine title.

3   In the Control panel, press the Character Formatting Controls button (A), and then set the font to Minion Pro Italic, the size to 12pt, and the leading (A) to Auto. Press the Paragraph Formatting Controls button (¶) and press the Align towards Spine button (≡).

4   Choose Type > Text Variables > Insert Variable > Magazine Title. The variable text <magazine Title> is placed into the frame. Press the space bar to separate this variable from the next variable that you will enter.

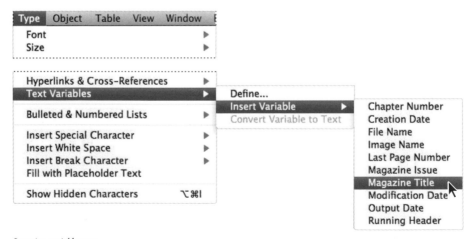

Inserting variable text.

5 In the Control panel, click the Character Formatting Controls button and change the font to Minion Pro Regular. Choose Type > Text Variables > Insert Variable > Magazine Issue. The variable text <magazine Issue> is placed into the frame.

6 Choose the Selection tool (↖) from the Tools panel and make sure the text frame that you drew in Step 2 is selected. Choose Object > Text Frame Options. In the Text Frame Options dialog box, select Bottom from the Align drop-down menu located in the Vertical Justification section in the General Tab. This causes the text to align to the bottom of the text frame. Press OK. You will now duplicate this box, moving the duplicate to the facing page.

7 Continuing to use the Selection tool, press and hold the Alt key (Windows) or Option key (Mac OS). While holding this key, click and drag the box you created to the page on the right side of the layout. The box duplicates as you drag it because of the key you are pressing.

As you are dragging an object such as the text frame in step 7, you can also add the Shift key while dragging. This constrains the movement of the object horizontally or vertically, ensuring that objects line up to one another.

8 Position the duplicate frame so that the left edge aligns with the left margin guide, and the bottom of the duplicate frame remains aligned to the ruler guide you created.

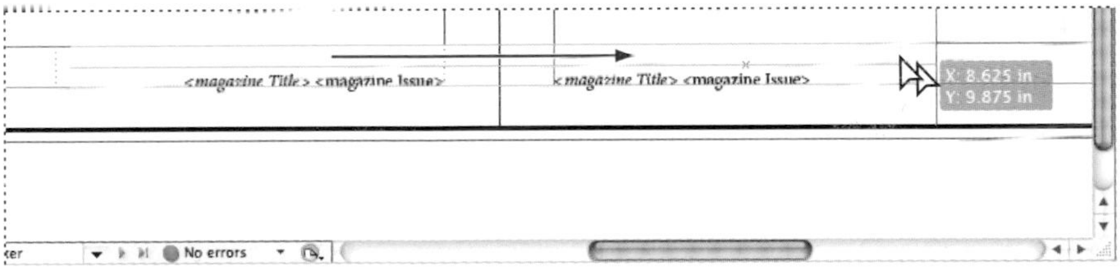

Position the duplicate text frame along the ruler guide, aligning the left edge with the left margin guide.

9 Choose the Type tool and click in the duplicated text frame. Press Ctrl+A (Windows) or Command+A (Mac OS) to select the type, and then press the Delete key.

10 Continuing to work in the same text frame, type **agitraining.com**.

11 Choose File > Save to save your work.

Basing master pages on other master pages

You can create additional master pages, and these pages can use the formatting and layout that you've already created for the A-Footer master page. In the next exercise, you'll import master pages that have already been created in another document. You'll then apply the A-Footer master page to these master pages that you import.

To create your own master pages, choose the New Master command from the Pages panel menu.

1   If necessary, open the Pages panel by pressing the Pages button (⊞) in the dock. In the Pages panel, press the panel menu button (·≡) and choose Load Master Pages. The Open a File dialog box appears.

2   In the Open a File dialog box, navigate to the id02lessons folder and select the file called id02styles.indd. Press Open. Four new master pages are added to your document. These pages correspond to the various sections of the magazine. Next, you'll apply the A-Footer master page you created earlier to these new master pages.

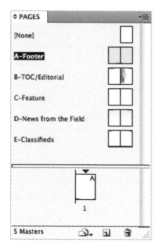

The Pages panel reflects the newly added master pages.

3   Double-click on the name B-TOC/Editorial master page in the Pages panel. By clicking the name instead of the icon, you can view the entire spread.

4   In the Pages panel menu, choose Master Options for B-TOC/Editorial. This opens the Master Options dialog box. You can also access the Master Options by holding down the Alt (Windows) or Option (Mac OS) key while clicking on the name of the master page.

5   In the Master Options dialog box, click the Based on Master drop-down menu and choose A-Footer. Press OK.

Notice that the B-TOC/Editorial master page now includes the footer you created. In the Pages panel, the page icons for B-TOC/Editorial display the letter A, indicating that these master pages are based on the master page A you created.

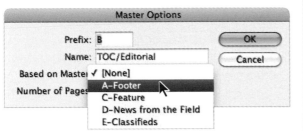
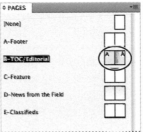

Base the page on the A-Footer master page.   The A indicates that a page is linked to this master.

6   In the Pages panel, click and drag the A-Footer master page onto the C-Feature master page. By dragging and dropping one master page icon onto another, you are applying the master page formatting to the destination page.

Drag the master page by its name instead of its icon to select the entire spread.

7   Drag and drop the A-Footer master page on top of the remaining master pages.

Overriding master page items

Master page items that appear on other pages are locked. The master page items are locked whether you apply a master page to another master page, or to a document page. This prevents you from accidentally modifying master page items that are intended to remain consistent on every page.

In the next exercise, you'll unlock some of the master page items that have been applied to another page, allowing you to selectively delete the footer information.

1   In the Pages panel, double-click the left B-TOC/Editorial master page. Notice that the text frames' edges appear as dotted lines. This indicates that these items are part of a master page that has been applied to this page. These items are locked and cannot be edited.

2   Choose the Selection tool (****) from the Tools panel. Place the cursor over the footer and click. Clicking the footer does not select the item, because it is attached to a master page. In order to modify these items, you must first override the item on the master page.

3 Continuing to use the Selection tool, press the Shift+Ctrl keys (Windows) or Shift+Command keys (Mac OS) and click the text frames containing the page number and footer. Use these modifier keys to select master page items. Press Delete to remove these frames from this page.

4 Choose File > Save to save your work.

Using Shift+Control+click (Windows) or Shift+Command+click (Mac OS) to select and change a master page item is referred to as a local override. The master page remains applied, and only the items you select are modified. To override all master page items on a page, choose Override All Master Page Items from the Pages panel menu (▾≡*).*

Adding placeholder frames to master pages

Creating text and image frames on master pages makes it easier to develop consistent layouts. You can also use frame-fitting options to control how images are sized after they are placed.

1 Select the Type tool (T) from the Tools panel and create a text frame on the In This Issue master page. The position and dimensions of the box are not important; you'll be setting these in the next step.

2 Choose the Selection tool (▸) from the Tools panel and make sure the text frame you drew in the last step is selected. In the Control panel, set the reference point (▦) to top left and type **2.9583"** for X and **1.4028"** for Y to set the location of the frame. Then type **4.6667"** for W and **3.6607"** for H to set the size.

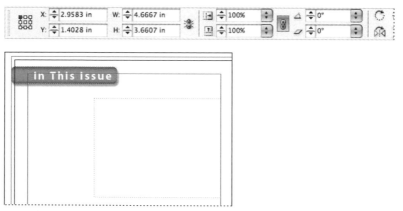

Use the Control panel to set the exact location of the text frame.

3 Now you'll add a number of image frames on the left side of the page. Select the Rectangle Frame tool (⊠) from the Tools panel and draw a small rectangle to the left of the text frame you created in the previous step. You'll use the Control panel to set the exact position and dimensions of this frame.

4 Choose the Selection tool from the Tools panel and make sure the frame you created in the last step is selected. In the Control panel, make sure the reference point (▦) is set to top-left and type the following values to set the dimensions and position: X: **-.125"** Y: **1.4028"** W: **2.3929"** H: **1.625"**.

You have created an image frame that is aligned to the top of the text frame and bleeds off the left side of the page. Next you will define how images placed in this frame will be sized.

5 Using the Selection tool, click to select the image frame you just created. From the menu bar at the top of the workspace, choose Object > Fitting > Frame Fitting Options. In the Frame Fitting Options dialog box, choose Fill Frame Proportionally from the Fitting drop-down menu in the Content Fitting section. Press OK.

You'll now duplicate the empty frame.

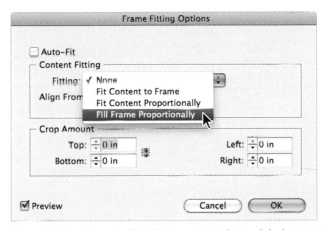

Choose Fill Frame Proportionally in the Frame Fitting Options dialog box to control how images placed in this frame will be sized.

6 With the image frame still selected, choose Edit > Step and Repeat. This allows you to duplicate an object multiple times, placing each duplicate in a specific location.

7 In the Step and Repeat dialog box, type **3** in the Repeat Count text field, type **2.0625"** in the Vertical Offset text field, and type **0** in the Horizontal Offset text field. Press OK. This creates three copies of the frame, and spaces them 2.0625 inches apart from each other.

Create three duplicates of the text frame using Step and Repeat.

8 Choose File > Save to save your file, and keep it open for the next part of the lesson.

Locking Master Items and setting text wrap

In the first lesson, you discovered how to wrap text around an object on a document page. Here you will wrap text around a shape on a master page.

1 Double-click the right page of the B-TOC/Editorial master page in the Pages panel. Using the Selection tool (⬉), select the oval shape on the left side of the page and right-click (Windows) or Ctrl+click (Mac OS) on the shape. In the contextual menu, deselect Allow Master Item Overrides. This prohibits designers from making changes to this master page object once it is part of a document page.

Deselect the Allow Master Item Overrides option to keep this item from being modified on a document page.

2 Choose Window > Text Wrap. This opens the Text Wrap panel. From the panel, select the Wrap around object shape option (▣) and set the Top Offset to **.25** inches, causing the text to wrap around the oval with ¼-inch distance between the text and the oval.

Use the Text Wrap panel to push text away from a frame or object. Here the text wraps above the image, offset by ¼ inch.

 When the Wrap around object shape option is chosen, all of the offset fields are grayed out except for the top value. This is because when you wrap text around an irregular shape, the wrap can't be identified by a specific side, only as an overall wrap based on the object's shape.

3 Close the Text Wrap panel.

Adding layout pages

Now that you have created and formatted all the master pages, you can start to lay out the document pages of the magazine. You'll begin by adding pages to the file.

When you create simple designs for one-time use, it may be easier to not create master pages. For longer documents or any documents that will repeat in a similar way, you should create master pages, as the time invested in defining the design saves time in the long run.

1 Double-click on page 1 in the Pages panel and choose Layout > Pages > Add Page, or use the keyboard shortcut Shift+Control+P (Windows) or Shift+Command+P (Mac OS), to add a page to the end of the document. Two pages are now displayed as icons in the Pages panel.

Next you'll insert the pages that will contain the Table of Contents and editorial content.

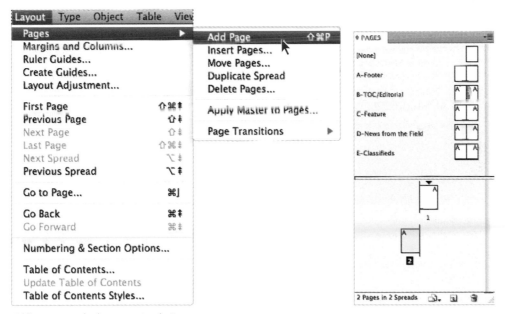

Adding a page to the document using the Layout menu.

2 In the Pages panel, Alt+click (Windows) or Option+click (Mac OS) on the Create new page button (◻) at the bottom of the Pages panel. This opens the Insert Pages dialog box.

3 In the Insert Pages dialog box, type **2** in the Pages text field, and from the Insert drop-down menu select After Page and type **1** in the text field. Select B–TOC/Editorial from the Master drop-down menu, then press OK.

This causes two pages to be added after page 1, and the new pages use the B–TOC/Editorial master page.

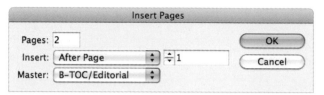

Adding multiple pages to the document. The new pages are based on a specific master page.

This inserts two pages between pages 1 and 2, and applies the B–TOC/Editorial master page to those new pages. This issue of the magazine will be 12 pages. You will now add the additional pages, but because they won't all be in the same section, you'll insert them without a master page assignment.

4 In the Pages panel, Alt+click (Windows) or Option+click (Mac OS) the Create new page button (⬛) at the bottom of the panel. The Insert Pages dialog box appears.

5 In the Insert Pages dialog box, type **9** in the Pages text field. Select After Page in the drop-down menu next to Insert, and type **4** in the text field. Choose None from the Master drop-down menu, then press OK. This inserts nine blank pages into your file after page 4. You now have 13 pages in the document. Because the document is only 12 pages, you'll practice deleting a page.

6 Select page 4 by double-clicking the page icon in the Pages panel. This highlights the page icon in the Pages panel and navigates to this page.

7 Click the Delete selected pages button (🗑) at the bottom of the Pages panel. This deletes page 4 and leaves you with the 12 pages you need for this issue.

8 Choose File > Save to save your work. Keep it open for the next exercise.

Setting numbering and section options

Now you have all the pages you need to set up the numbering and sections. Because you are using InDesign's automatic page numbering, the cover is considered to be page 1 in the document. You actually want page 1 of the magazine to be the third page of the file, with the first two pages considered to be the cover and inside front cover. Using numbering and section options, you will change the document's sections to reflect your desired numbering sequence.

1   In the Pages panel, double-click the section start icon, located above the first page in the Pages panel. This opens the Numbering & Section Options dialog box.

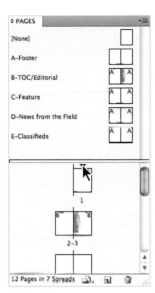

Double-click the section start icon in the Pages panel.

2   In the Numbering & Section Options dialog box, select I, II, III, IV from the Style drop-down menu in the Page Numbering section, then press OK.

This change adjusts the document's numbering to Roman numerals. You will now create a new section on the third page and have the new section start with page 1.

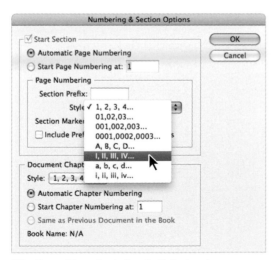

Select Roman Numeral style from the Styles drop-down menu.

3   In the Pages panel, double-click page III to select it. Press the panel menu button (‑≡) in the Pages panel and select Numbering & Section Options. Select the Start Page Numbering at radio button and type **1** in the text field. In the Page Numbering section, select 1, 2, 3, 4 from the Style drop-down menu and press OK.

This starts a new section on the third page of the document. The new section starts using the page number 1.

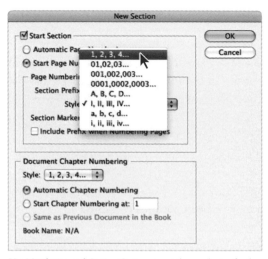

Use Numbering and Section Options to set the numbering for the new section of the magazine.

Placing formatted text

Now that the numbering and section options have been adjusted, you'll add some content to the editorial page. In this case, you'll import text from a document. The text uses placeholder copy and includes pre-formatted styles. You'll then complete the editorial page by adding a picture of the editor.

1   In the Pages panel, double-click the third page of the document. This is the page you set to page 1 in the previous exercise.

2   Select the Type tool (T) from the Tools panel and draw a small text frame on the right side of the page. The exact size and location isn't important; you'll use the Control panel to specify these values.

3   Choose the Selection tool (🖈) from the Tools panel—or you can press the Escape key on your keyboard to switch to the Selection tool—and make sure the text frame is selected. In the Control panel at the top of the workspace, make sure the reference point is set to top left. Type **11.0833"** in the X text field and **3"** in the Y text field. Also type **4.6667"** in the W text field and **6.875"** in the H text field.

Set the size of the text frame after you create it.

4   With the text frame still selected, choose File > Place. Navigate to the id02lessons folder and select the file Editorial.doc. At the bottom of the Place dialog box, make sure *Show Import Options* and *Replace Selected Item* are both checked. Click Open. The Microsoft Word Import Options dialog box appears.

5   In the Microsoft Word Import Options dialog box, make sure the Preserve Styles and Formatting from Text and Tables radio button is selected. Leave all other settings unchanged, then press OK. The Word document is placed into the text frame and all styles from the Word document are automatically mapped to the InDesign paragraph styles because the styles in each application have been identically named.

Use the Import Options to adjust the styles when importing a Microsoft Word document.

6   Because the editor probably won't get a new picture with each issue of the magazine, it makes sense to place this photo on the master page. Double-click on the right-hand page of the B-TOC/Editorial master page. Choose File > Place. In the Place dialog box, navigate to the id02lessons folder and select the file editor.jpg. Uncheck *Show Import Options* and also uncheck *Replace Selected Item*. Click Open to import this image. The cursor changes to a loaded cursor, indicating it has an image to place.

7   Move the loaded cursor to the top-right portion of the page, below the From the Editor text. Click once to place the photo. Choose the Selection tool from the Tools panel, and then drag the photo until the right side snaps to the right margin. If necessary, use the arrow keys to nudge the photo into place.

Place the editor's photo on the master page beneath the From the Editor text.

8   Choose File > Save to save your work.

Creating the classified page

Local goods and services are often advertised on a classified page located in the back of a magazine. Because most of the space is sold by number of words, characters, or column depth, these layouts typically involve narrow columns to pack as many ads as possible into the space. In this case, a four-column layout with an appropriate header has already been created for you. Next, you'll apply the master page and then add the classified text.

1   In the Pages panel, double-click page 9. Press the Pages panel menu button (⌄≣), and choose Apply Master to Pages. The Apply Master dialog box appears.

2   From the Apply Master drop-down menu, choose the master page E-Classifieds. The To Pages text field should reflect the current page number. If necessary, type **9** in this field. Click OK. The header, footer, and four-column layout of the E-Classifieds master page are applied to page 9.

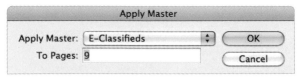

Use the Apply Master option to apply a master page to page 9 of the document.

3 To import the text into the page, choose File > Place. Navigate to the id02lessons folder and select the file named Classifieds.rtf. At the bottom of the Place dialog box, check *Show Import Options*, and leave *Replace Selected Item* unchecked. Click Open.

4 In the RTF Import Options dialog box, make sure the *Preserve Styles and Formatting from Text and Tables* radio button is selected. Leave all the other settings at their defaults and click OK.

InDesign remembers the last settings used in the Import Options dialog box. Settings you make will impact similar files you import until you change the import options.

5 On page 9, move the cursor anywhere within the first column. Press and hold the Shift key, and click to place the text.

Press and hold the Shift key to automatically flow the text as it is placed in the document.

6 Choose File > Save to save your work.

Adding images and text to the master frames

Earlier in this lesson, you added image and text frames to a master page. Next you will add content to these frames on the document pages.

1 Double-click the table of contents page icon in the Pages panel, which is now labeled with the Roman numeral II. The image and text frames you added earlier have dotted borders, indicating that these frames are located on a master page and cannot be selected.

2 Choose File > Place. In the Place dialog box, navigate to the id02lessons folder and locate the TOC images folder. Double-click the folder and select the file photo1.jpg. At the bottom of the Place dialog box, uncheck *Show Import Options* and *Replace Selected Item*. Click Open.

3 Move your cursor over the top image frame on the left side of the page and click to place the image. The image is placed inside the frame and automatically resized. This is because when you created this image frame on the master page, you applied fitting options to the frame. These options control how InDesign sizes and positions images placed into the empty frame.

After placing images and text in frames originally drawn on the master page, the frame is overridden, which means it can now be selected but it still retains all of the properties from the master page and will still update if a change is made to the master page. Properties that you change on a document page do not update if a change is made to the master page.

4 Choose File > Place and click on the image photo2.jpg. Now Shift+click on photo4.jpg to select all three images at the same time. Click Open.

5 Notice that the loaded cursor icon contains the number (3), indicating that there are three images to place in the document. Click the second frame from the top, placing the next photo. Continue clicking the empty frames to place the remaining photos.

If the photos in your loaded cursor don't appear in the order that you'd like, press the up or down arrow keys on your keyboard to cycle through the images that are loaded in your cursor to choose the next image that you'd like to place.

Now you'll finish the TOC/Editorial spread by adding the Table of Contents to the text frame on the right side of the page.

6 Choose File > Place. In the Place dialog box, navigate to the id02lessons folder. Select the TOC.rtf file. Make sure that *Show Import Options* and *Replace Selected Item* are still unchecked. Click Open.

7 Move your cursor over the text box on the right side of the Table of Contents page, and click to place the text into the layout.

Just like the Editorial and Classified sections, the TOC.rtf file is pre-formatted. In the next section of this exercise, you'll apply the remaining master pages and see how InDesign updates the content in the footer of each page.

The completed Table of Contents.

Applying master pages to multiple pages

Next you'll complete your work on this magazine by assigning master pages to the remaining pages in the magazine. The editorial content for this publication may not be complete, but you'll get the design ready for the final text to be placed as soon as it is ready.

1 In the Pages panel, press the panel menu button (-≡) and choose Apply Master to Pages. In the Apply Master dialog box, choose C-Feature from the Apply Master drop-down menu.

2 In the To Pages text field, type **2–4**. Be sure to add the hyphen (-) between the 2 and 4. Click OK. The C-Feature master page is applied to pages 2 to 4.

3 Click the Pages panel menu button again and choose Apply Master to Pages. In the resulting Apply Master dialog box, choose D-News from the Field from the Apply Master drop-down menu and type **5–8** in the To Pages text field. Click OK.

Scroll through the document pages. The text variables inserted in the footer have been automatically populated with the magazine title and issue. The master pages and text variables provide a convenient way to save time and maintain consistency throughout your design.

4   Choose File > Save to save your work.

Congratulations! You have finished this lesson.

Self study

Create a newsletter for your friends or family. Include a number of sections such as a page with profiles of people, stories relating to events or travels, favorite quotes, top ten lists, and photo galleries. Think about which of these sections share common elements, and design master pages to create a consistent design across these sections. Use headers, footers, guides, text frames, and picture frames on your master pages. If you find yourself repeating steps on multiple pages, consider how you can use features like master pages and text variables to streamline your design process.

Review

Questions

1   Do automatic page numbers always start with page 1?

2   If you want to modify content on a page that is linked to a master page, how do you select this locked content?

3   How can you access styles created in other InDesign documents?

Answers

1   No, you can start page numbering with any page number using the Numbering and Sections dialog box to specify where automatic page numbers start and end.

2   Using the Selection tool (⟨), Shift+Control+click (Windows) or Shift+Command+click (Mac OS) on content that is linked to a master page to break the link.

3   Use the Load Styles command found in the panel menu of the Paragraph or Character Styles panels, to import styles created in other documents.

Lesson 3

What you'll learn in this lesson:

- Creating and entering text
- Formatting and styling text
- Editing text in the Story Editor
- Customizing the dictionary
- Applying styles

Working with Text and Type

This lesson covers the essential capabilities for importing, formatting, and flowing text using InDesign CS5.

Starting up

Before starting, make sure that your tools and panels are consistent by resetting your preferences. See "Resetting the InDesign workspace and preferences" on page 3. It is important to use the Typography workspace for this lesson, as described on page 3.

You will work with several files from the id03lessons folder in this lesson. Make sure that you have copied the id03lessons folder onto your hard drive from the Digital Classroom DVD. See "Loading lesson files" on page 4. This lesson may be easier to follow if the id03lessons folder is on your desktop.

See Lesson 3 in action!

Use the accompanying video to gain a better understanding of how to use some of the features shown in this lesson. The video tutorial for this lesson can be found on the included DVD.

The project

You will explore InDesign's text controls by entering and flowing type into the layout for a fictitious magazine, *Tech*. You will explore a variety of text formatting tools. You will also create styles to easily format the text.

To view the finished project before starting, choose File > Open, navigate to the id03lessons folder, select id0301_done.indd, and then click Open. You can keep the lesson open for reference, or close it by choosing File > Close.

Adding text to your document

Text is almost always contained within a frame. You can use the Type tool, frame tools, or shape tools to draw a frame, and then click in the frame using the Type tool to add text. You can also add text that was created using other programs, such as Microsoft Word.

Creating a frame is usually the starting point for adding text to a layout. You'll use the most efficient way to define a new text frame: clicking and dragging with the Type tool.

Creating a text frame

You will start by creating a new text frame and entering text.

1 Choose File > Open. In the Open dialog box, navigate to the id03lessons folder, select the file id0301.indd, and then click Open. The document should open to the first page. If the document doesn't open to page 1, navigate to page one by double-clicking on page 1 in the Pages panel.

The lower-left section of page 1 has a listing of the stories featured in this issue. You will make a text frame above this box and type the text, **Inside this issue**.

If the document does not open to page 1, open the Pages panel and double-click on page 1.

2 Choose the Type tool (T) from the Tools panel. Position the cursor directly above the list of stories, then click and drag with the Type tool to define a text frame. Try to make the new frame approximately the same width as the existing text frame below it.

Click and drag with the Type tool to define a frame.

3   Type **Inside this issue:** into the text frame.

If you need to reposition the text frame, choose the Selection tool (↖) from the Tools panel, then click and drag the frame to move it, or use the frame handles to adjust the size of the frame.

When using the Selection tool, you can activate the Type tool (T) by double-clicking on any text frame.

4   Choose File > Save As. In the Save As dialog box, navigate to the id03lessons folder and type **id0301_work.indd** in the Name text field. Click Save.

Changing character attributes

The Control panel at the top of the workspace can be used to adjust the formatting of the text. At the far left of the Control panel, there are two buttons: the Character Formatting Controls button (A), and, below that, the Paragraph Formatting Controls button (¶).

You can use these buttons to toggle between Paragraph and Character Formatting controls. For this exercise, you will use the Control panel.

You can also use the Character and Paragraph panels to access many of the same controls. Choose Type > Character, or choose Type > Paragraph.

Changing font and type styles

You'll start by making some basic adjustments to text using the Control panel.

1   Make sure you have the Type tool (T) selected, then click and drag the *Inside this issue:* text to highlight it.

Type must be selected with the Type tool to make most text edits. You can select the frame with the Selection tool and click the Formatting Affects Text button (T) at the bottom of the Tools panel. This works well if you are changing the overall formatting of text.

2   In the Control panel at the top of the workspace, make sure the Character Formatting Controls icon (A) is selected.

The Character Formatting Controls.

3   Click the arrow to the right of the font name to see the drop-down menu listing all the fonts that InDesign is able to access. InDesign has a *WYSIWYG* (what you see is what you get) font menu, which shows the word *SAMPLE* displayed in the different fonts. Pick any font you'd like, just to see the font change.

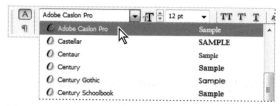

The WYSIWYG font menu.

You will now change the text to a different font. Instead of scrolling up and down the list to find a font you already know the name of, you can type it in the font name text field to get to the font more quickly.

4   In the Font drop-down menu in the Control panel, select the text in the font name text field and begin typing **Adobe Garamond Pro**. As soon as you get to the G in Garamond, the font name in the list changes; once Adobe Garamond Pro is displayed, press Enter (Windows) or Return (Mac OS). The text is formatted with the new font.

You will now change the type style to bold.

When text is selected, you can sample the appearance of different fonts by clicking to place the cursor in the Font drop-down menu in the Control panel. With the cursor positioned in the font name text field, use the up and down arrows on the keyboard to preview the selected text using different fonts.

5   With the text still selected, locate the Font Style drop-down menu, under the menu where you changed the font in the previous step. Choose Bold from the Font Style drop-down menu. Your type now appears as bold Adobe Garamond Pro. Keep the text selected.

You can use this drop-down menu to set the style of the font, such as bold, italic, or black. InDesign requires that the font style be installed before it will display the style option in the menu. For example, if you have Arial, but you don't have Arial Bold, Bold does not appear in the Font Style drop-down menu after you select Arial. This avoids possible problems when printing.

Changing the type style to bold.

Adjusting size

Next you will adjust the size of the selected text.

1   In the Control panel, select the font size (T) and replace it by typing **20** and then pressing Enter (Windows) or Return (Mac OS). The font size increases to 20 points.

2   Choose File > Save to save your work.

Adjusting line spacing

The space between lines of text is known as **leading**. Before computers were used to set type, original letter presses used bars of lead to separate the lines of type, and so the term leading remains, even though it is now only an adjustment made with a click of the mouse.

You will adjust the leading for the list of stories located below the text you were working with in the previous exercise.

1   Using the Type tool (T), click to insert the cursor in the frame listing the stories in this issue. Choose Edit > Select All to select all the text in the frame.

2   In the Control panel, set the Leading (ᴬ⁄ₐ) to 16 by selecting the existing value and typing **16**. Press Enter (Windows) or Return (Mac OS) to set the leading. Keep the text selected.

    If you had wanted to set the leading to one of the pre-set choices, you could select them from the drop-down menu.

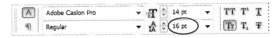

Changing the leading.

Adjusting character spacing: kerning and tracking

You can adjust the space between a group of characters, known as tracking, or the space between any pair of characters, known as kerning.

1   In the Tracking value (ᴬⱽ) in the Control panel, type **10**, and then press Enter (Windows) or Return (Mac OS) to increase the tracking.

    Tracking is measured using a fraction of an em space. A full em space is the width of the letter M of a particular font in a particular size—simply put, an em space varies depending upon the size and font you are using. In this case, the value 10 represents 10/1000ths of an em space.

Changing the tracking.

Next you will use the word *Tech* in the lower-left corner of the page to serve as a logo for the start of the High Tech Corner section. You will kern the letters closer together, and then use baseline shift to further adjust some of the letters.

2   Using the Type tool (T), click between the e and the c in the word *Tech* in the same block of text where you are currently working. The kerning value (AV) just above the tracking value displays 0. Select the 0 in the kerning value and then type **–120**, being certain to include the minus symbol to indicate a negative value. Press Enter (Windows) or Return (Mac OS) to set the kerning.

Changing the kerning.

Using a baseline shift

Text sits upon a line that is usually invisible, known as the baseline. Baseline shift allows you to change the vertical position of individual characters. This can be useful for fractions or symbols such as trademark or copyright symbols. Here you will use baseline shift to style the text.

1   Select the letters e and c of the word *Tech* and change their size to 10 using the Font Size drop-down menu in the Control panel.

2   Select only the letter *e* and in the Baseline Shift value (Aa) in the Control panel type **6 pt**, and then press Enter (Windows) or Return (Mac OS). The e is shifted upward, 6 points off the baseline.

Apply the baseline shift to the letter.

3   Choose File > Save to save your work.

Changing paragraph attributes

You have modified several character attributes that applied only to selected text. Now you will work with paragraph attributes, including text alignment, spacing, and tabs, that apply to an entire paragraph. As long as your cursor is within a given paragraph, you do not have to have any of the paragraph's text selected. You will make these adjustments using the paragraph controls section of the Control panel.

Horizontally aligning text

Text generally aligns to the left side of a text frame. You can change the alignment so that text aligns to the right side of the frame, is centered, or aligns along both sides of the frame (justified), or have InDesign adjust the alignment depending upon whether the text is on the left or right side of a publication.

1   Press the Pages button (⬚) to open the Pages panel. Double-click page 2 to navigate to it, and center this page in the workspace.

2   On page 2, click anywhere in the line of text that reads *Average Cell Phone Usage.* You don't need to highlight the line of text; simply place the cursor in this line.

3   In the Control panel, click the Paragraph Formatting Controls button (¶) to access the paragraph portion of the Control panel.

The paragraph formatting controls.

4   Press the Align Center button (≡) to align the text to the center of the text frame. The text is now centered. Keep the cursor in this text.

Changing the spacing before and after paragraphs

Adding space before or after paragraphs makes each paragraph stand out, making a clear transition between ideas or sections; it also provides much more control than simply inserting an additional return before or after the paragraph.

Next you will adjust all the city names to appear slightly lower than the top line. You will start by placing some extra space after the text *Average Cell Phone Usage.*

1   Using the Type tool, click anywhere within the line of text that reads *Average Cell Phone Usage.*

2   In the Control panel, locate the Space After text field (.≡), type **.0625**, and then press Enter (Windows) or Return (Mac OS).

3   Choose File > Save to save your work.

Using tabs

Tabs, or tab stops, are often used to align text. Tabs align words based on where you insert the tabs by pressing the Tab key on the keyboard. If you have seen a restaurant menu with prices aligned on the right side and a series of periods separating the menu item from the price, you've seen how tabs can be used. Similarly, if you've looked at a Table of Contents at the start of a book, you've seen how tabs can be used to align the page numbers and separate them from the contents. In this exercise, you will use tabs to separate the city name from the average hours of cellular phone usage.

1   Using the Type tool (T), select all the text in the Average Cell Phone Usage text frame by clicking in the text frame and choosing Edit > Select All. When this text was entered, a tab was placed between the city name and the hours.

2   Choose Type > Show Hidden Characters to see the tab, represented by a (>>). Choose Type > Hide Hidden Characters to hide these non-printing characters from view.

3   Choose Type > Tabs to open the Tabs panel. The Tabs panel appears aligned to the top of the selected text frame.

If the Tabs panel is not aligned to the top of the text frame, use the Zoom tool (⊙) to adjust the magnification so that the top of the text frame is visible. After adjusting the magnification, reselect the Type tool, click within the text frame, and select the text. In the right-hand corner of the Tabs panel, click the Position Panel above Text Frame button (⋒). If you move the Tabs panel, click the Position Panel above Text Frame button; the Tabs panel realigns to your text frame. The Position Panel above Text Frame button will position the Tabs panel over the text frame if the entire width of the frame is visible in the display.

Understanding the Tabs panel

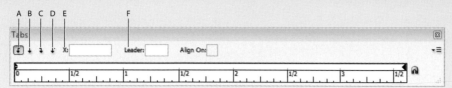

A. Left-Justified Tab. B. Center-Justified Tab. C. Right-Justified Tab. D. Align to Decimal (or Other Specified Character) Tab. E. X text field. F. Leader text field.

There are four ways to align tabs within the Tabs panel. Located at the top left are the Left-Justified Tab (↓), Center-Justified Tab (↓), Right-Justified Tab (↓), and Align to Decimal (or Other Specified Character) Tab (↓) buttons.

Next to the tab buttons is the X text field. This value represents where the tab sits relative to the ruler. The Leader text field allows you to insert a period, for example, to have leader dots between your tabbed items, as you would find in a Table of Contents or a menu. The Align On text field allows you to set the tab to align on a special character, such as a decimal point for currency or a colon for time. You can also insert and move tabs visually, by clicking to insert them directly above the ruler. The triangles on the left and right sides of the ruler also control the left, right, and first-line indents for the active paragraph where the cursor is inserted.

Creating hanging indents

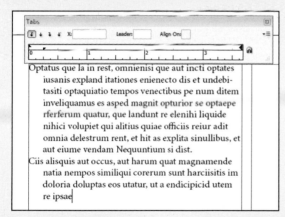

An example of a hanging indent.

A hanging indent is created when the first line of the paragraph starts at the left margin, but the second and subsequent lines are indented. This is called hanging indentation because the first line hangs out over the rest of the paragraph. To make a hanging indent, make your First line indent a negative value, and the Left indent a positive value.

4   In the Tabs panel, press the Right-Justified Tab button (⤵), then click in the space above the ruler toward the right edge of the tab area. In the selected text, the time values now align to the right of the frame at the location where you placed the tab.

5   With the tab stop you entered in the previous step still selected above the ruler, highlight the X value in the Tabs panel and type **3.3611**. Press Enter (Windows) or Return (Mac OS) to set this as the new location for this tab stop. The text is repositioned to this location.

6   With the tab stop still selected in the ruler, type a period (.) into the Leader text field, and then press Enter (Windows) or Return (Mac OS). A series of periods now connect the cities with the time values.

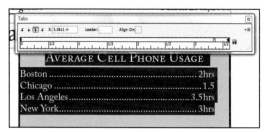

Add leader dots to the listing.

7   Close the Tabs panel, and then choose File > Save to save your work.

Adding rules above or below paragraphs

Rules are lines that you can place above or below a paragraph. You can use rules to separate paragraphs or call attention to headlines. Rules move with the text, and so the rule and the associated text move together. You will add a rule below the words *Average Cell Phone Usage*.

1   Using the Type tool (T), click anywhere inside the text *Average Cell Phone Usage*.

2   Press the pancl menu button (▾≡) located at the far-right side of the Control panel, and choose Paragraph Rules from the drop-down menu.

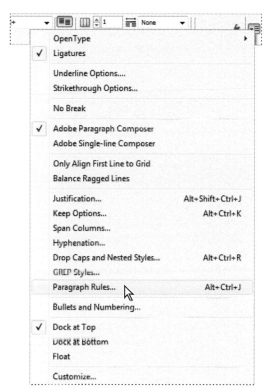

Choose Paragraph Rules from the panel drop-down menu in the Control panel.

3   In the Paragraph Rules dialog box, choose Rule Below from the drop-down menu and select the *Rule On* checkbox to enable the rule. Select the *Preview* checkbox in the lower-left corner of the dialog box to see the rule applied. Keep the dialog box open.

The line appears and is automatically aligned relative to the baseline of the text. Next you will examine the offset value, allowing you to move the rule vertically.

4   In the Offset text field, make sure the offset value is set to 0.0625. This shifts the line below the baseline. When the offset is set to 0, it should align on the baseline, but you can use the offset value to move the rule up or down by entering negative or positive values.

5 If necessary, choose Text from the Width drop-down menu so that the line appears only beneath the selected text. Click OK.

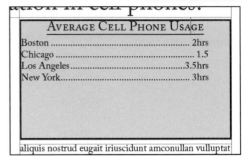

The Paragraph Rules dialog box with the correct settings.

Changing text color

You can change the color of text to make it stand out or appear more visually appealing. When changing text color, you can adjust either the fill or stroke of the text.

1 Using the Type tool (T), select the words *Average Cell Phone Usage*, making sure that the return at the end of the line is also selected.

2 Press the Swatches button (▦) in the panel docking area to open the Swatches panel. You can also access the Swatches panel by choosing Window > Swatches.

3 In the top-left corner of the Swatches panel, make certain the fill icon (T) is in the foreground. If not, click to select it so that color adjustments affect the fill of the selected object.

The Fill and Stroke controls in the Swatches panel.

4   With the words *Average Cell Phone Usage* still selected, locate the color Blue in the
Swatches panel, and then click to select it. The color of the text is changed, as is the rule
below the text. The rule changes because the rule was defined to be the same color as
the text. If the rule color does not change with the text color, make sure that the return
at the end of the line was also selected as described in step 1.

Select the blue swatch in the Swatches panel.

5   Choose File > Save to save your work.

Creating drop caps

Drop caps, or initial caps, help to draw a reader's attention to the start of a story. You will create
a drop cap for the beginning of a story on the second page of the magazine.

1   Using the Type tool (T), click anywhere in the first paragraph of the story on page 2. You
do not need to highlight the text.

2   In the Paragraph Formatting Controls area of the Control panel (¶), locate the Drop Cap
Number of Lines text field (⫶) and change the value to 3. Press Enter (Windows) or
Return (Mac OS) to commit the change.

The character *I* now appears as a three-line drop cap.

3   Press the panel menu button (▾≡) in the Control panel and choose Drop Caps and
Nested Styles.

4 When the Drop Caps and Nested Styles dialog box appears, select the *Preview* checkbox on the right side to view the changes as they are made. Notice that the I is not aligned to the side of the text box. Select the *Align Left Edge* checkbox to align the I to the text box, and then click OK. The drop-capped I is now aligned against the text frame on the left side.

The drop cap's left edge is aligned to the edge of the text box.

Checking and correcting spelling

Checking spelling is an important part of creating a professional-looking document, and InDesign has several capabilities that can help correct typographical errors or help you identify spelling mistakes.

The Dynamic Spelling and Autocorrect options alert you to misspelled words and can automatically change them for you. In this exercise, you will take a closer look at some of these options, including the ability to find and change words across an entire document or group of documents.

Finding and changing text and text attributes

Let's say you want to change the name *Tech Magazine* in the top folio of each page to be bold. Instead of making the change on each page, you can use Find/Change to modify the formatting of every instance of the word or phrase.

As you learned in Lesson 2, you could also use a master page to adjust an object with a consistent location on many pages. So there are many time-saving ways to create and modify your layout.

1 Choose the Zoom tool (⌕) from the Tools panel and increase the magnification on the top of page 2 so that the words *Tech Magazine* are clearly visible. After the words are visible, switch to the Type tool.

You can also press and hold Ctrl+space bar (Windows) or Command+space bar (Mac OS) to temporarily activate the Zoom tool while working with the Type tool.

2 Choose Edit > Find/Change to open the Find/Change dialog box. In the Find/Change dialog box, type **Tech Magazine** in the Find what text field. Next you'll identify the changes to make to this text.

Using Find/Change.

3 In the Change Format text field at the bottom of the Find/Change dialog box, press the Specify Attributes to Change button (*A*). The Change Format Settings dialog box appears.

4 On the left side of the dialog box, choose Basic Character Formats. Select Bold from the Font Style drop-down menu, and then click OK. This changes text that meets the Find criteria to bold.

You can also have InDesign search for text based upon style attributes. For example, you could have InDesign locate all text that uses a certain font, style, or color, and have it changed to another font, style, or color. This is accomplished by using the Specify Attributes to Find button in the Find Format section of the Find/Change dialog box.

5 In the Find/Change dialog box, make sure the Search drop-down menu is set to Document so that the entire document is searched. While you can have InDesign search smaller, more refined areas of a document, here you want to search the entire document.

6 Click Change All. A dialog box appears, indicating that the search is complete and that four replacements were made.

7 Click OK to accept the changes, and then click Done. All four instances of the words *Tech Magazine* are now bold. If desired, you can scroll or use the Pages panel to navigate to the other pages to confirm the changes.

8 Choose File > Save to save your work.

Finding and changing text using GREP

As powerful as the Find/Change feature is, InDesign offers an even more powerful Find/Change tool called GREP. GREP stands for Global Regular Expression Print. It's not important to know what it stands for but it is important to understand how powerful and useful GREP can be when you need it. Think of GREP as your typical Find/Change times ten!

In the exercise that follows, you'll use GREP to standardize the formatting of some phone numbers that appear on the last page of the document.

1 In the Pages panel, double-click on page 6 to make that the active page, and zoom in on the Information box in the lower-right corner of the page.

This box lists companies and their phone numbers so that customers can contact them. Notice that the phone numbers have been entered in a variety of formats and are inconsistent. You'll fix that in the next steps.

2 Select the Type tool (T) and select the entries that contain phone numbers. There are a total of five lines to select.

3 Choose Edit > Find/Change to open the Find/Change dialog box, and click on the GREP tab to make it active. Note that because you selected text prior to entering the Find/Change dialog box, the Search defaults to only the Selection as opposed to the entire document. This is a useful technique to restrict a search to a given area.

4 For this exercise, you'll use a built-in GREP search that is included with InDesign. From the Query drop-down menu, choose Phone Number Conversion (dot format). The Find what and Change to fields are automatically populated.

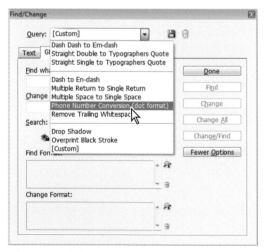

Choosing a predefined GREP search from the Query drop-down menu.

5   Click the Change All button. A window is displayed, indicating that five replacements have been made. Click OK and notice that all of the phone numbers in the information box have been standardized.

As powerful as that is, not everyone wants this format for phone numbers. Let's change it to a different format.

6   With the Find/Change dialog box still open, go to the Change to text field, put parentheses around the $1 text, and replace the period after the 1 with a space. In addition, replace the remaining periods with hyphens so that the text in the Change to field looks like this: ($1) $2-$3. Click the Change All button. A window appears indicating that five replacements have been made. Click OK, then click Done.

The GREP expression used in the Find/Change dialog box and the text after applying the GREP search.

This is simply one example of how powerful GREP can be. Can you imagine several pages of contact information where the phone numbers were not consistently entered? GREP to the rescue.

GREP Explained

GREP requires a bit of practice and experimentation to become proficient with the language. In the GREP exercise that you performed in this lesson, you may have wondered what all of those characters meant in the Find what and Change to fields. Let's break it down to help you understand what was happening:

\(?(\d\d\d)\)?[-.]

The beginning text \(is how you search for a specific character in GREP. The backslash is called an escape character and forces GREP to search for the character immediately following it. In this case the \(is searching for an open parenthesis. The ? that follows the open parenthesis indicates that the parenthesis that you are searching for may or may not be there. If it exists, GREP acknowledges it; if it doesn't exist, GREP ignores it. The next section (\d\d\d) is looking for three numeric digits in a row. These three digits are wrapped in parentheses so that they can be protected when the change is performed. The next three characters \)? are essentially the same as the beginning section, only GREP is looking for a closed parenthesis that may or may not be there. Finally, [-.] looks for a hyphen, a period, or a space. Any one will be acceptable. The remainder of the expression is just a repeated variation on the first section.

Now in the Change to field, you see $1.$2.$3. This is where GREP does some amazing work. Each $ followed by a number is a variable. $1 is capturing whatever was found in the first section of text that was surrounded by parentheses—in this case (\d\d\d). So whatever numbers GREP found as those first three digits, it will retain in the change expression so that the found numbers and the changed numbers remain the same. Now you can put whatever characters you want between those groups to format the text to your liking, just like you did in the exercise by replacing the periods with spaces or hyphens.

Checking spelling

InDesign can help you locate misspelled words, repeated words, uncapitalized words, and uncapitalized sentences.

1 In the Pages panel, double-click on page 2 to center the page in the workspace.

2 Select the Type tool (T) from the Tools panel, and then click anywhere in the *What is the next inovation in cell phones?* headline at the top of page 2.

The word *innovation* is intentionally misspelled to help you gain an understanding of the spelling features available within InDesign.

3 Choose Edit > Spelling > Check Spelling. The Check Spelling dialog box appears.

4 Select Story from the Search drop-down menu at the bottom of the dialog box so that only this text frame is searched. A story is a text frame and any linked text frames.

5 *Inovation* is displayed at the top of the dialog box, and listed as not being in the dictionary. The correct spelling of innovation appears in the Suggested Corrections field. Select the correct spelling, innovation, and then click Change.

Checking and correcting spelling.

The Start button is available once again, indicating that InDesign has searched the entire story, and that all errors have been corrected.

6 Click Done.

Adding words to the dictionary

You can provide InDesign with a list of common terms, proper names, or industry-specific terms that should be ignored when checking spelling. You can add these words to your dictionary so that InDesign does not indicate that these words are misspelled.

1 Using the Type tool (T), insert the cursor at the start of the first paragraph at the top of page 2.

2 Choose Edit > Spelling > Check Spelling.

In the Not in Dictionary section, *Blippa* appears. This is the name of a new product that appears throughout this document.

3   Click Add to place *Blippa* in your user dictionary, and then click Done.

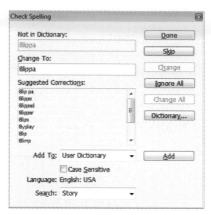

Adding a word to the dictionary.

 You can add or remove words from your user dictionary by choosing Edit > Spelling > Dictionary. You can add or remove individual words, or use the Import option to import a list of words to add to the dictionary.

4   Choose File > Save to save your work.

Centralized user dictionary

You can also create a central user dictionary to share with colleagues.

To create and share a dictionary, choose Edit > Preferences > Dictionary (Windows), or InDesign > Preferences > Dictionary (Mac OS). Click the New User Dictionary button (⊐). When the New User Dictionary dialog box appears, name the new dictionary. The location and name of the new dictionary file appear listed under the Language drop-down menu.

After adding your commonly used words to the new dictionary, access the new dictionary file on another user's InDesign program using the Add User Dictionary button (⊕) in their Preferences > Dictionary dialog box.

Checking spelling as you type

Another way to avoid spelling errors is to use InDesign's Dynamic Spelling option, which checks spelling as you type. Words not found in the InDesign dictionaries are marked with a red underline in your layout, as is common in word processing applications such as Microsoft Word.

1   Press the Pages button (⊞) in the dock to open the Pages panel. Locate page 3 and double-click the page 3 icon to center the page in the workspace.

2 Using the Type tool (T), click inside the text frame containing the headline *When is the best time to update equpment?*

3 Choose Edit > Spelling > Dynamic Spelling to activate the Dynamic Spelling feature. A red line appears under the word *equpment*. This may take a moment to occur, as InDesign will review the entire document once Dynamic Spelling is enabled.

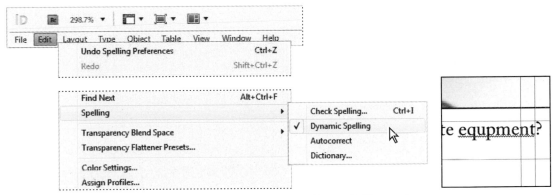

Accessing Dynamic Spelling through the Edit menu.   *Dynamic Spelling turned on.*

4 Right-click (Windows) or Ctrl+click (Mac OS) the word *equpment*. A list of suggested corrections appears in the contextual menu. Choose the word *equipment* from the list, and the misspelled word is corrected.

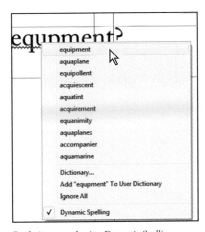

Replacing a word using Dynamic Spelling.

5 Disable Dynamic Spelling by choosing Edit > Spelling > Dynamic Spelling.

Automatically correcting spelling

You can use the Autocorrect feature to correct commonly misspelled words as you type. For example, if you type **hte** when you intend to type **the**, you can have InDesign automatically correct this error as you enter text while typing. You will now enable Autocorrect and add a word to the list of those that are automatically corrected.

1 Using the Pages panel, navigate to page 2 by double-clicking the page 2 icon.

2 Choose Edit > Preferences > Autocorrect (Windows), or InDesign > Preferences > Autocorrect (Mac OS).

3 When the Preferences dialog box appears, select the *Enable Autocorrect* checkbox, if it is not already selected.

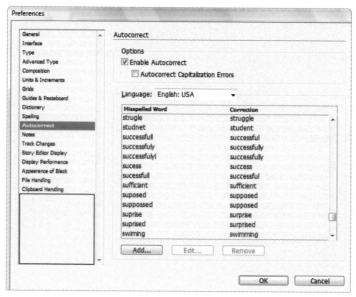

The Autocorrect Preferences dialog box.

4 Click the Add button at the bottom of the dialog box to add your own word to be automatically corrected.

5 In the Add to Autocorrect List dialog box, type **useage** in the Misspelled Word text field, and **usage** in the Correction text field.

This provides InDesign with the incorrect spelling that should be changed and the correct spelling that should be used instead.

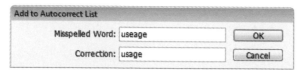

Entering a word into Autocorrect.

6   Click OK, then click OK again to close the Preferences dialog box.

7   In the *Average Cell Phone Usage* text frame on page 2, highlight the word Usage and delete it from the text frame. You will now re-type this word, intentionally spelling it incorrectly.

8   Type **Useage**, and then press the space bar. The Autocorrect feature corrects the misspelled word. Press the Backspace (Windows) or Delete (Mac OS) key to remove the extra space.

Editing text using the Story Editor

In some projects, a story might be spread across several pages. You may find yourself moving from one page to another to edit text, which can distract you from the editing process. When stories are placed across multiple pages, you can use the Story Editor to more easily view all text in one location.

The Story Editor also displays text that does not fit into existing frames, known as overset text. Overset text is indicated by a red plus sign that appears at the bottom-right corner of a frame when there is more text than fits into the frame.

1   In the Pages panel, double-click on page 5 to center the page in the workspace. Using the Type tool (T), click anywhere inside the text frame on page 5 containing the story.

2   Choose Edit > Edit in Story Editor to open the Story Editor window. This allows you to view the entire story across several pages.

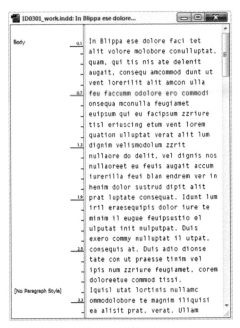

Viewing text using the Story Editor.

3 Use the scroll bar on the right side of the window to navigate to the bottom of the story. The Story Editor allows you to view the overset text.

The Story Editor identifies overset text, which does not fit in the current text frames.

4 Highlight from the word *eugue* to the end of the document and delete the overset text; then close the Story Editor.

In addition to deleting the text, you can also address overset text in a number of ways: For example, make edits to the existing text, to create space for the overset text to move into the existing frames. You can also create more space for the text, either by expanding the existing frames or by linking the text to a new frame, or you can reduce the size, leading, or tracking of the current text to allow for more text to fit in the same area.

5 Notice that the red plus sign at the end of the text frame has disappeared.

6 Choose File > Save to save your work.

Using the Track Changes feature

If you work in an environment where you collaborate with other users, the new Track Changes feature in InDesign CS5 provides a wonderful tool for displaying changes made to a document by yourself or other users, and permits the approval or rejection of those changes. Let's take a look at this new feature.

1 If, necessary, click on the Pages panel button to display the Pages panel, and double-click on page 3. Zoom in on the text frame below the photo.

2 Choose Window > Editorial > Track Changes to display the Track Changes panel.

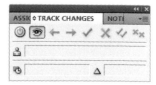

The Track Changes panel.

3 Select the Type tool (T), and click anywhere within the text frame on page 3.

4 Click on the Enable Track Changes in Current Story button (◉). This enables the Track Changes feature for the current story only. You can enable all stories at once by choosing the option from the Track Changes panel menu (•≡).

5 Highlight the word *ultimate* and change it to *best*. Also, highlight the word *update* and change it to *replace*.

Although Track Changes is enabled, the appearance of the changed text isn't apparent in layout view. In order to see any of the changed text, you need to view it using the Story Editor.

6 Choose Edit > Edit in Story Editor to display the Story Editor. Note that all of the text changes made within this story are highlighted.

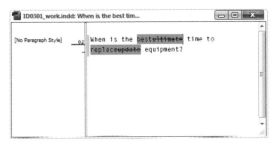

Changes highlighted in the Story Editor.

7 Click at the very beginning of the text in the Story Editor and click the Next Change button (→) in the Track Changes panel to highlight the first change displayed in the current story. The word *best* is highlighted.

8 Click the Accept Change button (✔) to accept the insertion of the word *best* into the final text of the story.

9 Click the Next Change button again to highlight the next change, which is the deletion of the word *ultimate*.

10 This time, hold down the Alt key (Windows) or Option key (Mac OS) when accepting the change. The next change will automatically highlight in the Story Editor. The word *replace* is highlighted.

11 You've decided that this was not a good change and would like to change this word to its original state. Hold down the Alt key (Windows) or Option key (Mac OS) and click the Reject Change button (✘) to reject the change and automatically highlight the next change.

12 Finally, click the Reject Change button to reject the deletion of the word *update*.

After accepting or rejecting changes in the Story Editor, the changes are automatically displayed in layout view within InDesign. It's important to note, however, that any changes made to the text in your document automatically appear in the layout view, whether the changes have been accepted or not. The Track Changes feature simply allows you to monitor those changes in a document.

13 Close the Story Editor window and view the final text as it appears in your document. Close the Track Changes panel as well.

Drag-and-drop text editing

When editing text, it can be faster to use your mouse to relocate text instead of using the menu commands to cut, copy, and paste text. Use drag-and-drop text editing to highlight words or characters, and then drag them to a different location. You can use this option in both the Story Editor and in layout view, although you need to enable it in layout view, as it is turned off by default.

1 Choose Edit > Preferences > Type (Windows), or InDesign > Preferences > Type (Mac OS).

2 When the Type Preferences dialog box appears, in the Drag and Drop Text Editing section, select the *Enable in layout view* checkbox, then click OK.

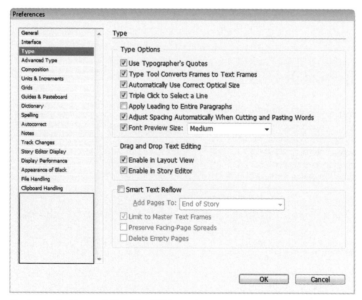

Turning on the Drag and Drop Text Editing option.

3   Click and drag to select the words *cell phone,* without the s, in the headline on page 5. With the text selected, click and drag the highlighted words so that they are placed before the word *innovation.* Release the mouse to relocate these words.

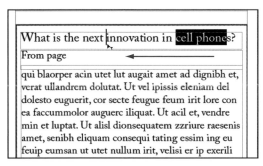

*Once text is highlighted, click and drag the highlighted text to a
new location to reposition it.*

4   Delete the word *in* and also the letter *s.* Also add a space after *phone,* if necessary. The question mark now follows the word *innovation*

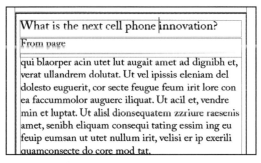

The final text after editing.

5   Choose File > Save to save your work.

Special characters and glyphs

Symbols such as those used for dollars, cents, bullets, copyrights, and registered trademarks can be difficult to insert if you don't remember the appropriate keystrokes.

You can use the Glyphs panel in InDesign to see all the characters, known as *glyphs,* within every font. You will work with the Glyphs panel to add a trademark symbol to the words Tech Magazine, and you will then use the Find/Change feature to add the symbol to all instances of the name throughout the layout.

1   Choose the Zoom tool (q) from the Tools panel and increase the magnification so you can clearly see the words *Tech Magazine* in the top text frame on page 5.

2   Choose the Type tool (T) from the Tools panel and click after the word *Magazine* to insert the cursor.

3 Choose Type > Glyphs to open the Glyphs panel. From the Show drop-down menu, choose Symbols and scroll down until you see the trademark glyph (™).

4 In the Glyphs panel, double-click the trademark symbol to place it after the word *Magazine*.

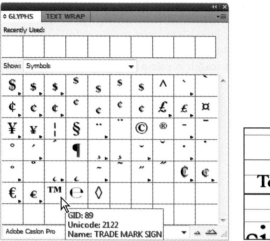

Insert the trademark glyph from the Glyphs panel into the layout.

5 Using the Type tool, highlight the word Magazine along with the trademark glyph you just inserted.

6 Choose Edit > Copy to copy these characters.

7 Choose Edit > Find/Change to open the Find/Change dialog box. Click on the Text tab to make it active.

8 In the Find what text field, type **Magazine**.

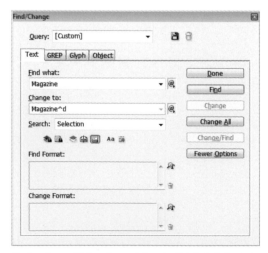

Finding the word Magazine, and changing it to include the trademark symbol.

9 Click inside the Change to text field and choose Edit > Paste. The notation for the symbol is pasted.

10 If you've been following along with the lessons in this chapter, you may notice that Bold is still specified in the Change Format section of the Find/Change dialog box. Although it won't make a difference in this example, it's important to note that those attributes are "sticky" and remain specified until you remove them. Click the Clear Specified Attributes icon (🗑) to the right of the Change Format section to remove these attributes.

11 Make sure that Document is chosen from the Search drop-down menu and click Change All. A dialog box appears, indicating that the search is complete and that five changes have been made. Click OK.

12 Click Done. All instances of the words *Tech Magazine* now include a trademark symbol.

13 Delete the extra trademark symbol from the Tech Magazine text on page 5, and then choose File > Save to save your work.

Using the Glyphs panel and glyph sets

The Glyphs panel also allows you to create a set of commonly used glyphs, making it easy to access the special characters and symbols you use most frequently.

1 In the Glyphs panel, press the panel menu button (▾≡), and then choose New Glyph Set. In the New Glyph Set dialog box, type **Adobe Caslon Pro** in the Name text field. Leave the Insert Order drop-down menu at its default, and then click OK.

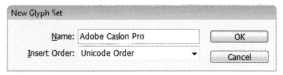

Creating a new glyph set.

2 In the Glyphs panel, select the trademark symbol, if it is not selected. Click the panel menu button and choose Add to Glyph Set; then choose Adobe Caslon Pro from the menu that appears.

3 In the Glyphs panel, click the Show drop-down menu, and choose Adobe Caslon Pro from the top of the list. You can add as many glyphs as you like to this glyph set. InDesign allows you to add different glyphs from different fonts to a set. You should add only those glyphs from one font to each set so that you know you are inserting the correct version of a glyph.

A custom glyph set.

4 Close the Glyphs panel.

Text frame options

InDesign includes options for formatting text frames. These options control the vertical alignment of type, the distance text is inset from the edge of the frame, and the number of columns inside the frame. Some of these options are accessible only within the Text Frame Option dialog box, while others are also accessible in the Control panel. In this exercise, you will change some of the text frame options for a text frame on page 2.

Adjusting text inset

Inside the *Average Cell Phone Usage* text frame, the text touches the side of the text frame. Because there is a border on the frame, this looks unappealing, and you will adjust the position of the text.

1 In the Pages panel, double-click the page 2 icon to center the page on the workspace.

2 Using the Type tool (T), click inside the *Average Cell Phone Usage* text frame on page 2.

3 Choose Object > Text Frame Options to access the Text Frame Options dialog box.

The keyboard shortcut to open the Text Frame Options dialog box is Ctrl+B (Windows) or Command+B (Mac OS).

4 When the Text Frame Options dialog box appears, make sure the Make all settings the same button (●) in the Inset Spacing section is selected.

5 In the Top text field, highlight the current value, and then type **.125**. Press the Tab key, and the cursor moves to the next text field. Click to select the *Preview* checkbox, and the text is inset by .125 inches.

6 Click OK. The text has moved and is no longer touching the sides of the frame. Keep the cursor in the same location for the next part of this lesson.

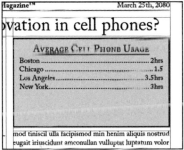

Setting a text inset.

Vertically aligning text

You can align text inside a frame both horizontally and vertically. With vertical alignment, you determine whether text aligns with the top, bottom, or center of a frame. You can also justify the type so that multiple lines of type are evenly distributed between the top and bottom of a text frame. This time, you'll access the Text Frame Options dialog box using a slightly quicker method.

1 With the Selection tool (▸) active, hold down the Alt (Windows) or Option (Mac OS) key and double-click on the text frame for Average Cell Phone Usage.

2   In the Vertical Justification section, choose Justify from the Align drop-down menu.

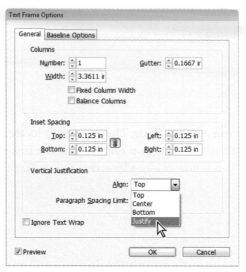

Using text frame options to set the text to be vertically justified.

3   Click OK. Notice that the text now snaps to the top and bottom of the frame. Leading is changed, but the text inset is still retained.

4   Choose File > Save to save your work.

Importing text

There are three ways to flow text into an InDesign document: You can flow text manually, and link the text boxes yourself. You can also flow text semi-automatically, which reloads your cursor with text. And you can flow text into a document that automatically makes new frames and pages for you.

Flowing text manually

In this first exercise, you will manually flow text and practice threading text between frames.

1   In the Pages panel, locate page 3 and double-click the page 3 icon to navigate to the page, and then choose Edit > Deselect All to make certain nothing is selected.

2   Choose File > Place. In the Place dialog box, navigate to the id03lessons folder, select the id0301.doc file, make sure *Show Import Options* is checked, and click Open. The Microsoft Word Import Options dialog box appears.

3 In the Microsoft Word Import Options dialog box, confirm that the *Remove Styles and Formatting from Text and Tables* option is selected, and directly under this option, that *Preserve Local Overrides* is not checked. Click OK to close the dialog box.

These steps make sure that none of the styles used in the Microsoft Word document accidentally find their way into your document.

If you accidentally flow text into your previously selected frame, choose Edit > Undo.

4 InDesign CS5 displays a preview of the file you are importing. The preview is located inside the loaded cursor. With the cursor loaded with text, you can preview the first few sentences of the text being imported. Click just below the headline text frame. Text fills the column.

Flowing text into a column.

You have successfully placed a story in the first column, but there is more type than fits into this frame. You can tell this because a red plus sign that appears in the bottom-right corner of the text frame indicating that there is overset text. In the next exercise, you will thread the text from this frame to another frame.

Threading text between frames

As you discovered in Lesson 1, text frames contain two small boxes that let you link text between frames, allowing stories to flow between columns or between pages. At the top-left corner of a text frame is the In Port, and at the bottom-right corner of the text frame is the Out Port. You will be using the Out Port of this text frame to thread it to another frame.

Anatomy of a Text Frame

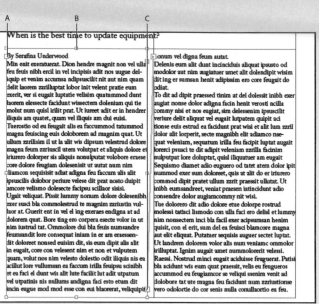

*A. In Port. **B**. Handles for resizing frame. **C**. Out Port.*

The arrow within the In Port or Out Port indicates that text flows from another frame. Choose View > Show Text Threads to display links connected to the selected frame. The arrow shows that text continues in another frame. The Out Port may also display a red plus sign (+), indicating that there is overset text that does not fit in the frame, or it may be empty, indicating that all text fits within this frame.

1 Choose the Selection tool (⬉) from the Tools panel.

2 Click the red plus sign in the bottom-right corner of the text frame. This is the Out Port, and the red plus sign indicates that there is overset text that does not fit in this frame. After clicking the Out Port, the cursor is ready to link to another text frame so that the story can continue.

The Out Port showing overset text.

3 Move the cursor to the second column, positioning the cursor under the headline. Starting in the top-left side of the column on the right side of the page, click and drag to the bottom-right side of the column. The two text frames are now linked.

4 If necessary, choose View > Extras > Show Text Threads. InDesign displays the link between the two frames. Choose View > Extras > Hide Text Threads to stop displaying the linked frames. Linked frames are visible only when one of the frames in the link is selected.

5 Choose File > Save to save your work.

Using semi-autoflow to link several text frames

Clicking the Out Port to link every text frame is not efficient with longer documents. You can hold down the Alt (Windows) or Option (Mac OS) key when linking or importing text so that you can place text into one frame, then move to the next frame to continue linking. This allows you to link multiple text frames without needing to click the Out Port of each frame.

1 In the Pages panel, double-click the page 4 icon to center the page in the workspace.

2 Choose the Selection tool (✹) from the Tools panel and click anywhere in the pasteboard to make sure that there is nothing selected, or choose Edit > Deselect All.

3 Choose File > Place. In the Place dialog box, navigate to the id03lessons folder and select the id0302.doc file. Deselect the *Show Import Options* checkbox, and then click Open.

4 With the loaded cursor, press and hold down Alt (Windows) or Option (Mac OS), and then click in the first column, just below the headline. Release the Alt or Option key.

The text flows into the first column and the cursor is automatically loaded, so that you can link this column to another frame without needing to click the Out Port.

5 In the second column, click and drag to draw a new frame below the image of the Data Center Server. The text flows into the new frame.

Linking to an existing text frame

If you have an existing frame that you want to link text into, first click the Out Port in the frame containing the overset text. Then move the cursor over the existing text frame and click anywhere within the frame. This is common if you are linking to frames created on master pages.

Linking the text to a new frame.

Changing the number of columns in a text frame

You can change the size and shape of a text frame at any time. You will start by making a new text frame, and then you will resize it.

1   Choose the Selection tool (⬚). Click to select the frame you created in the previous exercise, on the right side of the page below the image. Press the Delete key. The first column displays the symbol for overset text.

2   Continuing to use the Selection tool, click to select the text frame in the first column. Move the cursor to the center handle along the right side of the first column. Click and drag to the right, expanding the size of the column so that it overlaps the picture and extends into the right side of the page.

The text now spans the entire width of the page. You will divide this single text frame into two columns.

3   Choose the Type tool (T) from the Tools panel. In the Paragraph Formatting Options section of the Control panel, type **2** for the number of columns (▥), then press Enter (Windows) or Return (Mac OS).

4   Still in the Paragraph Formatting Options section of the Control panel, type **.167 in** in the gutter field (▥), which sets the distance between the columns. Press Enter/Return.

Setting the number of columns
and gutter distance.

5   The text does not flow over the image because the image has text wrap applied to it, causing the text to flow around the image. See Lesson 5, "Working with Graphics," for more on text wrap.

6   Choose File > Save to save your work.

When you automatically flow text, InDesign creates new frames based on where you click inside the margin guides. To flow text automatically, press and hold the Shift key as you place or flow text. InDesign automatically generates enough frames to flow all the text based on the column guides defined for each page.

Baseline grid

The baseline grid allows you to align text in a layout so that text in various columns has a consistent position on the page. You will view the baseline grid, change the grid settings, and align the text to the baseline grid.

Viewing and changing the baseline grid

1 To view the baseline grid, choose View > Grids & Guides > Show Baseline Grid.

The baseline grid guides may not be visible when viewing the document below 100 percent.

Viewing the baseline grid.

It is a good idea to create the baseline grid with an increment or line using the same space as the leading of your body copy. You will now change the increment for the baseline grid.

2 Select the Type tool (T) from the Tools panel and click in the body text in either of the columns on page 4.

3 In the Control panel, press the Character Formatting Controls button; notice that the Leading (⒜) is set to 14.4 pt. You will enter this value inside the Baseline Grid Preferences.

4 Choose Edit > Preferences > Grids (Windows), or InDesign > Preferences > Grids (Mac OS). In the Grids Preferences dialog box, type **14.4 pt** in the Increment Every text field. Click OK to close the Preferences dialog box.

The grid now increments at the same interval as the leading. You will now align the text to the baseline grid.

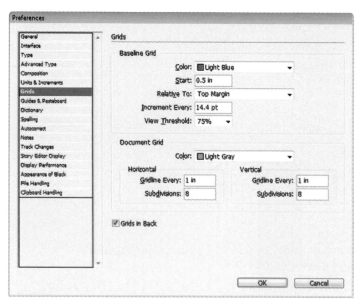

Changing the Increment Every value defines the spacing for the baseline grid.

5 Choose Edit > Select All, then press the Paragraph Formatting Controls button (¶) in the Control panel.

6 In the Control panel, press the Align to Baseline Grid button (≡). The selected text in both columns aligns to the baseline grid.

7 Choose View > Grids & Guides > Hide Baseline Grid, and then choose File > Save to save your work.

Adding story jumps

If stories continue from one page to another within a document, you will want to direct the reader to the appropriate page where the story continues. If you type in **Please see page**, and then manually enter a page number, there is room for error, especially if the page changes.

You will use a page marker on page 2 showing that the story continues on page 5. There are text frames prepared for you to enter the marker. These frames with the Previous and Next page markers need to touch the linked text frames, and they have already been created for you. You will enter in the marker and see how InDesign displays the linked page information.

1   In the Pages panel, navigate to page 2 by double-clicking the page 2 icon.

2   At the bottom-right corner of the text frame is a small frame containing the text *Please see page*. Select the Type tool (T) from the Tools panel and place the cursor directly after the word page in this text frame.

3   Press the space bar once to put a space between the word page and the marker you will insert.

4   Choose Type > Insert Special Character > Markers > Next Page Number. This marker displays the number 5 because the larger text frame it is touching links to page 5. Now you will add the Previous page number to advise the readers where the story originates.

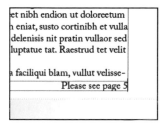

et nibh endion ut doloreetum
h eniat, susto cortinibh et vulla
delenisis nit pratin vullaor sed
luptatue tat. Raestrud tet velit

a faciliqui blam, vullut velisse–
Please see page 5

The text frame with the Next Page marker.

5   In the lower-left corner of the workspace, click the page drop-down menu to navigate to page 5. You can use this method or the Pages panel to easily move between pages.

6   Using the Type tool, place the cursor after the word *page* in the *From page* text frame.

7   Press the space bar to put a space between the words and the marker.

8   Choose Type > Insert Special Character > Markers > Previous Page Number. The number 2 appears because the text in the adjacent frame is linked from page 2.

9   Choose File > Save to save your work.

Using styles to format text

Styles save time when you're working with text that shares the same look and feel across a document. If you decide that your body text should be a different size or font, styles let you make the change in one location, avoiding the need to make changes on every page. Additionally, styles make it easy to keep a consistent design, as you can use styles to apply multiple text attributes in a single click.

Creating a headline and applying a style

In this exercise, you will create a style and apply it to a headline.

1   In the Pages panel, double-click the page 2 icon.

2   Select the Type tool (T) from the Tools panel.

3   Highlight the headline *What is the next cell phone innovation?*

4 Choose Type > Paragraph Styles or click the Paragraph Styles button in the panel docking area. The Paragraph Styles panel opens.

5 Press the panel menu button (▾≣) in the upper corner of the Paragraph Styles panel and choose New Paragraph Style. In the Style Name text field, type **Headline**, and then click OK.

The new style contains the text attributes from where the cursor was located when you created the new style, including font, style, color, and spacing.

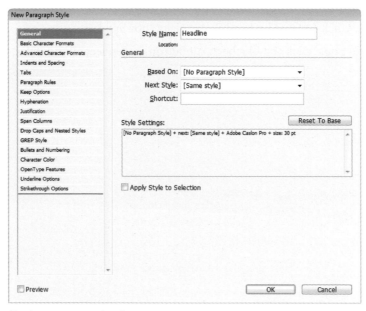

Creating a new paragraph style.

6 Select the Headline style in the Paragraph Styles panel to apply the style to the text. The appearance of the text does not change, but the text is now attached to the style. If the style is updated, the appearance of this headline will also update.

When you create a new style, you can also have InDesign apply it to the current selection. In the General section of the New Paragraph Style dialog box, select the Apply Style to Selection checkbox.

7 Click to place the cursor in the headline *When is the best time to update equipment?* located on page 3. In the Paragraph Styles panel, select the Headline style to apply it. The headline is formatted with the paragraph style you created.

Importing styles from other documents

You can import styles from one InDesign document to another, making it possible to share formatting across various documents, and keeping your brand identity and style consistent across multiple types of documents. In this exercise, you will import a Drop Cap style from another document and use the style in this document.

1 In the Paragraph Styles panel, press the panel menu button (▾≣) and choose Load Paragraph Styles. You will locate a file from which to import a style.

2 In the Open a File dialog box, navigate to the id03lessons folder and select the id0301_done.indd file. Click Open. The Load Styles dialog box appears.

3 In the Load Styles dialog box, click the Uncheck All button to deselect all the styles, because you will only import one specific style. Select the *Drop Cap* checkbox to select only this one style.

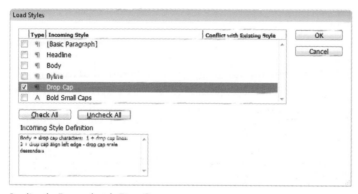

Loading the Paragraph style Drop Cap.

4 Click OK. Drop Cap is now added to the styles in the Paragraph Styles panel in your document. In the next exercise, you will update an existing style, and then apply the Drop Cap style.

Redefining styles

You will now update the Body paragraph style to contain a new attribute, which will align the text to the baseline grid.

1 If necessary, navigate or scroll to view page 2.

2 Choose the Type tool (T) and click in the text frame containing the story on page 2; then choose Edit > Select All.

3 Select the Body style in the Paragraph Styles panel to apply this style to all the selected paragraphs.

4   Move your cursor over the top center of the oval until you see a plus sign appear next to the cursor, and then click once.

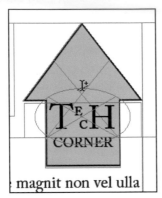

The cursor changes to indicate that you are able to place text on the path.

5   Type **HIGH**, and then highlight the text using the Type on a Path tool by clicking and dragging or double-clicking to select the word.

6   In the Paragraph Formatting Controls section of the Control panel, press the Align Center button (≡). You will adjust the exact position of the text in the next steps, as the text is likely upside-down along the bottom of the circle.

7   Choose the Selection tool (ⸯ) from the Tools panel. Notice that there are two vertical handles that appear directly to the left of where you clicked on the path. These handles mark the starting and ending points for the text on the path.

8   Select the left-most line and drag it clockwise, stopping when the line is vertically centered along the right half of the oval. If the text moves inside the oval, choose Edit > Undo and repeat the process, carefully following the oval as you drag clockwise. Be careful to not click the boxes when you move the handles, as these boxes are the In and Out Ports, which are used for flowing text, as you learned earlier in this lesson.

9   Take the top line that marks where the text starts, and drag it counterclockwise, positioning it so it is vertically centered along the left half of the oval.

Because you had already centered the text, aligning the start and end points of the text to the opposite sides of the circle lets you know that the text is centered correctly.

The new start and end points of the text.

10   Choose File > Save to save your work.

When placing text on an oval or circle as you did in the previous exercise, if you ultimately want the text centered on the path, begin the process by clicking on the bottom of the circle with the Type on a Path tool (⤳). Because doing so causes the text to begin and end at the bottom of the shape, you can quickly center the text by simply setting the paragraph alignment to align center.

Importing text from Microsoft Word

When flowing a Microsoft Word document into InDesign, the default setting, *Remove Styles and Formatting from Text and Tables,* automatically eliminates all the styles applied to the file in Word. The text comes into your document using the style set in the Paragraph Styles panel.

1   Navigate to page 6 in the document.

2 Choose File > Place. In the Place dialog box, navigate to the id03lessons folder and select the id0302.doc file. Select the *Show Import Options* checkbox, which is located toward the bottom of the Place dialog box, and then click Open. The Microsoft Word Import Options dialog box opens.

The Show Import Options and Replace Selected Item check box.

To open the Import Options dialog box automatically when opening a file, hold down the Shift key while you click Open.

3 In the Microsoft Word Import Options dialog box, select the *Preserve Styles and Formatting from Text and Tables* radio button. This maintains styles and other text formatting in the imported file. Also select the *Customize Style Import* radio button.

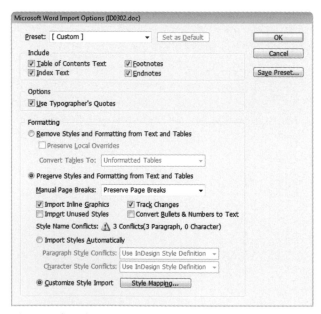

The Microsoft Word Import Options dialog box.

About Microsoft Word import options

Any Table of Contents text, index text, footnotes, and endnotes can be brought from Microsoft Word into InDesign. By default, the *Use Typographer's Quotes* option is checked, which changes all quotes to typographer's (curly) quotes. This means that every inch- and foot-mark quote will be converted as well.

If the *Remove Styles and Formatting from Text and Tables* radio button is selected, all text will be imported and formatted using the default Paragraph style (usually Basic Paragraph) for that document. If you want to keep all the character attributes that were applied in Word, select the *Preserve Local Overrides* checkbox.

If you select the *Preserve Styles and Formatting from Text and Tables* radio button, the styles created in Word are imported into your document, and the text adopts the imported styles, trying to mimic the styles from Word. However, if you create a template in Word that contains styles with the same names as the styles in your InDesign document, there will be paragraph style conflicts upon importing, and the imported text will use InDesign's style definition by default. This means that, regardless of how text looked in Word, once imported into InDesign, the text is formatted with InDesign's styles if the Word document and the InDesign document have styles with the same names.

4   Click the Style Mapping button at the bottom of the dialog box, next to the *Customize Style Import* radio button. The Style Mapping dialog box appears.

Microsoft Word Import Options should show that the Body and Byline styles from the Word document have mapped to the InDesign styles with the same names. Identically named styles are automatically mapped when you use Style Mapping.

5   The dialog box shows that the Microsoft Word style *Normal* is mapped to a style in this InDesign document. Next to Normal, select the New Paragraph Style and choose Basic Paragraph style from the drop-down menu. This causes the text in the Word document that uses the style Normal to be formatted using the Basic Paragraph style once it is imported into InDesign.

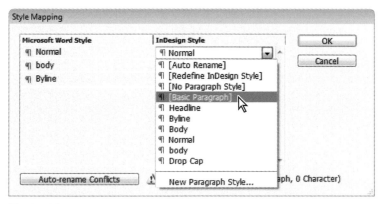

Mapping styles.

6 Click OK to close the Style Mapping dialog box. Click OK again to accept the Microsoft Word Import Options. The cursor is loaded with text that is ready to be placed with already-applied paragraph styles.

7 Click in the left column on page 6 to place the text.

Missing fonts

Fonts, like graphics, are not embedded within an InDesign document. If you receive an InDesign document from a colleague, you need the same fonts that they used when creating the document. In this exercise, you will import text from a Microsoft Word document that uses a font that you probably do not have on your computer, and you will fix the font errors that occur as a result of the font not being available.

By default, InDesign highlights missing fonts in pink to alert you to the fact that the font being displayed is not the same as what was used when the text was originally formatted.

Finding and fixing missing fonts

1 In the Pages panel, double-click the page 5 icon to navigate to it.

2 Select the Type tool (T) in the Tools panel.

3 Click inside the empty text frame at the top of page 5.

4 Choose File > Place. In the Place dialog box, navigate to the id03lessons folder and select the id0303.doc file. Select the *Show Import Options* checkbox if it is not selected, and then click Open.

5 Confirm the *Preserve Styles and Formatting from Text and Tables* radio button is selected. Click OK.

The Missing Font dialog box appears because you do not have the font Futura Bold installed on your computer.

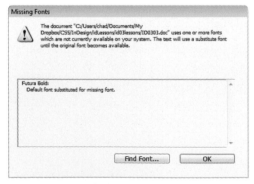

The Missing Font dialog box.

6 Click the Find Font button. The Find Font dialog box opens. Highlight the font Futura Bold by clicking on it in the Fonts in Document section. Notice the warning icon (⚠) next to the font name. This indicates that the font is missing.

7 In the Replace With section at the bottom of the dialog box, highlight the text in the Font Family text field and type **Adobe Caslon Pro**. You are going to replace Futura Bold with Adobe Caslon Pro Regular. If you do not have Adobe Caslon Pro Regular, you may use another font that is available on your computer.

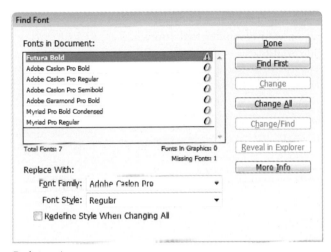

Replacing a font.

8 Click Change All. To see the missing font replaced, click Done.

9 Choose File > Save to save your work, and then choose File > Close.

Congratulations! You have completed the lesson.

Self study

1 Starting on page 1, navigate through the document and apply styles to all text, including body, byline, drop cap, and headline.

2 Change the color of the body text and redefine the style.

3 Turn on Show Text Threads and using the Selection tool (⬉) to select the linked text frames on page 5, create a new page at the end of the document and drag the frames to the new page. Return to page 2 and see if the story jump automatically updates.

4 Make a new headline box on page 7 and type in a fictitious headline. Format the headline using the headline style as a starting point. You may need to adjust the size depending on how many words you enter.

Review

Questions

1 If you have a font that doesn't have the style of italic, can you make it italic?

2 Can you flow text into an existing frame?

3 Can you divide one text frame into multiple columns?

4 How can you add Previous and Next page markers?

5 What is the best way to see changes that have been made to text in a given story?

Answers

1 No, you cannot create a false italic style using InDesign. You need the actual font with the italic style to make this change, which is also true for other styles, including bold or outline. One exception to this is the ability to apply a skew or false italic using the Skew button (*T*) in the Character formatting panel. Although this is possible, it's typically not recommended because it is not a true italic font.

2 Yes, you can flow text into existing frames, including frames that already contain text.

3 Yes, you can have many columns in a single frame. You make column adjustments in the Control panel or by choosing Object > Text Frame Options.

4 Choose Type > Insert Special Characters > Markers or use the context menus when entering the text.

5 Use the new Track Changes feature in InDesign CS5. Enable Track Changes for a story using the Track Changes panel, and view changes made in the Story Editor.

Lesson 4

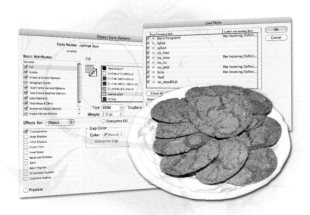

What you'll learn in this lesson:

- Defining and applying paragraph, character, and object styles

- Using nested styles

- Globally updating styles

- Loading styles from another document

- Using Quick Apply

- Organizing styles into groups

Working with Styles

Styles streamline the formatting of your documents, making it easier to create a consistent design across text and objects. Styles also help simplify adjustments, as you can change a style and update all items that use the style.

Starting up

Before starting, make sure that your tools and panels are consistent by resetting your preferences. See "Resetting the InDesign workspace and preferences" on page 3.

You will work with several files from the id04lessons folder in this lesson. Make sure that you have copied the id04lessons folder onto your hard drive from the Digital Classroom DVD. See "Loading lesson files" on page 4. This lesson may be easier to follow if the id04lessons folder is on your desktop.

See Lesson 4 in action!

Use the accompanying video to gain a better understanding of how to use some of the features shown in this lesson. The video tutorial for this lesson can be found on the included DVD.

The project

You will discover how styles simplify the design process by using them to enhance the look of a two-page recipe layout. You will work with paragraph, character, and object styles.

Creating styles adds a bit of work at the start of a project, but the planning saves an enormous amount of time and effort as you design and format your document. If you need to make changes, styles make it a quick and easy process.

You will also discover how to import styles from other documents, allowing you to re-use design work done in those other documents, or keep a consistent identity across multiple files. You will also learn how to organize your styles using style sets, along with techniques for quickly applying styles.

Style types

There are several types of styles you can use when designing and formatting your documents: these include paragraph, character, object, and GREP, as well as table and cell styles. Each type of style applies to a different page element. All these style types speed up the process of formatting and changing the appearance of text and page elements, especially when creating larger documents.

- **Paragraph styles** define text attributes that affect an entire paragraph of text, including line spacing (leading), indents, and alignment. They may also include character attributes, and apply to an entire paragraph. These styles are used for things like headlines or body copy.

- **Character styles** contain only character formatting attributes, such as typeface, size, and color. These attributes apply only to selected text. Character styles are used for things such as proper names that are formatted uniquely, or technical terms that might have a different style to call attention to them within a document.

- **Object styles** apply to page elements such as boxes and lines in a layout. Sidebars or picture frames can use object styles to make them consistent.

- **GREP styles** use GREP expressions to format specific content within a paragraph. For example, using a GREP style, you could find a text pattern such as a phone number, and format it using a character style to make the text a specific color. GREP styles are extremely powerful, as they can format text that appears anywhere within a given paragraph.

- **Table and Cell styles** apply to various portions of a table. This lesson is focused primarily on using paragraph, character, and object styles. Table styles are covered in more detail in Lesson 6, "Creating and Using Tables."

InDesign includes only one style for each style type, so you will create customized style definitions for your documents. Once you create styles, you can import them into other documents, allowing you to define the formatting one time and re-use it across multiple files. You can even define the styles to be available for all future documents you create.

Paragraph styles

Paragraph styles generally include both character and paragraph attributes. When you apply a paragraph style to text, all text within a paragraph is formatted. With one click you can use a paragraph style to specify the font, size, alignment, spacing, and other attributes used in the paragraph. Keep in mind that InDesign uses a paragraph return to identify each paragraph. This is why you shouldn't use a standard return to force a word to the next line in a paragraph, as InDesign treats this as a completely separate paragraph and can cause your styles to "break" or work improperly. In this lesson, you'll start by defining the style, and then you'll apply it to text.

Defining a paragraph style

When building styles, it is useful to see what the style will look like when it is applied. You can format a paragraph, and then use the formatting as the foundation for an InDesign paragraph style. You'll start by building a paragraph style for the body text used in a cookie recipe.

1   Choose File > Open. In the Open dialog box, navigate to the id04lessons folder and select the id0401.indd file. Click Open. A two-page spread from a cookbook opens, displaying pages 72 and 73, as noted in the Pages panel and in the bottom-left corner of the workspace.

2   Choose Advanced from the workspace drop-down menu, or choose Window > Workspace > Advanced, to display the panels and menu options used in this lesson.

3   Choose File > Save As. In the Save As dialog box, navigate to the id04lessons folder and type **id0401_work.indd** in the Name text field. Click Save.

4   Click the Paragraph Styles button in the dock on the right side of the workspace to open the Paragraph Styles panel. The styles used in this document are listed. This document contains four styles: basic paragraph and callout large, along with two recipe-specific styles, rec_steps and rec_yield.

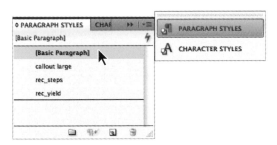

The Paragraph Styles panel lists all available styles for formatting paragraphs.

5   Select the Type tool (T) from the Tools panel. Position the cursor over the first paragraph of text located in the middle column on the left-hand page. The paragraph starts with the text, *The smell of fresh baked cookies...* Click four times to select the entire paragraph.

6 Press the Character Formatting Controls button (**A**) in the top-left corner of the Control panel located at the top of the workspace, to display the character options. Choose Minion Pro from the Font drop-down menu, and, if necessary, choose Regular from the Font Style drop-down menu. Set the size to 10 points from the Font Size drop-down menu.

Setting the character formatting options in the Control panel.

7 Press the Paragraph Formatting Controls button (¶) in the Control panel to display the paragraph formatting options, and type **0.2** in the First Line Left Indent (⁺≣) text field. Press Enter (Windows) or Return (Mac OS) to indent the paragraph by 0.2 inches.

*In the paragraph formatting options section, type **0.2** in the First Line Left Indent text field.*

8 With the paragraph still selected, press the panel menu button (•≣) in the upper-right corner of the Paragraph Styles panel and choose New Paragraph Style.

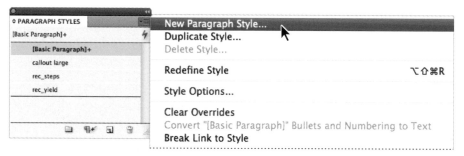

Use the Paragraph Styles panel menu to create a new style.

9 The New Paragraph Style dialog box appears. In the New Paragraph Style dialog box, type **body** in the Style Name text field, click to select the Apply Style to Selection check box, and then click OK to establish the name of the new style. The body style is added to the list of styles in the Paragraph Styles panel.

Choosing the *Apply Style to Selection* option also links the selected text to the new style. If the style is updated, the original text will reflect any formatting changes.

10 Save the file by choosing File > Save.

Applying a paragraph style

You will now apply this new paragraph style to text in the document. To format a single paragraph, use the Type tool to place the cursor within the paragraph, then choose the paragraph style from the Paragraph Styles panel. To format multiple paragraphs, select them and then select the style you want to apply.

1   With the cursor still within the recipe, choose Edit > Select All, or use the keyboard shortcut Ctrl+A (Windows) or Command+A (Mac OS), to select all the text in the frame.

2   In the Paragraph Styles panel, select the body style to apply the style to all selected text. The entire recipe now uses the same character and paragraph formatting as the initial paragraph you formatted.

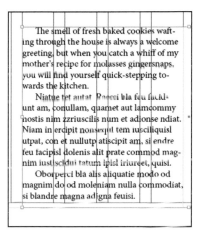

Format all the text within the text frame with the body style.

Character styles

Building character styles is similar to creating paragraph styles. You'll start by formatting text, and then you'll define the character style based upon the attributes of the text you have formatted. Character styles affect only character attributes, such as font and point size. Character styles are typically used for words that need special treatment, such as bold, italics, or a unique font, and only apply to selected text.

Defining a character style

On the right page of the document (page 73), you will make the text bold at the start of each step. You'll format the first two steps, and then define a style to apply to the others.

1   Using the Type tool (T), highlight the word *Create* under the Yield section on page 73 of the recipe layout.

2   Press the Character Format Controls button (A) in the Control panel, and then choose Bold from the Font Style drop-down menu. Keep the text selected.

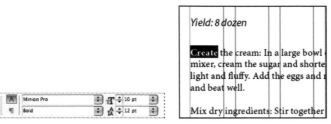

Use the character portion of the Control panel to set the type style.

3   Press the Character Styles button (A) in the dock on the right side of the workspace to open the Character Styles panel.

4   With the bold text still highlighted on the page, press the panel menu button (-≡) in the upper-right corner of the Character Styles panel, and choose New Character Style.

5   In the New Character Style dialog box, type **Bold** in the Style name text field. Note that the only attribute being defined by this style in the Style Settings section is "bold". This is because this is the only attribute that is different from the paragraph style that is also applied to this text. This concept makes the character style very powerful because it can be applied to any text regardless of what font is currently applied to the text. Click OK to create a new style. The new style name appears in the Character Styles panel.

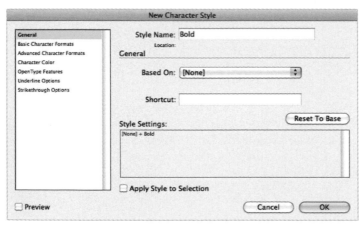

Bold is the only attribute being defined in the character style because that is the only attribute that is different from the paragraph style that was previously applied to the text.

6   Choose File > Save to save your work.

Applying a character style

Applying character styles is similar to applying paragraph styles. You highlight the text you want to format, and then click the style name to apply the style.

1 On page 73 of the layout, highlight *Create the cream:*.

2 In the Character Styles panel, select the style Bold to apply the new style to the selected text.

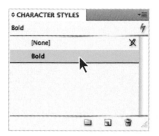 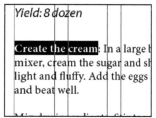

Apply the character style.

3 Highlight the phrase *Mix dry ingredients:* and apply the Bold style by selecting it in the Character Styles panel.

Note that character styles have more strength or weight than Paragraph Styles. That is to say, when both a character and a paragraph style are applied to the same text, the attributes defined in the character style will take precedence over the attributes defined in the paragraph style, as shown in the exercise above where the rec_steps paragraph style and the Bold character style are both applied to the same text. The Bold attribute of the character style is being applied even though the rec_steps paragraph style is formatting the text using the Regular attribute.

Using nested styles

Nested styles combine character styles with paragraph styles, allowing you to apply both character and paragraph styles in a single step. For example, you can use a nested style to make the first word of an introductory paragraph bold and blue, while the rest of the paragraph is regular and black.

You will modify one of the paragraph styles so it also includes a character style for the initial portion of the paragraph, creating a nested style.

1 With the Type tool (T) selected, click in the bottom paragraph on the right page, which starts with the text, *Bake in oven*. If the Paragraph Styles panel is closed, click the Paragraph Styles button to open it, or choose Type > Paragraph Styles.

2 In the Paragraph Styles panel, double-click on the rec_steps style to open the Paragraph Style Options dialog box.

3 Select the *Drop Caps and Nested Styles* option along the left side of the Paragraph Style Options dialog box, and then click the New Nested Style button.

4 In the Nested Styles section's drop–down menu, choose Bold.

5 Click to select *Words* next to *Through 1*, located to the right of the Bold style you added in the Nested Styles section of the dialog box. In the text field that appears, change the word *Words* to *:* by pressing the Colon key.

The Bold style will apply to all text up to, and including, the colon (:). You can define where nested styles stop, or you can string together multiple nested styles so that different list entries can be formatted automatically.

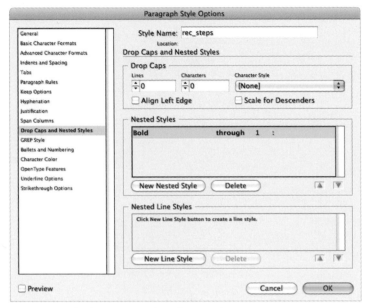

Creating a nested style automates applying character styles.

If you do not replace Words with a colon, only the first word of the recipe step will be bold.

6 Click the *Preview* checkbox in the lower-left corner of the dialog box to view the changes in your document. If necessary, reposition the dialog box to view your page.

7 Click OK to close the dialog box.

8 To ensure that all of the formatting is being applied using the nested style, select all four paragraphs under the Yield: 8 dozen heading and choose none from the Character Styles panel. A common problem made by many users when working with nested styles is manually applying character styles to the text. This will prevent the nested style from being able to format the text within a paragraph properly.

9 Choose File > Save to save your work. Keep the file open for the next part of the lesson.

Globally updating styles

As you have seen, styles make it easier to apply consistent formatting to your text. You have seen how to apply multiple attributes to text in a single click. Styles also save time when you need to change or update formatting. You can modify a style definition and automatically update all text that is associated with a style. In this exercise, you will change the size of the recipe steps. By making a single update, all text using the rec_steps style will be updated. Although you are working with two pages in this example, the same time-saving technique works just as easily on documents with hundreds of pages.

1 Click in the bottom paragraph on the right page, which starts with the text, *Bake in oven*.

2 In the Paragraph Styles panel, the rec_steps paragraph style should be highlighted, indicating that the style is applied to the paragraph where the cursor is positioned. Double-click the style to open the Paragraph Style Options dialog box.

3 Click to select Basic Character Formats on the left side of the Paragraph Style Options dialog box.

4 Choose 11 points from the Size drop-down menu, and then choose Auto from the Leading drop-down menu to change the vertical line spacing.

5 Select the *Character Color* option along the left side of the dialog box, and then choose *cookie color* from the list of available colors.

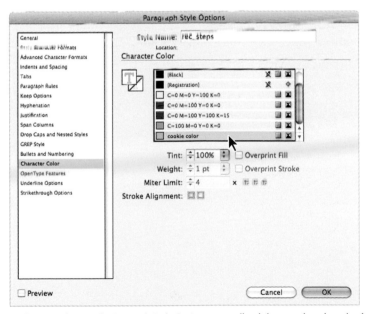

Updating attributes in the Paragraph Style Options causes all styled paragraphs to be updated.

6 If necessary, click the *Preview* checkbox in the lower-left corner to see the changes in the document as you make them.

7 Click OK to commit the changes and close the dialog box. All text formatted with the rec_steps style has been changed.

The updated text after the paragraph style is changed.

Loading styles from another document

After you create a style, you can use it in other InDesign documents. This lets you reuse your work in other files, keeping their appearance consistent, or simply saving time. The Paragraph Styles and Character Styles panel menus both include an option to load text styles from other documents. Here you will import previously created styles used in another recipe.

In this exercise, you'll import some new styles into the gingersnaps recipe as practice.

1 With the document open, choose Load All Text Styles from the Paragraph Styles panel menu (·≡). The Open a File dialog box appears.

In cases when you only want to use paragraph or character styles, you can choose to load only these styles by selecting either Load Paragraph Styles or Load Character Styles from the respective panel menus. For this example, you will continue to load all styles.

2 In the Open a File dialog box, choose the file id0402.indd from the id04lessons folder. This is the document from which you'll import the styles. Click Open, and the Load Styles dialog box appears.

To see the entire contents of the Load Styles dialog box, you may need to click and drag the lower-right corner until all the options are visible.

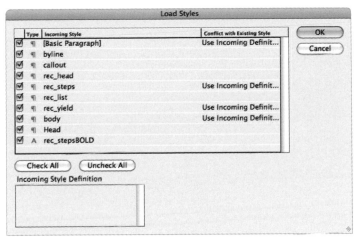

The Load Styles dialog box appears after selecting a document from which you want to import styles.

If you want to import styles that use the same name as existing styles in your document, the Load Styles dialog box lets you choose how to handle the conflicting names. The Use Incoming Definition option causes the imported style definition to be used. The Auto-Rename option causes the imported style to be renamed, allowing you to use both the existing and imported styles. Click the words Use Incoming Definition to see the drop-down list, where you can change it to the Auto-Rename option.

The Incoming Style Definition box below each style's name displays the highlighted style's definition for easy comparison.

3 Click the Uncheck All button, as this deselects all the styles in the Load Styles dialog box. Select the rec_head, rec_list, and Head styles by clicking the check box next to each respective style.

You can import all the styles in a document or only a few. By deselecting certain styles, you prevent them from being imported into your document.

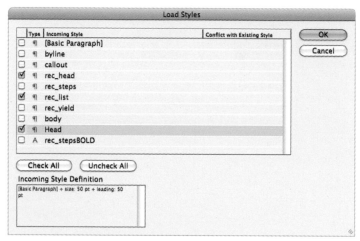

Check the styles you want to import into your document.

4 Click OK to close the Load Styles dialog box. The Paragraph Styles panel now includes the imported styles rec_head, rec_list, and Head, which can be used in this document.

5 Choose File > Save to save your work.

Quick Apply

As your list of styles grows, navigating to find a specific style can be time-consuming. If you perform editing work, you'll appreciate the ability to efficiently apply styles using Quick Apply. Using a special key command, you'll type the first few letters of a style's name and be able to quickly apply the style.

1 Using the Type tool (T), click in the *Molasses Won't Slow Eating These Gingersnaps* text box at the top of the left page.

2 Press Ctrl+Enter (Windows) or Command+Return (Mac OS) to open the Quick Apply window.

You can also use the Quick Apply button (✦) located in the upper-right corner of the Paragraph Styles, Character Styles, or Control panels.

3 Type **hea** in the window's search field. The Head style appears at the top of the list. Press the Enter (Windows) or Return (Mac OS) key on your keyboard to apply the style to the text. The Quick Apply window closes.

Because paragraph styles format an entire paragraph, you don't have to highlight the text. Simply click in the paragraph, and then apply the paragraph style.

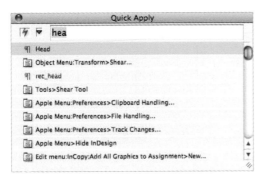

The Quick Apply window makes applying styles faster and easier.

4 Click in the box at the top of the right page, placing the cursor within the phrase, *Cookie Color*.

5 Click the Quick Apply button in the Control panel and type **rec** in the text field. Three styles starting with rec appear in the list. If necessary, use the arrow keys on your keyboard to highlight the rec_head style if it isn't already highlighted, and then press Enter (Windows) or Return (Mac OS) to apply the style.

You can also use Quick Apply to access many commands. Quick Apply lets you access a command even if you have forgotten the menu or panel where the command is located—you need to know only the name of the command you want to access.

3 In the Vertical Justification section of the Text Frame Options dialog box, choose Center from the Align drop-down menu to center the text vertically within the frame. Click OK to apply the formatting.

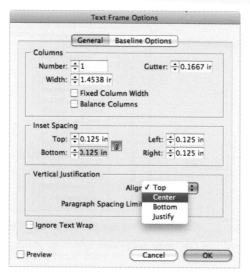

The Text Frame Options dialog box lets you format your objects.

4 Click the Object Styles button in the dock on the right side of the workspace or choose Window > Object Styles to open the Object Styles panel.

You can click and drag the bottom-right corner of the Object Styles panel to display more of the available styles.

5 With the Cookie Color frame still selected, click the Object Styles panel menu button (-≡) and choose New Object Style. The New Object Style dialog box opens.

6 In the New Object Style dialog box, type **callout box** in the Style Name text field and click the *Apply Style to Selection* checkbox.

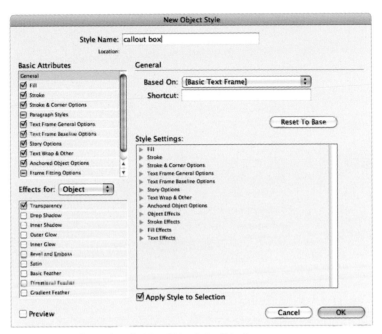

Name your new object style in the New Object Style dialog box.

7 Click OK to create the new object style, and then choose File > Save to save your work. Keep the file open.

Applying an object style

Applying an object style is similar to applying text styles. You start by selecting the object to be formatted, and then choose the style to apply to the object. You will apply the callout box style to another frame in the layout.

1   Using the Selection tool (⭡), select the frames containing the headline and byline on the left page of the layout.

2   Apply the callout box style to the frame by clicking the style in the Object Styles panel.

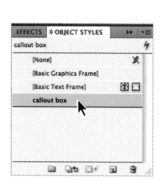

Applying the object style to the text frame containing the headline and byline.

3   Choose File > Save, or press Ctrl+S (Windows) or Command+S (Mac OS), to save your work.

Changing an object style

As with text styles, when you change an object style's definition, you update all elements to which the style is applied. In the following steps, you will update the object style by changing the background color of the frames.

1   With the headline and byline frames still selected, double-click the callout box style name in the Object Styles panel to open the Object Style Options dialog box.

2   In the Basic Attributes section, select the *Fill* option. The available color swatches for this document appear in the Fill section.

3   Choose the swatch named cookie color to add it to the callout box object style. You may
need to scroll through the swatches list to see this color.

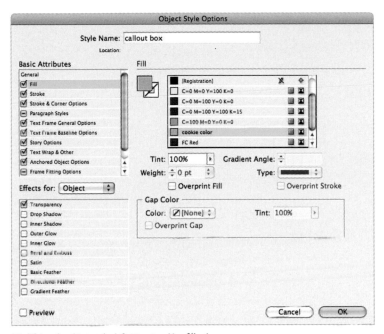

Modifying the object style definition to add a fill color.

4   Click OK. Both frames now reflect the changes to the background color.

Finishing up

As a review, you'll import some more styles and review the process of applying them to
your document.

1   With the id0401_work.indd document open, choose Load All Text Styles from the
Paragraph Styles panel menu. The Open a File dialog box appears.

2   In the Open a File dialog box, choose the file id0402.indd from the id04lessons folder.
Click Open, and the Load Styles dialog box appears.

3   In the Load Styles dialog box, select only the styles named callout and byline to import
these into your document. Click OK to close the dialog box and import the styles.

4   Choose the Type tool (T) from the Tools panel, and then click and drag to select
the ingredients on the right side of the document, selecting from sugar through
cinnamon. In the Paragraph Styles panel, click to apply the paragraph style rec_list to
the ingredients.

5 Click to place the cursor within the words *Molasses Gingersnaps* located above the ingredients; then click the rec_head style in the Paragraph Styles panel to apply the style to this text.

6 Click and place the cursor within the words *by Larry Happy* located at the bottom of the left page, then click the byline style to apply it to this text.

7 Choose File > Save to save your work.

GREP Styles

GREP was discussed in the lesson titled "Working with Text and Type," where you discovered how powerful GREP can be for finding and changing text in an intelligent way. GREP styles use the same expressions that GREP uses in the Find/Change dialog box; however, GREP styles don't change the content of text, but rather the formatting. In the following exercise, you'll modify an existing style to cause key numbers within text to be displayed in bold to make it easier for the baker to read the baking instructions.

1 Zoom in on the Molasses Gingersnaps recipe, where you'll make a change to the rec_steps paragraph style for the steps in this recipe.

2 Right-click on the rec_steps paragraph style in the Paragraph Styles panel, and choose Edit "rec_steps" to display the Paragraph Style Options dialog box.

3 Click on the GREP Style category on the left side of the dialog box, and then click the New Grep Style button. A new entry is created in the GREP Style section of the dialog box.

4 Next to Apply Style, choose New Character Style from the drop-down menu. Name the Style **Myriad Bold**, then click on the Basic Character Formats section and set the Font Family to Myriad Pro and the Font Style to Bold. Click OK. The new character style you created now displays next to Apply Style.

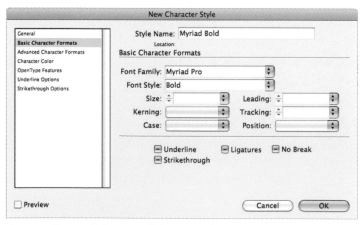

Creating a Character Style dynamically from within the Paragraph Style Options dialog box.

5 Click on the area to the right of To Text and delete any content that is there. Click on the @ symbol to the right and choose Wildcards > Any Digit. This will search for any digit within the text that has the rec_steps Paragraph Style applied to it.

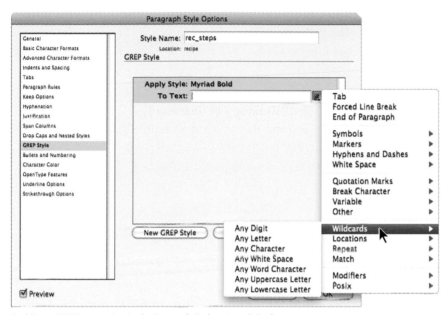

Building a GREP expression in the Paragraph Style options dialog box.

6 Click on the @ symbol again and choose Repeat > One or More Times. This GREP expression looks for any digit that occurs one or more times in a row within the rec_steps styled text. Click OK.

Note that any numeric character that appears within the recipe steps is now bold and uses the font Myriad Pro to make it easier to identify key areas in the steps of the recipe that need special attention. GREP Styles are an amazing way to automatically format text in your document.

Paragraph Style Options

General
Basic Character Formats
Advanced Character Formats
Indents and Spacing
Tabs
Paragraph Rules
Keep Options
Hyphenation
Justification
Span Columns
Drop Caps and Nested Styles
GREP Style
Bullets and Numbering

Style Name: rec_steps
Location: recipe
GREP Style

Apply Style: Myriad Bold
      To Text: \d+

This GREP Style formats any digit within text that has this Paragraph Style applied as Myriad Pro Bold.

7 Choose File > Save to save your work, and then choose File > Close.

Congratulations! You have finished the lesson.

Self study

To practice creating styles, create your own layout using your favorite family recipes. Import the styles from this lesson and apply them to the text and frames in your own recipes. Import the object styles as well.

Review

Questions

1 What is the difference between character and paragraph styles?

2 What is a nested style and why is it used?

3 What is the keyboard shortcut to access the Quick Apply option?

4 If there are multiple styles in a document and scrolling becomes tedious, how can you organize the styles?

Answers

1 Paragraph styles apply to all text between paragraph returns, while character styles apply only to selected text. Character styles do not include paragraph attributes such as indenting or line spacing.

2 A nested style is a paragraph style that also includes one or more character styles, that formats specific areas of a paragraph style. Nested styles allow you to combine multiple formatting steps into a single click.

3 You can apply the Quick Apply option by pressing Ctrl+Enter (Windows) or Command+Return (Mac OS).

4 You can use style groups to organize your styles. They allow you to group together styles and determine which styles are displayed or hidden.

What you'll learn in this lesson:

- Adding graphics to your layout
- Managing links to imported files
- Updating changed graphics
- Using graphics with clipping paths and alpha channels

Working with Graphics

Graphics add depth and style to your documents. You can use InDesign's powerful controls to place and enhance graphics using most common file formats, as well as integrate images from Adobe Illustrator and Photoshop.

Starting up

Before starting, make sure that your tools and panels are consistent by resetting your preferences. See "Resetting the InDesign workspace and preferences" on page 3.

You will work with several files from the id05lessons folder in this lesson. Make sure that you have copied the id05lessons folder onto your hard drive from the Digital Classroom DVD. See "Loading lesson files" on page 4. This lesson may be easier to follow if the id05lessons folder is on your desktop.

See Lesson 5 in action!

Use the accompanying video to gain a better understanding of how to use some of the features shown in this lesson. The video tutorial for this lesson can be found on the included DVD.

The project

In this lesson, you will work on a fictional travel magazine called SoJournal, adding graphics to the layout using different techniques. You will learn how to resize graphics, precisely change positioning, set display quality, and wrap text around graphics. You will also learn how to manage graphics that have been updated, replaced, or are missing.

Understanding how InDesign handles graphics

When you place a graphic into an InDesign layout, the graphic file remains a separate file. Imported images or illustrations are not embedded into the InDesign document, so both the separate graphic files and the InDesign document are necessary for printing, archiving, or sharing your document with collaborators who might need to otherwise manipulate the original files. InDesign keeps track of graphic files used in your InDesign documents using the Links panel, as image files are considered to be linked. This is different from text files that are imported from programs like Microsoft Word or Excel. Text files are placed into the InDesign layout, and the original file is no longer needed to manipulate the text. For every rule there are exceptions, and graphic files can be embedded within an InDesign layout—although this is generally not advisable because it increases the size of the InDesign document and limits the ability to share a graphic for use in other media, such as on the Web or as part of an interactive campaign.

You'll start this lesson by opening a document where images have been imported, but InDesign can no longer locate the image files. You will help InDesign locate the missing files.

Locating missing images

If an image is renamed or moved from its original location after you import it into an InDesign file, InDesign loses the link to the image. Likewise, if you copy an InDesign document to a different computer, and don't transfer the images, InDesign will alert you that linked files are missing.

You'll use the Links panel to reconnect the InDesign layout with a missing image. In the Links panel, missing links display a red warning icon (◉) next to their names, and links that have been updated or edited since they were originally placed in the layout display a yellow warning icon (▲), indicating the original image has been modified. In this exercise, you will fix a link that was broken because the associated files were moved, and also fix a link to a graphic in the layout that was modified.

1   Choose File > Open. In the Open dialog box, navigate to the id05lessons folder and select id0501.indd. Click Open. As the file opens, InDesign displays a message informing you that the document contains links to missing or modified files.

2 Click the Update Links button to update the one modified link.

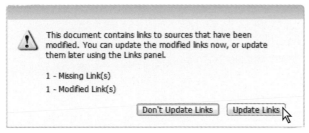

When opening a file with missing or modified links, you can choose Update Links to help reconnect the linked image files with the InDesign layout.

Depending on which workspace you have active, the Links panel will display in the middle of your screen or on the right side of the screen in the panel dock. Notice the citytravel.psd file displays a red warning icon—indicating that the link is missing—while the id0507.psd file displays no icons. If you had not updated the links, it would display a yellow warning icon—indicating that the link had been changed since it was placed into the layout. In the next part of the lesson, you will work with the Links panel to discover how to update image files that are missing.

When using the Update Links option, any other broken links located in the folder are also updated when you update the first linked item. For example, if an entire folder containing images is relocated, you can update the link to the first missing item using the Update Links option, eliminating the need to update multiple broken links individually. You can also use the Relink to folder command from the Links panel menu.

3 Choose File > Save As. In the Save As dialog box, navigate to the id05lessons folder and type **id0501_work.indd** in the File name text field. Click Save and keep the file open.

Working with the Links panel

When you import an image into your layout, InDesign doesn't copy the complete image into your document file. Instead, it saves a reference, or a link, to the location of the original graphic file so it can access the image when necessary. This process lets you import many files into your layout without significantly increasing the file size of the document. For example, you can create a catalog with hundreds of images, but the InDesign document remains a small file with many linked images.

Because graphic files are generally linked, and not embedded within the InDesign file, you need to know how to manage linked graphic files. The Links panel lets you manage these links, find files in the document, find missing files, and update graphics in the document when changes are made to the image file. In this exercise, you will fix a link to a previously imported image that has been moved and is missing.

1   If the Links panel isn't open, choose Window > Links to display it or click the Links button (∿) in the panel docking area on the right side of the workspace.

2   Click once on citytravel.psd, and then click the Go To Link button (⟶) at the bottom of the Links panel.

InDesign navigates to the selected image that accompanies the City Travel article.

*The Go To Link button displays a
selected link within the layout.*

3   With the citytravel.psd option still selected in the Links panel, click the Relink button (⟲) at the bottom of the Links panel. In the Locate dialog box that appears, navigate to the links folder in the id05lessons folder and select the citytravel.psd file. Click Open.

The Links panel now displays the list of links without any warning icons. You've updated both a missing link and a modified link.

4   Choose File > Save, or press Ctrl+S (Windows) or Command+S (Mac OS), to save your work. Keep the file open for the next part of the lesson.

When you click the Relink button (⟲) in the Links panel, the Relink All Instances *checkbox appears at the bottom of the Links dialog box. Click this check box, and all instances of the image throughout the document are relinked.*

Understanding the Links Panel

The Links panel displays all imported objects, the color space they use, and where they are used within the file.

A. *Show/Hide Link Information.* B. *Number of Links Selected.*
C. *Relink.* D. *Go to Link.* E. *Update Link.* F. *Edit Original.*

Customizing the Links panel

You can choose to have the Links panel display additional information regarding the links used in your layout.

1 From the Links panel menu (-≡), choose Panel Options.

Use the Panel Options command to customize the display of the Links panel.

2 In the Panel Options dialog box, click to select the *Size* and *Color Space* options in the Show Column located in the center of the dialog box. These options determine which information is displayed in a column within the Links panel.

3 Click OK to close the Panel Options window. The additional information is now displayed within the Links panel.

4 To view the additional information, click the tab at the top of the Links panel, and drag it away from the panel docking area. Click in the lower-right corner of the Links panel and then drag to the right, expanding the width of the panel.

5 Click the heading of each of the items displayed in the Links panel, including Name, Page, Size, and Color Space. As you click each item, the links sort by the selected criteria.

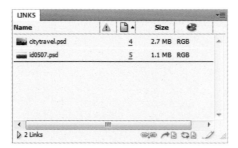

You can customize the information displayed in the Links panel and sort the display by clicking the column titles.

6 Click the Links panel tab and drag the panel over the Pages panel in the dock. When a blue border appears around the edge of the Pages panel, release the mouse to dock the Links panel with the Pages panel.

Adding graphics to your layout

You can add graphics that are created using a number of different programs or use a variety of graphic file types, such as JPEG, EPS, PSD, TIFF, AI, and many others. InDesign lets you import native Photoshop, PDF, and Illustrator files into your layouts. You can also import other InDesign documents (.indd format) into your layouts. In all, InDesign supports more than a dozen graphic file formats.

The most common way to add graphics to your InDesign layouts is to use the Place command, located under the File menu. In this exercise, you'll use the Place command to add an image to the front page of your travel magazine.

You can also import movies and audio in QuickTime, .avi, .wav, .aif, and .swf formats, as well as .au sound clips, into InDesign. These can be exported to the PDF and SWF file formats.

1 If necessary, use the pages drop-down menu in the lower-left corner of the page to navigate to page 1 of the file id0501_work.indd, and then choose View > Fit Page in Window. This page displays the magazine title SoJournal at the top of the page.

*Use the page drop-down menu
to navigate to page 1.*

2 To make certain that nothing is selected, choose Edit > Deselect All. If the Deselect All option is unavailable, nothing is currently selected; proceed to the next step.

3 Choose File > Place and navigate to the id05lessons folder. Select the id0501.psd file to import this image. In the Place dialog box, make sure the *Show Import Options* checkbox is unchecked, and then click Open to import the image.

Importing an image and selecting the Show Import Options checkbox.

4   The cursor displays a thumbnail of the image you are importing. Position the thumbnail image in the upper-left corner of the red bleed guides, positioned outside the edge of the page, and then click to place the image. InDesign imports the image, the SoJournal masthead, at its original size.

If you accidentally clicked in a different spot on the page and need to reposition the image, use the Selection tool (k) to drag the image until it snaps to the upper-left corner of the red bleed guides.

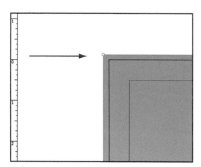

Place the image in the upper-left corner of page 1 so it extends above and to the left of the edge of the page.

5   Scroll down to the bottom of page 1. Notice that the image frame extends beyond the edge of the bleed guides. You will resize the image frame to fit within these guides.

6   Position the Selection tool over the lower-right corner of the image frame. When the pointer becomes a diagonal arrow (⤡), click and drag the corner of the frame to reduce the size of the frame. Stop when it snaps to the lower-right corner of the bleed. The arrowheads turn white when they are positioned over the corner of the bleed guides.

Using the Selection tool to resize the image.

7 Adjust the image by clicking on the Content Indicator in the middle of the image with the Selection tool. This targets the photo itself and your cursor changes to a hand icon (🖑). Click and drag to reposition the image and change how it is cropped by the frame.

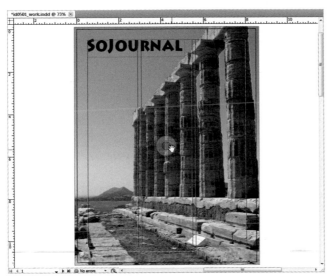

Adjusting the position of an image within a frame using the Content Indicator.

The Content Indicator is new in InDesign CS5 and provides an easier and more efficient method of adjusting an image within its frame. You can still adjust an image with the tried-and-true method of using the Direct Selection tool (⬚) to click on an image and adjust its position.

8 With the cover image still selected, choose Object > Arrange > Send Backward. The cover image moves behind the magazine title.

9 Choose File > Save to save your work. Keep the file open for the next part of the lesson.

Fitting options

You can use several options to get images to fit correctly to the frames on your page, including the following:

Object > Fitting > Fit Content Proportionally resizes the image to fit inside the frame, maintaining the original image proportions. If the proportions of the box do not match the proportions of the image, extra space will display around one or more of the frame edges.

Object > Fitting > Fill Frame Proportionally causes the smallest size to become larger or smaller to fit within the frame, eliminating any additional space around the edge of the frame.

Object > Fitting > Fit Frame to Content causes the frame to snap to the edges of the image. The frame either reduces or enlarges to fit the exact size of the image.

Be careful when using **Fit Content to Frame**, because it distorts the image to fit the frame. The proportional options are generally a better choice for most images.

These options are also available from the context menu, either by right-clicking (Windows) or Ctrl+clicking (Mac OS) with the mouse.

Fitting an image within an existing frame

You will now explore options for controlling where graphics are placed within your layouts.

1   Navigate to page 2 using the page drop-down menu in the lower-left corner of the document window.

Page 2 includes four image frames for pictures to accompany the paragraphs about Athens, Austin, Chicago, and Honolulu.

2   If necessary, choose the Selection tool (k) from the Tools panel and click the empty picture frame accompanying the Athens story at the top of the page. Handles appear around the edge of the frame, indicating the frame is selected.

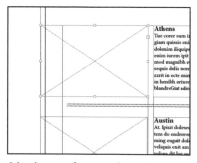

Select the empty frame to make it active.

3 Choose File > Place to import an image into the selected frame. In the Place dialog box, confirm that *Replace Selected Item* is selected. Navigate to the id05lessons folder, select the id0502.psd image, and click Open. The image appears in the selected frame, but only a part of the image is visible. You will reposition the graphic within the frame in the next part of this exercise.

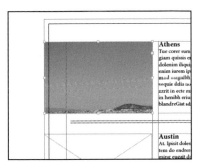

Importing an image into the selected frame.

4 Choose the Direct Selection tool (⦅) from the Tools panel and position the cursor over the image. The cursor changes to a hand icon. Click and drag the image inside the frame until the image is relatively centered in the frame.

While dragging the image, a light-brown bounding box appears around the edge of the image that is outside the cropping area, and InDesign also displays any part of the image that is cropped by the frame. This "live" screen drawing is an improved feature in InDesign CS5 that allows you to see the entire image as you drag it, "ghosting" the image where it is being cropped by the frame.

When clicking and dragging an image with the Direct Selection tool, InDesign displays the complete size, even any part outside of the frame.

5 Right-click (Windows) or Ctrl+click (Mac OS) the graphic and choose Fitting > Center Content. The image is centered within the frame.

6 Using the Selection tool, right-click (Windows) or Ctrl+click (Mac OS) the graphic, and choose Fitting > Fill Frame Proportionally.

These fitting options provide different ways to reposition the image. After using the Fill Frame Proportionally option, you may want to manually refine the image position using the Direct Selection tool (☝).

Auto Fitting

You can use the Frame Fitting Options to choose settings and create default options for whenever you place graphics inside existing frames. In this part of the exercise, you will create default fitting options for frames.

1 Choose Edit > Deselect All, or press Shift+Ctrl+A (Windows) or Shift+Command+A (Mac OS), to make sure nothing in your document is selected.

2 Using the Selection tool (▸), Shift+click the three remaining empty frames on page 2 of the layout.

3 Choose Object > Fitting > Frame Fitting Options.

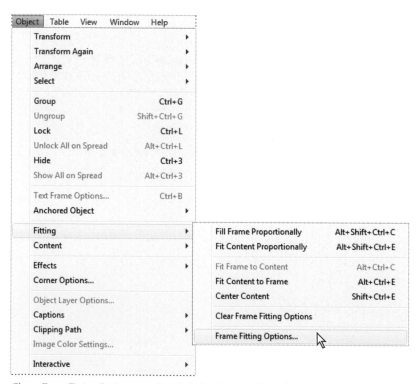

Choose Frame Fitting Options to set the defaults for placing graphics in frames.

4   Choose Fill Frame Proportionally from the Fitting drop-down menu and click the center box on the Align from icon; then click OK. Graphics placed into these frames will fill each frame proportionally.

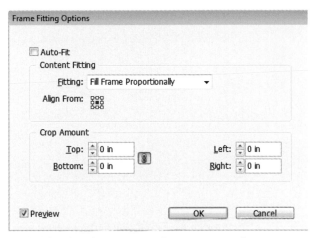

Set the default frame fitting option to Fill Frame Proportionally.

5   Choose File > Save.

Using Adobe Bridge to import graphics

Adobe Bridge is a separate application that ships with InDesign. It provides a way to manage and view your digital assets, including images and InDesign documents. You can use Bridge to get previews of your documents, and view information about files before you even open them. Bridge works like a specialized version of your operating system for managing and arranging the files you import into an InDesign layout, and files you have created using InDesign.

In this section, you will import an image into the document by dragging it from the Bridge window directly into the InDesign document.

1   With id0501.indd still open, choose File > Browse in Bridge, or click the Go to Bridge button (Br) in the Control panel to launch Adobe Bridge.

2   When Adobe Bridge opens, click the Favorites tab in the upper-left corner to bring it forward, and then click once on the Desktop listing, or click the location where you placed the files for this lesson.

3 In the Content tab at the center of the Bridge window, locate the id05lessons folder and double-click to open the folder.

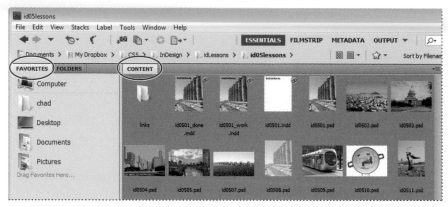

Open the lessons folder using Adobe Bridge.

4 In the upper-right corner of the Bridge window, click the Switch to Compact Mode button (⊟). This results in a smaller version of Bridge that allows you to work simultaneously with Bridge and your InDesign document.

5 Position the compact Bridge window so you can see the empty frame next to the second city description, Austin, located on page 2 of the InDesign document.

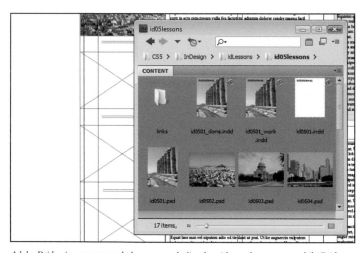

Adobe Bridge in compact mode lets you work directly with another program while Bridge remains visible.

6 Using the Bridge window, locate the Photoshop image id0503.psd, an image of the Austin Capitol building. Click and hold, then drag the image into the empty Austin frame on page 2 of the InDesign document. When your cursor is positioned inside the frame, release the mouse. The photo is placed into the frame.

7 Close the Bridge window, and click anywhere within the InDesign document window to make it active; then choose File > Save.

Placing multiple graphics using Mini Bridge

You can place multiple graphics into your InDesign layouts in a single step. InDesign CS5 introduces a new feature called Mini Bridge. Mini Bridge offers features found in the Adobe Bridge application, but is built into Adobe InDesign as a panel. This alleviates the need to view images on your computer using a completely separate application. In this section, you will place two graphics in the remaining frames on page 2 of the layout.

1 If necessary, choose Edit > Deselect All so that nothing is selected, and then choose Window > Mini Bridge.

2 In the Mini Bridge panel, click the Browse Files button. If this button is not available, click the Home Page button (⌂), and then click the Browse Files button.

3 Click on Favorites on the left column of the Navigation section, and then click on Desktop or select the folder where you placed the files for this lesson.

4 In the Content area at the bottom of the Mini Bridge panel, navigate to the id05lessons folder by double-clicking on the folders to open them.

5 In the Mini Bridge panel, Ctrl+click (Windows) or Command+click (Mac OS) to select both the id0504.psd and id0505.psd images; then click and drag either of the selected images anywhere in the InDesign document. The cursor changes to a paintbrush icon (🖌) and displays the number 2 in parentheses, along with a thumbnail of the first image. Click inside the empty frame to the left of the Chicago entry to place the first graphic. The paintbrush's number disappears, and a thumbnail of the Honolulu image appears.

6 Position your cursor over the remaining empty frame and click to place id0505.psd in the frame.

You can place multiple graphics in multiple frames using the Mini Bridge panel or by choosing File > Place.

When you have multiple images loaded in the place cursor, you can use the arrow keys on the keyboard to cycle through the various images. As you press the arrow keys, the preview of the image to be placed changes, letting you choose which image will be placed. Press the Esc key to remove an image from the list of images that are being placed.

Contact Sheet place

You can have InDesign create multiple frames and place images into a grid, known as a contact sheet. After choosing multiple images to place, click and drag to define the area for the grid. As you drag, use the left and right arrow keys to add or reduce the number of columns in the grid, and use the up and down arrow keys to add or reduce the number of rows in the grid.

7 Close the Mini Bridge panel and choose File > Save to save your work. Keep the file open for the next part of the lesson.

Adjusting the display quality of images

InDesign typically provides a low-resolution preview of placed graphics. The higher-resolution information is not displayed, as the high-quality information is often unnecessary for layout, and displaying many high-quality images can slow the performance of InDesign.

You may need to view the high-quality images, and you can choose to display high-quality image data for specific images, or for all images.

To change the display quality of an individual image, right-click (Windows) or Control+click (Mac OS) and choose Display Performance. Choose Fast Display to display a gray box instead of the image preview. Choose Typical to display a medium resolution for the image and choose High Quality display to show the high-resolution image information—the same data you would see in programs like Photoshop or Illustrator.

To change the display performance for all images in a document, choose View > Display Performance and select the desired quality level to use for the document.

Using object styles for images

In Lesson 4, "Working with Styles," you applied object styles to frames. You can also apply object styles to frames that contain images, quickly giving them a consistent, finished appearance. In this exercise, you'll create and apply an object style that adds a black stroke and applies rounded corners to all the frames on page 2.

1 Zoom in on the first image, the picture of Athens, on page 2 of the layout. Press Shift+Ctrl+A (Windows) or Shift+Command+A (Mac OS) to deselect all items on the page.

2 Click the Stroke button (■) in the Control panel and drag and drop it onto the frame edge of the picture of Athens to apply the default stroke to the frame. Your cursor will change to indicate that you are applying the stroke to the frame (▶/).

3 In the panel dock on the right side of the workspace, click the Stroke button (≡). In the Stroke panel, click the Align Stroke to Inside button (▣) to set the stroke to align to the inside of the frame, and make sure that the stroke weight is set to 1 point.

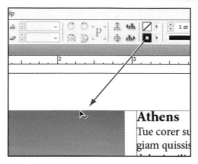

Applying a stroke to the frame by dragging and dropping the Stroke icon onto the frame edge.

4 Click on the Stroke button in the panel dock to collapse it back into a button.

5 Click on the yellow square in the upper-right corner of the Athens photo frame to enable Live Corner Effects edit mode. Diamonds appear in each corner of the frame, indicating that the Live Corner Effects have been enabled.

6 Hold down the Shift+Alt (Windows) or Shift+Option (Mac OS) keys and drag the diamond in the upper-right corner of the frame to the left to change the radius of that corner. Drag to about .25 inches by monitoring the smart guide for that corner. Repeat this step for the diamond in the lower-right corner of the frame. You can also precisely adjust each corner by choosing Object > Corner Options and changing the values using the Corner Options dialog box.

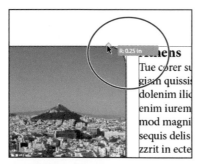

Drag the corner of the frame to adjust the Live Corner Effects.

You will now use the formatting of this initial frame to create an object style, and then apply it to the other frames.

7 In the dock, click the Object Styles button (▣). If the button is not visible, choose Window > Styles > Object Styles to open the Object Styles panel.

8 With the Athens image on page 2 still selected, Alt+click (Windows) or Option+click (Mac OS) on the Create New Style button (⊒) at the bottom of the Object Styles panel to create a new object style.

Pressing the Alt/Option key when creating a new style causes the New Style dialog box to open, making it easy to confirm the settings and name the style. If you do not press the Alt/Option key, the new style is created and given a generic name.

Alt/Option+click the Create New Style button.

9 In the New Object Style dialog box, click the *Apply Style to Selection* checkbox to link the new style to the selected object.

10 Make sure the checkbox for Frame Fitting Options is selected (it is located along the left side of the dialog box). Next, click the words Frame Fitting Options to highlight it and display the Frame Fitting Options.

11 From the Fitting drop-down menu, choose Fill Frame Proportionally, and then click on the center box of the Align From icon.

12 In the Style Name text field, enter the name **Image Frame** to name the style, and then click OK. InDesign saves the attributes of the selected object as a new style and applies them to the selected frame.

13 Shift+click to select the remaining three images on page 2 that have not yet been formatted.

14 In the Object Styles panel, click the Image Frame style, applying it to all four images simultaneously.

To better view the 1-point strokes and rounded corners on the four image frames, you may need to press Ctrl+(plus sign) (Windows) or Command+(plus sign) (Mac OS) to zoom in. This shortcut brings you progressively closer to the page. After you view the final result, choose View > Fit Page in Window to bring you back to a broad view of your file.

15 Choose Edit > Deselect All to deselect the images, and then choose File > Save. Keep the document open.

Wrapping text around images

To force text away from graphics, you can use text wrap to determine how far text should be pushed away from an object.

Wrapping text around the bounding box

When you place a graphic on a page, you might want the text to wrap around the frame that contains the graphic.

1 With the Selection tool (⬐), select the image of Athens on page 2. Click, hold, and drag it to the right so the upper-left corner of the image fits into the corner where the top and left margins intersect. Part of the image overlaps the text because the image frame is positioned above the text frame at the half-inch mark.

2 Move the remaining three photos to the right so that the left edge of the frame is aligned with the left margin of the page. Holding down the Shift key while moving these frames will constrain their movement horizontally.

Move the image to the intersection of the top and left margins.

3 Choose Window > Text Wrap. The Text Wrap panel opens.

4 Click the Wrap Around Bounding Box button (▣), which causes the text to wrap around the edge of the frame.

Wrapping text around the image frame.

5   In the middle of the panel are the offset values, which determine how closely the text wraps around the image. Confirm that the Make All Settings the Same button (◉) in the middle of the offset values is selected. Click the up arrow, next to any one of the offset options, twice to set the offset to 0.125 inches. The text is positioned at least .125 inches away from the image frame.

6   Click the Object Styles button to display the Object Styles panel. Notice that the Object Style Image Frame that was applied to this image in the previous exercise contains a plus sign next to it. This indicates that a change has been made to the selected object beyond what the Object Style defines. Right-click on the Image Frame object style and choose Redefine Style. This applies the changes made to the object to the Object style, and the remaining three images on the page update to reflect the updated Object style and now have the text wrap applied as well.

7   Choose File > Save to save your work. Keep the file open for the next exercise.

Using graphics with clipping paths and alpha channels

Some images contain clipping paths or alpha channels. Clipping paths and alpha channels can be used to hide information in an image, typically the background, enabling users to wrap text around part of the image. Clipping paths are stored in the Paths panel in Photoshop, and alpha channels are saved selections stored in the Channels panel in Photoshop.

The formats that utilize paths and channels include .psd, .eps, and .tif. These formats can hide parts of the image that are outside the path or channel when they are used in an InDesign layout. You will add a graphic to your layout that contains a clipping path from Photoshop, and then use the text wrap option to wrap text around the object's shape. You will place the next image in the Transportation article on page 3 of the InDesign document.

1   Click the Pages button in the dock to open the Pages panel. Double-click on the page 3 icon, and page 3 centers in the workspace.

2   Choose Edit > Deselect to make sure nothing is selected; then choose File > Place, and navigate to the id05lessons folder. Click once to select the image id0509.psd, and click to select the *Show Import Options* checkbox at the bottom of the Place dialog box. Click Open. The Image Import Options dialog box appears.

3 In the Image Import Options dialog box, click the Image tab. If necessary, click the *Apply Photoshop Clipping Path* checkbox so that it is checked, and confirm that Alpha Channel is set to None. Click OK to import the image.

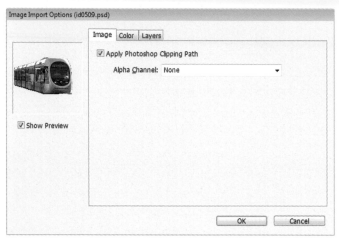

Choosing the import options when placing an image with a clipping path.

4 Position the paintbrush-and-thumbnail cursor (⌖) at the top of the left column in the Transportation article, and then click to place the graphic. The train image, without a background, appears over the text. By selecting the *Apply Photoshop Clipping Path* option, you set the image to appear without its background.

When placing the image, be certain the cursor does not display the paintbrush inside parentheses as this indicates the image will be placed into an existing frame on the page. If you unintentionally place the image into a frame, choose Edit > Undo and repeat the process.

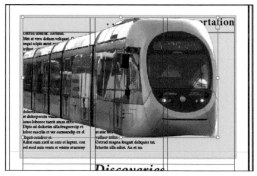

When Apply Photoshop Clipping Path is enabled, images display only the information inside a clipping path that was created in Photoshop.

5　With the image still selected, click the lower-left reference point locator (▦) in the Control panel.

Set the train image's lower-left corner as the reference point.

6　In the Control panel, make sure that the Constrain Proportions for Scaling button (⊗) is selected. This constrains the proportions to keep them equal when the image is scaled.

7　Choose 50% from the Scale X percentage drop-down menu (▣). The resulting image is a smaller train positioned in the lower-left corner of the Transportation article.

8　Choose Window > Text Wrap to open the Text Wrap panel, if it is not already open. Click the Wrap Around Object Shape button (▦) to wrap the text around the shape of the image, and then change the offset amount to **0.1875** inches.

The text now wraps around the clipping path that was created using Photoshop.

Wrap text around the object shape.

9　Choose File > Save to save your work. Keep the file open for the next part of the lesson.

Removing an image background using InDesign

You don't have to use Photoshop to remove the background from an image. You can use InDesign to create and apply a clipping path to an image. Clipping paths added to images using InDesign impact only the image in the InDesign document, and are not saved back into the original image file.

1　Choose Edit > Deselect All, to make sure nothing is selected. This keeps you from accidentally editing items in your layout. You will place a new image in the Discoveries article on page 3.

2　Choose File > Place. In the Place dialog box, navigate to the id05lessons folder. Select the id0510.psd image. At the bottom of the dialog box, make sure the Show Import Options check box is selected, and then click Open.

4   Choose File > Place. At the bottom of the Place dialog box, click to uncheck the *Show Import Options* checkbox. Navigate to the id05lessons folder, select id0513.psd, make sure the Replace Selected Item check box is selected, and then click Open. InDesign imports the image to the location where the cursor was inserted.

Import the image next to the word CHICAGO, *creating an anchored object.*

5   Continuing to use the Type tool, click to position the text cursor at the end of the paragraph, immediately above the image you imported in the previous step, and then press Enter (Windows) or Return (Mac OS) one time. The text moves down, and the graphic moves with the text.

The anchored image moves with its text.

6   Press Ctrl+Z (Windows) or Command+Z (Mac OS) to undo the paragraph return, bringing the image back to its original position.

You repositioned the text to understand how the image is attached to the text, but you will want it back in its original position for the remainder of this exercise.

7   To manually control the positioning of the anchored image, switch to the Selection tool and then click once on the anchored image to select it. Choose Object > Anchored Object > Options. The Anchored Object Options dialog box appears.

8   In the Anchored Object Options dialog box, click to select the *Preview* checkbox in the lower-left corner. Choose Custom from the Position drop-down menu, and click the *Relative to Spine* checkbox. This causes the image position to remain consistent to the spine of the document if pages are added or deleted and the page on which it is placed reflows.

Although the image is now positioned outside the text frame, it remains linked to the text. If the text position changes, the image will continue to flow with the text. Leave all the other settings at their defaults, then click OK to close the dialog box.

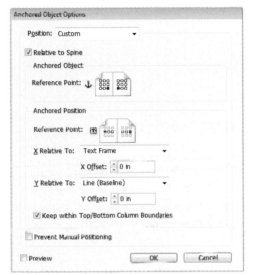 

Set the anchored image to Custom and Relative to Spine to place the image outside the text frame.

9   With the Selection tool, click and drag the graphic into the upper-right corner of the City Art box.

Reposition the anchored image manually using the Selection tool.

10 To test the spine-sensitive options, choose View > Fit Spread In Window. Use the Selection tool to select the City Art frame. Drag the frame to the empty column on the right side of the City Music box on page 5. Notice how the graphic automatically adjusts its position within the City Art box relative to the spread's spine. Likewise, if the text flowed from a left page to a right page, the anchored object would reposition itself automatically.

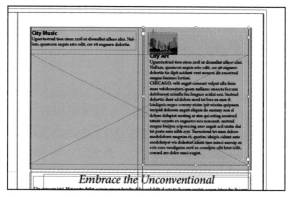

When you reposition the City Art frame to page 5, the graphic adjusts its position relative to the spine.

11 Press Ctrl+Z (Windows) or Command+Z (Mac OS) to undo the repositioning of the text frame, or simply drag the City Art frame back to its original position.

12 Save the file by choosing File > Save. Keep the file open for the next part of the lesson.

Applying a text wrap to anchored graphics is the same as applying a text wrap to any object. Click the anchored graphic with the Selection tool, choose the desired option from the Text Wrap panel, and set your offset value accordingly. In addition, Object Styles can be created and applied to inline graphics for consistent positioning of Anchored Objects in your document.

Advanced importing

You can import more advanced graphics into your layouts, including Photoshop files that use layers, and InDesign documents, without converting them to any other file type. Even if you don't work extensively with Photoshop, you can still follow along with these steps.

Importing layered Photoshop files

In this exercise, you'll work with an imported Photoshop file that uses a group of layers that have been organized using a layer comp. Layer comps are a snapshot of the current state of the Photoshop Layers palette. Within Photoshop, you can change the visibility, position, and appearance of the layers to create different versions of a file. When you create a layer comp, it saves these settings by remembering the state of each layer at the time the layer comp was saved. You can use layer comps to create multiple compositions from a single Photoshop file.

When you import a .psd document into InDesign and select the *Show Import Options* checkbox, you can choose which layer comp to use from the Photoshop file within the InDesign document.

When you use layered Photoshop files in your InDesign layouts, you can change the visibility of the layers directly within InDesign. You do not need to go back to Photoshop to create or save different versions of an image. In this exercise, you will display different versions of an image by changing the visibility of the Photoshop layers and layer comps.

1 With the Zoom tool (⊘), click and drag to draw a box around the empty frame under the Sculpture article on page 4 of the InDesign document. This increases the magnification of the page, making the frame more clearly visible.

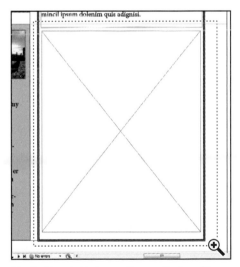

Use the Zoom tool to increase the magnification of the empty frame.

2 With the Selection tool (⊁), click to select the empty frame under the Sculpture article. Choose File > Place, and at the bottom of the Place dialog box, click to select both the *Replace Selected Item* checkbox and the *Show Import Options* checkbox so that both options are enabled. Navigate to the id05lessons folder, select id0511.psd, and then click Open. The Image Import Options dialog box opens.

3 In the resulting Image Import Options dialog box, click the Layers tab to bring the layers options forward. Notice that several layers are listed in the Show Layers section. Make sure the *Show Preview* checkbox is selected, and then click the box next to the hsbGray layer to display that layer's option. The appearance of the image changes when you display the hsbGray layer.

4 Choose 3w/hsbGray from the Layer Comp drop-down menu to display a number of layer visibility changes that were defined by this layer comp when the image was edited in Photoshop.

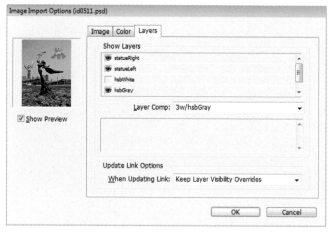

Use the layer comp visibility options to change the visibility of layers in placed Photoshop files.

5 Click OK. The image imports into the InDesign layout and displays the layers from the Photoshop image that you selected in the Image Import Options dialog box.

Now you'll explore how to change layer visibility of images after they've been placed in a layout.

6 If necessary, click the image with the Selection tool. With the image selected, choose Object > Object Layer Options. Choose Last Document State from the Layer Comp drop-down menu to return the image to its original settings, and then click OK.

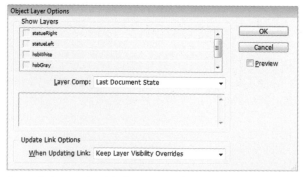

Return the image to its original state using Object Layer Options.

7 Continuing to use the Selection tool, right-click (Windows) or Ctrl+click (Mac OS) the image, and from the contextual menu, choose Fitting > Fill Frame Proportionally so the image fits nicely inside the frame.

8 Choose File > Save to save your work.

Importing InDesign layouts as graphics

Along with traditional image formats, you can also import other InDesign layouts into your document, placing them as graphics. You may have an ad or a flyer that was created in InDesign that you want to use in another InDesign layout. By importing an InDesign file as a graphic, you can make changes to the imported file and the modifications are automatically updated in your layout. In this exercise, you will import a CD booklet design, created using InDesign, into the layout.

1 Open the Pages panel from the dock on the right side of the workspace and, in the panel, double-click on page 5 to navigate to this page; then choose View > Fit Page in Window. Use the Selection tool (↖) to select the frame beneath the City Music headline.

2 Choose File > Place or press the keyboard shortcut, Ctrl+D (Windows) or Command+D (Mac OS). At the bottom of the Place dialog box, make sure that both the *Replace Selected Item* and the *Show Import Options* checkboxes are checked, navigate to the id05lessons folder, and select the id0514.indd file. Click Open. The Place InDesign Document dialog box appears.

3 In the Place InDesign Document dialog box, click the General tab to bring it forward, and make sure the Crop to drop-down menu is set to Page bounding box, this determines how much of the page is displayed. The other two crop options for bleed and slug would be used if you wanted those additional layout options to be visible. Leave the Layers tab options unchanged, and then click OK.

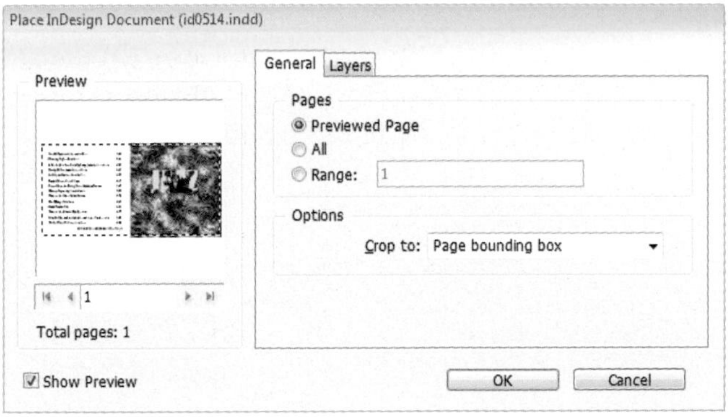

Set the Crop options to Page bounding box when importing the InDesign document into your layout.

When you import InDesign files that have links, you need to have those links available for the new layout as well. In order to print or export the layout properly, those links need to be available at that time.

4   The CD booklet design fills the frame. Because it doesn't fit entirely in the frame, right-click (Windows) or Ctrl+click (Mac OS), and from the contextual menu, choose Fitting > Fit Content Proportionally.

5   Choose File > Save.

At the very bottom of the Tools panel, click and hold the Normal button (▣) to reveal more viewing options. Choose Preview, and then scroll through your completed layout. When you're finished, choose File > Close to close the document.

Congratulations! You've finished Lesson 5, "Working with Graphics."

Self study

For a different text wrap option, try placing id0509.psd in a block of text and, using the Text Wrap panel, select the Wrap around Object Shape button and choose Alpha Channel from the Contour Options drop-down menu. Make sure to go to the Object menu and choose Clipping Path > Options. Change the Type field to Alpha Channel, and set Alpha to trainOpenWindow.

Use Adobe Bridge or Mini Bridge to add more images to your document. Once you get used to this workflow, you will find that it can speed up the design process.

Create additional anchored images in the text frames of your document. Explore the offset options to change the positioning of anchored objects.

Customize the display of the Links panel, and change the sorting order of the links. Then use the Links panel to collect the links used in the document by using the Utilities > Copy Links To option in the Links panel menu.

Review

Questions

1 How can you have InDesign automatically fit images to frames or frames to images?

2 To flow text around the shape of a clipping path, which panel can you use?

3 How do you reposition a graphic inside its frame?

4 Which graphic format supports the visibility of layer comps?

5 Once a layered graphic is placed in an InDesign document, how do you change the layer visibility?

Answers

1 You can do this by using the Object > Fitting command.

2 You can use the Text Wrap panel.

3 You can reposition the graphic by using the new Content Indicator or by using the Direct Selection tool (⬆).

4 The Photoshop .psd file format supports the visibility of layer comps.

5 With the graphic selected, choose Object > Object Layer Options, or right-click (Windows) or Ctrl+click (Mac OS), and choose Object Layer Options from the contextual menu.

Lesson 6

What you'll learn in this lesson:

- Creating and importing tables
- Pasting text into a table
- Editing tables and table options
- Formatting cells, rows, and text
- Defining a header cell
- Using graphics in tables

Creating and Using Tables

Tables are an effective way to convey large amounts of data in an organized manner. Whether you import a table from Microsoft Word or Excel, or build a new one using InDesign, you can use many powerful methods for designing impressive, professional-looking tables. After designing a table, you can save all the attributes as a style and quickly apply those attributes to another table with just one click using table styles.

Starting up

Before starting, make sure that your tools and panels are consistent by resetting your preferences. See "Resetting the InDesign workspace and preferences" on page 3.

You will work with several files from the id06lessons folder in this lesson. Make sure that you have copied the id06lessons folder onto your hard drive from the Digital Classroom DVD. See "Loading lesson files" on page 4. This lesson may be easier to follow if the id06lessons folder is on your desktop.

See Lesson 6 in action!

Use the accompanying video to gain a better understanding of how to use some of the features shown in this lesson. The video tutorial for this lesson can be found on the included DVD.

The project

In this lesson, you will add tables to a brochure for Bella's Bakery. The first page of the brochure is complete, but the second page needs tables to list the products for sale. To preview the results you'll be working toward, navigate to the id06lessons folder and open id0601_done.indd. Once you've looked over the layout, you can close the file by choosing File > Close, or keep it open for reference as you work.

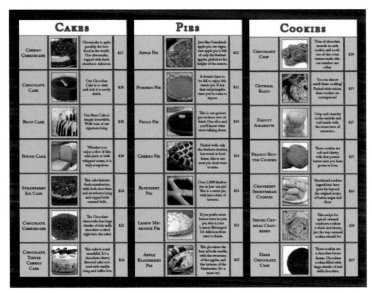

This is what the final layout should look like.

Creating a table

You can create a table using one of three methods: from scratch by typing in your data, by copying and pasting information from another table, or by converting tabbed text into a table. In this section, you'll start with creating a table from scratch, and then explore the other two options as well. Tables exist inside text frames, so to create a table you must first make a text frame. To select or modify a table, you must use the Type tool.

Creating new tables

The Bella's Bakery brochure needs multiple tables. For this first one, you'll use the Insert Table control to design your own tables.

1   Within InDesign, choose Window > Mini Bridge to display the Mini Bridge panel. Click the Browse Files button, navigate to the id06lessons folder, and open the file id0601.indd. The file opens in InDesign.

2   Click the Pages button (⊞) in the dock on the right side of the workspace to open the Pages panel. Page 2 should be highlighted in blue to indicate that it's the active page. If it's not highlighted, double-click page 2 in the Pages panel to make it the active page.

3   Choose View > Fit Page in Window so that you can see all of page 2 of your document.

4   Activate the Type tool (T) from the Tools panel, then click and drag to create a new text frame starting in the upper-left corner of the layout's middle column to the lower-right corner of the same column.

5   Choose Table > Insert Table.

Choose Insert Table from the Table menu.

6   In the Insert Table dialog box that appears, type **7** for the Body Rows, and **4** for the Columns.

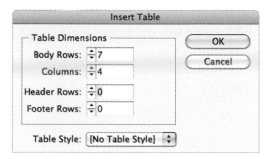

The Insert Table dialog box with the correct settings.

7 Click OK to close the dialog box and insert the table. A table with four columns and seven rows appears in the second column's text frame.

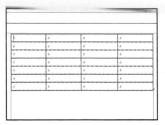

The resulting table has four columns and seven rows.

Copying and pasting table information

You now have a table with no data. You could type the information into the table, but InDesign offers an easier way: cutting and pasting data from another table. InDesign CS5 provides great flexibility when copying information by allowing you to copy data from a Microsoft Excel or Word table and paste those entries into a selected table in InDesign. Using the Clipboard Handling section of the InDesign Preferences, you can specify whether the text pasted from another application retains its original formatting or not. If you check *Text Only*, the information appears as unformatted text, which you can then flow into a selected table. If *All Information* is selected, the pasted text appears as the table looked in Word or Excel, and InDesign imports the styles from those programs. You must select the destination table's cells prior to pasting.

Because you may or may not have Word or Excel, for this exercise you will practice copying and pasting just between InDesign tables.

1 With the id0601.indd file still open, choose Window > Layers, or click the Layers button (◉) in the dock to reveal the Layers panel. If you can't find the panel under the Window menu, choose Window > Workspace > Advanced.

Open the Layers panel.

2   Within the Layers panel, click to select the Pies layer. To the left of the Pies listing, click in the left-hand box to reveal the visibility icon (👁), which makes the layer's contents visible. The layer's contents appear on the pasteboard to the right of the page.

Click the gray square to reveal the layer's contents.

3   Select the Hand tool (✋) from the Tools panel. Click the page with the Hand tool, and drag left to reveal the pasteboard on the right side of the page. Next to the pie images is a table with information on the bakery's pies. Use the Hand tool to position this area so that you can see both the table and the pie images.

4   Select the Type tool (T) from the Tools panel. You edit a table by selecting either the table or its cells with the Type tool, as they reside in text frames.

5   Hover over the top-left corner of the pies table until you see an arrow that points diagonally toward the lower-right corner. Click to select the entire table.

Click when the arrow in the upper-left corner is displayed to select the entire table.

When hovering over a table, the cursor image indicates which parts of the table you can select. The diagonal arrow means you can select the whole table. An arrow pointing to the right indicates that clicking selects a row. Click when the arrow points straight down, and you select a single column.

6 Choose Edit > Copy to copy the selected table to the clipboard.

7 On page 2, you need to selct the table you created in the previous exercise, which is the destination table. Double-click the Hand tool to fit the page to the window. Select the whole table by moving the Type tool over the top-left corner of the table, and clicking when you see the diagonal arrow.

8 Choose Edit > Paste to paste the information from the existing pies table into your new table. You have successfully moved table information from an existing table to another new table.

9 Choose File > Save As. In the Save As dialog box, navigate to the id06lessons folder and type **id0601_work.indd** in the File name text field. Click Save.

Converting text to a table and a table to text

If you prefer, you can bypass the step of creating a table grid, and simply paste data from an existing table into a text frame in your document. The information appears as tab-delimited text, which you can then convert into a table using the Table menu's Convert Text to Table command. You can also perform this process in the opposite direction using Convert Table to Text. When you choose this command, InDesign removes the table lines and inserts the separators you specify at the end of each row and column.

To demonstrate both commands, you will convert the table you just created to text and then convert the text back to a table.

1 With the table on page 2 still selected, choose Table > Convert Table to Text.

2 In the Convert Table to Text dialog box, Tab should be set as the Column Separator and Paragraph should be set as the Row Separator.

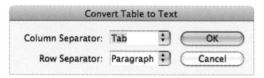

Specify your item separators in the Convert Table to Text dialog box.

3 Click OK. InDesign inserts tabs between each column entry, and paragraph returns after each row, removing all table lines.

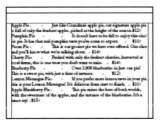

The table is now tab-delimited text.

You will now take this mess of text and turn it back into a table.

4 With the Type tool (T), click inside the text frame, and then choose Edit > Select All, or press Ctrl+A (Windows) or Command+A (Mac OS), to highlight all the text.

5 Choose Table > Convert Text to Table. In the resulting Convert Text to Table dialog box, keep the default separator settings and click OK to display the selected text as a table again.

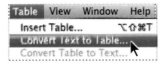

Choose Table > Convert Text to Table to display the selected text as a table.

6 Press Shift+Ctrl+A (Windows) or Shift+Command+A (Mac OS) to deselect everything in the document. Choose File > Save to save your work.

Importing a table

For some projects, you may need to incorporate an existing table created in Microsoft Word or Excel into your layout. Instead of simply pasting a table into the document, the better approach is to use the Place command, which gives you more control over formatting. When you place a Word or Excel document, you can edit the resulting table in InDesign using its Microsoft Word Import options to control the formatting.

1 With id0601_work.indd still open, activate the Type tool (T) and choose File > Place to insert the Microsoft Word document with a table into page 2 of your InDesign file.

2 Click to turn on the *Show Import Options* checkbox at the bottom-left of the Place dialog box. Navigate to the id06lessons folder, select id0601.docx, and click Open. InDesign supports the latest XML-based open format from Word and Excel.

3 The Microsoft Word Import Options dialog box appears. Click the *Remove Styles and Formatting from Text and Tables* radio button, located in the Formatting section of the dialog box, to strip the incoming document of all Word formatting and replace it with the InDesign Basic Paragraph style. This is a good idea if you don't want any of the styles, colors, or other formatting from Word in your InDesign document. Later in this lesson, you will format the text and save the results as your own styles.

For more on importing text, see Lesson 3, "Working with Text and Type."

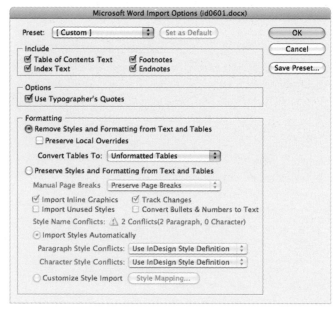

Strip the Word document of its formatting to avoid any inconsistencies once it's in InDesign.

4 Click OK in the Microsoft Word Import Options dialog box. It closes, and to the right of the cursor is a miniature preview of the text.

5 In the left-hand column on page 2, click and drag from the top-left margin to the bottom-right corner to designate the area in which to place the table. You can also just click in the upper-left corner of the margin area to flow the text into the first column. If you see a red overflow box at the bottom-right corner of the text frame, which indicates that there is more placed text than the column can hold, don't worry: you'll fix the proportions of the frame soon.

Click to place the table on the InDesign page.

6 Choose File > Save to save your work.

Editing tables and table options

InDesign CS5 has all the same table tools you've come to rely on to make your table presentations visually pleasing. In this series of exercises, you will concentrate on ways to adjust the entire Word table you imported. First you'll change the height of the top row, and then you will explore Table Options to change the border row strokes, column strokes, and fill of the table.

Changing row height

If your rows are too short to hold your entries, you can easily expand them.

1   With the Type tool (T) selected, click inside the table you imported in the left-hand column.

2   Hover between the top row, which holds the word *Cakes*, and the row below it, which contains *Cherry Cheesecake* in its left-most cell. When the cursor is directly over the row separator, it becomes a double arrow.

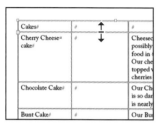

The cursor changes to a double arrow when it is directly over a row separator.

3   Click the row separator with the double-arrow cursor, and drag it to resize the top row. Drag up or down enough so that the height of the row is at a desired size.

To change just the size of a row or column without affecting the entire table, hold the Shift key as you drag. You can do this for all rows and columns except the rightmost row and bottommost column, where holding the Shift key alters all the rows at the same time.

Editing the border

Now you will change the size of the table border.

1   With the Type tool still active, click once inside the cell holding the Cakes heading, and then choose Table > Table Options > Table Setup. The Table Options dialog box opens.

Choose Table Options > Table Setup in the Table menu to open the Table Options dialog box.

2 In the Table Options dialog box, type **3** in the Weight text field in the Table Border section. Check the *Preview* checkbox in the bottom-left corner of the dialog box to see the change take effect. Your bottom row may disappear. If not, keep the dialog box open and jump down to the next section. If it does disappear, click OK; then, with the Type tool selected (T), click the divider between the first and second rows, drag it up to resize the top row again, and then choose Table > Table Options > Table Setup. The Table Options dialog box opens again.

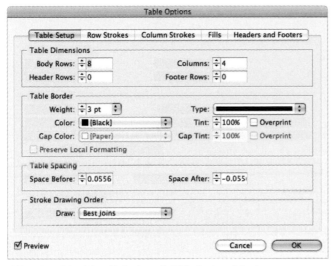

Adjust the weight of the table border in the Table Options dialog box.

Formatting rows and columns

In the previous section, you have changed the border size, and now you will change the color and size of the row and column separators.

1 With the table still selected, and the Table Options dialog box still open, click on the Row Strokes tab at the top of the dialog box.

2 From the Alternating Pattern drop-down menu, choose Every Other Row. This setting allows you to control the appearance of the rows. The options on the left side of the Alternating section are for the first row, and the options on the right side are for the next row. It repeats this pattern throughout the table's rows.

3 In the Alternating section, beneath the First text field, type **3** in the Weight text field, and choose Dark Blue from the Color drop-down menu. These settings affect the first row and every alternating row beneath it.

4 Type **3** in the Weight text field beneath the Next text field, and choose Light Blue from the Color drop-down menu. This setting affects the second row and every second row beneath that.

After you're done changing the row settings, you will adjust the column settings in the Table Options dialog box as well.

5 Click the Column Strokes tab in the Table Options dialog box.

6 Choose Every Other Column from the Alternating Pattern drop-down menu.

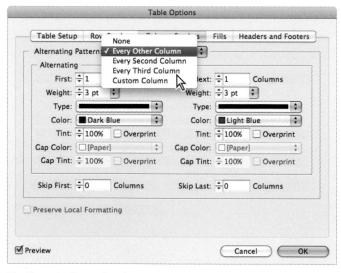

The Alternating Pattern drop-down menu.

7 In the Alternating section, beneath the First text field, type **3** for Weight, and choose Dark Blue from the Color drop-down menu. These settings affect the first column and every alternating column after it.

8 Beneath the Next text field, type **3** for Weight, and choose Light Blue from the Color drop-down menu. Click OK to apply the changes. Choose the Selection tool. Then press **W** on your keyboard to toggle into Preview mode to see how the table will appear when printed. Press **W** again to return to Normal view.

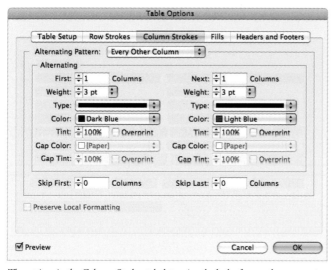

The settings in the Column Strokes tab determine the look of your column separators.

Using fills

To put the finishing touch on your table, you will fill it with color.

1 Select the Type tool (T) and click inside any cell; then choose Table > Select > Table. Choose Table > Table Options > Alternating Fills. This opens the Fills section of the Table Options dialog box.

2 Choose Every Other Row from the Alternating Pattern drop-down menu.

3 In the Alternating section, beneath the First text field, choose Light Chocolate from the Color drop-down menu and type **20** in the Tint Percentage text field.

4   In the color section beneath the Next text field, choose Light Blue from the Color drop-down menu and type **20** for Tint Percentage. With *Preview* checked, you should see the changes happen instantaneously.

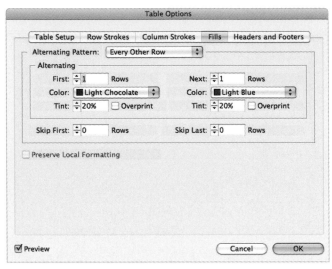

Set the fill color and tint percentage in the Fill section of the Table Options dialog box.

5   Click OK to apply all your fill colors. Press the Esc key to deselect the table. Note that when a table is highlighted, the colors applied to the table appear to be the inverse of their actual color. You need to deselect the table in order to view the actual colors.

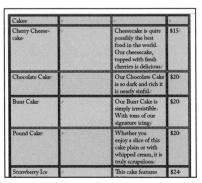

The table now reflects all the Table Options changes.

6   Choose File > Save to save your work.

Formatting cells and text

Unlike the Table Options settings that apply to the whole table, your cell styles and Cell Options settings can be different for each cell in the table. You can select and format one cell at a time, an entire row, an entire column, or any other group of cells. You will now format the table on a cell-by-cell basis. You will start by resetting the cell style of all the cells in the table. You will then change the vertical alignment of type within all cells. Finally, you will make four paragraph styles, one each for the table's header, name, description, and price sections. In later exercises, you'll use these paragraph styles to create cell styles that will speed the rest of the table's formatting, and ultimately you'll use the cell styles to create a table style with which you'll format the entire Pies table.

Resetting the cell styles within a table

Soon you will make both cell and table styles so that you can quickly apply all the attributes of a table and also the cells within a table using a single click of the mouse. But as we start this lesson, this table has mixed cell styles, which means that some of the settings from Microsoft Word have remained with the table. You'll start by clearing the additional formatting.

1   With the Type tool (T) selected, hover over the top-left corner of the cakes frame until you see a diagonal arrow, then click to select the Cakes table.

2   Choose Window > Styles > Cell Styles to open the Cell Styles panel. Notice the plus sign next to None in the panel's list of styles. This means that the selected table contains *overrides*, which are Word styles left over from the original document.

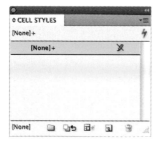

Manage the styles used in your table cells from the Cell Styles panel.

3   Hover your cursor over the plus sign to prompt a small yellow box listing all the items on your page that are formatted using settings not defined in the None style. Alt+click (Windows) or Option+click (Mac OS) the word *None* to clear the overrides. This ensures that the cells are not using any additional formatting.

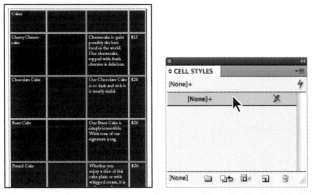

Clear the overrides to ensure consistent formatting of the table cells. Alt+click (Windows) or Option+click (Mac OS) to remove any style overrides from the selected cells.

4   Choose File > Save.

Text alignment and inset within a cell

Some cell formatting options are similar to the Text frame options you worked with in previous lessons. For example, you can use the same alignment options within a cell—top, center, bottom, and justified—as you can in a text box. You also have the same text inset settings that control how far from the edge of a cell text is inset. You will now change these settings for the whole table. You can also change these options one cell at a time, for a range of cells, or for all the cells at once. For the Bella's Bakery table, you will change the alignment and inset settings for all the cells at once.

1   Make sure the whole table is selected, and then choose Table > Cell Options > Text to open the Cell Options dialog box.

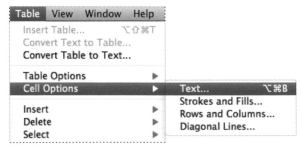

After you select the table, choose Cell Options > Text from the Table menu.

2   In the Cell Insets section of the Cell Options dialog box, type **0.0625** in the Top text field. Press the Tab key to apply the settings to all the insets. If this does not insert 0.0625 automatically in the Bottom, Left, and Right fields, type **0.0625** again and click the Make All Settings the Same button (◉) to the immediate right of the top and bottom inset values.

3   In the Vertical Justification section, choose Align Center from the Align drop-down menu.

4   Click the *Preview* checkbox to see your changes. The text in each cell is centered and inset from each edge. Click OK to apply the settings.

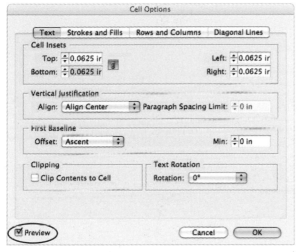

Set the text alignment and inset in the Cell Options dialog box.

Formatting text within a cell and saving paragraph styles

You can also format the text color and font size in your cells. You can then save these settings as a paragraph style for reuse later; applying styles to cells is as easy as applying them to text frames. In this exercise, you'll create several paragraph styles from your cell formatting. In the next section, you'll apply these styles to other cells and see how much time you can save by using styles.

1   With the Type tool (T), click inside the first cell of the second row, and then choose Edit > Select All to highlight the cell's contents (the words *Cherry Cheesecake*).

2   Type **10** in the Font Size field in the character formatting section of the Control panel, and then click the Small Caps button (Tᴛ) to apply small caps.

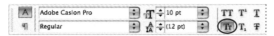

Set the font size and toggle on Small Caps in the Control panel.

3 Open the Swatches panel. Select the Dark Chocolate swatch to make the text dark brown. Make sure your text fill icon is in the foreground.

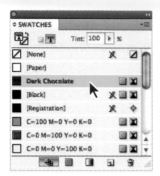

Select Dark Chocolate from the Swatches panel.

4 Press Shift+Ctrl+C (Windows) or Shift+Command+C (Mac OS) to center the type in its box.

5 Choose Type > Paragraph Styles to open the Paragraph Styles panel. Click the panel menu button (▾☰) in the Paragraph Styles panel and choose New Paragraph Style from the contextual menu.

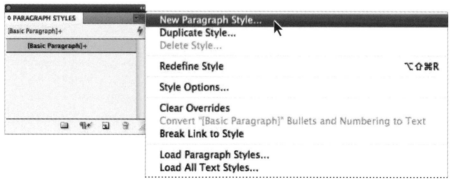

Create a new paragraph style in the Paragraph Styles panel.

6 In the resulting New Paragraph Style dialog box, type **Name** in the Style Name text field, click the *Apply Style to Selection* checkbox, then click OK to create a new style based upon the attributes from the selected text. You'll use the Name style to format the names of all the baked goods listed for Bella's Bakery.

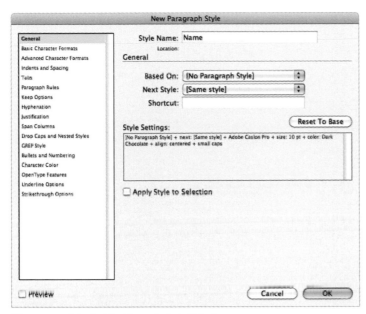

Name your style in the New Paragraph Style dialog box.

Making a style does not automatically apply that style. By checking Apply Style to Selection in the New Paragraph Style dialog box, InDesign applies the newly created style to the selected text, linking the selected text to the style. If the style is updated, the text that was selected when the style was created will also be updated.

7 Select the Name listing in the Paragraph Styles panel. If a plus sign appears next to it, Alt+click (Windows) or Option+click (Mac OS) it to clear all overrides.

The Paragraph Styles panel automatically lists your new style.

You will now make a paragraph style for the cake's descriptions.

8 Repeat steps 1 to 6, using the text in the third-from-left cell in the second row, the paragraph that starts with the sentence, *Cheesecake is quite possibly the best food in the world.* Set the font size to 8 points if it isn't already, and leave Small Caps toggled off. Set the paragraph alignment to center and name this new style **Description**.

9 Click Description in the Paragraph Styles panel to apply the style to the selected cell. If a plus sign appears next to the style name, Alt+click (Windows) or Option+click (Mac OS) Description to clear all overrides.

You will now make a paragraph style for the price listings.

10 With the Type tool, click inside the last cell on the right in the second row (the one containing *$15*). Choose Edit > Select All, and repeat steps 3 to 6, naming the new style **Price**.

11 Select the Price listing in the Paragraph Styles panel to apply the style to the selected cell. If necessary, clear all overrides.

The Paragraph Styles panel now includes three new styles, and the Cakes table is taking shape.

12 Choose File > Save to save your work.

Formatting text in tables by column

You can easily apply paragraph styles to groups of cells, such as a column. The process involves selecting the group and then applying a paragraph style. You will now select the first column of the table and apply one of the paragraph styles created in the last exercise.

1 With the Type tool (T), click in the Cherry Cheesecake cell (second row, first cell), and drag down until all the cells below it in the column are highlighted.

2 Click on the paragraph style Name in the Paragraph Styles panel to apply it to all the selected cells.

Highlight the first column's cells, and apply the Name paragraph style.

3 Now click in the top cell of the third column (*Cheesecake is quite possibly…*), drag to select all the cells below it, and select Description in the Paragraph Styles panel to apply the Description style.

Select the third column, and apply the Description style.

4 Click the $15 cell, drag down until all the price column's cells are highlighted, and select the Price style in the Paragraph Styles panel.

Working with tables in Story Editor

InDesign CS5 lets you view tables in the Story Editor. You can use the Story Editor to make sure you have applied the correct paragraph styles to the selected columns.

1 Click anywhere inside the table with the Type tool (T).

2 Choose Edit > Edit in Story Editor. The Story Editor opens up and allows you to view the table away from the page, while you can still see which styles are applied to each row and column.

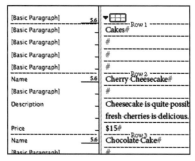

The Story Editor in InDesign CS5 displays tables and identifies styles applied to them.

Make sure that the correct styles are applied. You can make edits directly in the Story Editor and the changes are immediately applied to the layout. Close the Story Editor by clicking the "X" in the top-right corner (Windows), or the red circle in the top-left corner (Mac OS).

Merging cells

You can merge multiple cells in the same row or column into a single cell. To demonstrate, you will merge the top four cells of the example table so that the top row (with the word *Cakes* in it) looks more like a title. In the next section, you'll format it to stand out even more.

1 Select the cells in the first row by hovering your cursor over the left edge of the box until you see an arrow pointing to the right. Click to select the entire row.

2   Choose Table > Merge Cells or click the Merge Cells button (⊠) in the Control panel to make the top four cells into a single cell.

Merge the top four cells into one cell
for the Cakes *header.*

Defining a header cell

For a large table that spans multiple columns, frames, or pages, you can designate header or footer rows in order to repeat identifying information at the top or bottom of each portion of the divided table. If your table breaks over several pages, headers are vital to orienting readers with the table's data. For instance, if the number of cakes sold by Bella's Bakery increased enough to require two columns in its brochure, the next linked column would automatically be a header row. This saves you the time of inserting the header on each subsequent page.

Because it treats header cells as special cases, InDesign enables you to color and format them independently, without changing the features of the rest of the table. You can take advantage of this to help the headers stand out from the body of your table. Your header will be instantly identifiable when repeated in a multi-page, -column, or -frame layout, and your readers will be able to more easily decipher the information in the table. In this exercise, you will convert the Cakes cell into a header cell, apply unique formatting, and create a new paragraph style from it. Then you'll create a header for the Pies table.

If you just click in a cell or even highlight its contents, InDesign thinks you want to color the text. Either click with the right-pointing arrow or press the Esc key to select an entire cell.

1   Making sure the top row is still selected, choose Table > Convert Rows > To Header to make the top cell a header cell. Click once inside the cell with the Type tool (T), and notice how the color drops out of the cell. It's a header cell now, so InDesign strips the normal cell formatting. You'll now add some header-specific formatting.

2   The cell's fill should automatically change to None because it is now separate from the rest of the table. Select the cell in the first row by hovering your cursor over the left edge of the box until you see an arrow pointing to the right. Click to select the entire row. In the Swatches panel, make sure the Fill icon (▢) is in the foreground and click the Paper swatch to color the topmost cell.

Paper is opaque and represents the background on which the document will print. By contrast, the None option is transparent and displays any objects beneath it.

Choose Paper for the fill in the Swatches panel.

3   With the Type tool, click anywhere in the header cell to activate the cell, and then double-click on the word *Cakes* to select only the text.

Now you will stylize the type and make a paragraph style.

4   Center the type in the cell by pressing Shift+Ctrl+C (Windows) or Shift+Command+C (Mac OS). In the Control panel, click on the Small Caps button (ᴛ) to convert the title to a mix of large and small caps, and type **24** in the Font Size text field. Press Enter (Windows) or Return (Mac OS) to increase the size of the text.

If the type disappears from the cell, the type is too large for the cell to contain it. Hover over the bottom of the header cell until you see the double-arrow cursor, and then click and drag down. Make sure you don't lose any of the table at the bottom because of overflow.

5 Choose Type > Character to reveal the Character panel. Type **100** in the Tracking text field and press Enter (Windows) or Return (Mac OS). You can use either the Character panel or the Control panel to control character formatting.

Change the tracking in the Character panel.

6 Click the Swatches button (▦) in the dock to open the Swatches panel. Bring Fill to the foreground and click Light Blue to choose it for the fill color. Click the Stroke icon to bring it to the foreground, then choose Black to add a black stroke around the text.

7 With the formatting finished, you can now save it as a paragraph style. Choose Window > Styles > Paragraph Styles to reveal the Paragraph Styles panel. Alt+click (Windows) or Option+click (Mac OS) the Create New Style button (⊒) to open the New Paragraph Style dialog box. Type **Header** in the Style Name text field, and click OK.

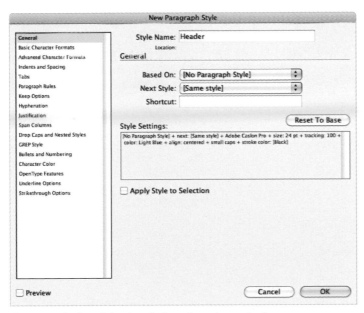

Create a new header style based on the formatting settings you've chosen.

8 In the Paragraph Styles panel's list, click Header to apply the style to the selected text.

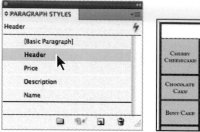 

The title Cakes stands out from the rest of the table thanks to its Header style.

9 The Pies table in the second column on page 2 needs a header as well. Click anywhere in the table with the Type tool.

10 Choose Table > Table Options > Headers and Footers to open the Table Options dialog box.

11 In the Table Dimensions section, type **1** in the Header Rows text field. Click OK to create a header row.

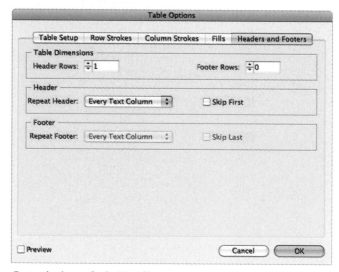

Create a header row for the Pies table.

12 Select the header row in the Pies table, and then choose Table > Merge Cells to convert the row to a single title cell.

13   Click inside the header row with the Type tool, then type **Pies**.

Add the title Pies *to the second table's header cell.*

14   Choose File > Save to save your work.

Setting column and row dimensions

At this point, you've adjusted the contents of rows and columns, but you haven't modified the row height or column width directly. By default, row height is determined by the height of the current font. Tables imported from Microsoft Word or Excel, however, can retain their original, exact row heights. If neither of these options fits your layout, InDesign enables you to change row height and column width in the Cell Options dialog box. Here you can specify whether you want a fixed row height that does not change when you add to or delete from the row, or, if you prefer, a variable height. For a fixed height, choose Exactly from the Row Height drop-down menu, and then specify the height you need. Choose At Least to specify a minimum row height; with this setting, rows increase in height as you add text or increase the font size, but will not be smaller than the minimum you set. Try out these cell options on the Cakes and Pies tables.

Setting a fixed row height

For the Cakes and Pies tables, a fixed row height works best. In the steps that follow, you'll adjust the size of the cells and also change their Row height to be an exact value. Then you will do the same for the Pies table.

1   Using the Type tool (T), click in the Cakes header cell, and then press the Esc key to select the cell.

2 Choose Table > Cell Options > Rows and Columns to open the Cell Options dialog box. In the Row Height section, choose Exactly from the drop-down menu. Type **0.5** in the Row Height text field, and then click OK. The height of the header row changes.

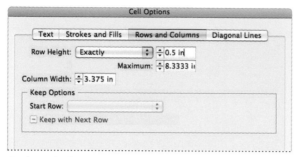

Set the row height to exactly 0.5 in the Cell Options dialog box.

3 Click and drag from the Cherry Cheesecake cell in the top-left corner to the $24 cell in the bottom-right corner to select the rest of the table.

4 Choose Table > Cell Options > Rows and Columns. Choose Exactly from the Row Height drop-down menu, type **1.0625** in the Row Height field, and click OK.

5 Now you need to set the row height for the Pies table. Click and drag from the Apple Pie cell in the top-left corner to the $15 cell in the bottom-right corner to select the rest of the table.

If the table is overset, use the Selection tool (▸) to extend the boundaries of the text frame down below the page. Setting row height fits the table into the column.

6 Choose Table > Cell Options > Rows and Columns to open the Cell Options dialog box. If it is not already selected, choose Exactly from the Row Height drop-down menu. Type **1.0625** in the Row Height text field, and then click OK.

7 Using the Type tool, click in the Pies header cell, and then press the Esc key to select the cell.

8   Choose Table > Cell Options > Rows and Columns. In the resulting Cell Options dialog box, choose Exactly from the Row Height drop-down menu and type **0.5** in the Row Height field. Click OK.

The Pies table now has a header row height of 0.5 and a body row height of 1.0625.

9   Choose File > Save to save your work.

Setting column width

You will now fix the column width for the Pies table.

1   Activate the Type tool (T), and then click inside the $12 cell, to the right of, or after, the text. Press Shift+down arrow to select the current cell, and then press Shift+down arrow six more times to select the whole column.

2   Choose Window > Type & Tables > Table to open the Table panel, and make the same changes you made earlier in the Cell Options dialog box. Type **0.4215** in the Column Width text field and press Enter (Windows) or Return (Mac OS).

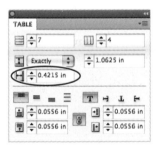

Enter the desired width in the Column Width text field of the Table panel.

3   Click inside the cell in the top-right part of the table containing the paragraph that starts with *Just like Grandma's*. Press Shift+down arrow seven times to select the entire column.

4   In the Table panel, type **1.0438** in the Column Width text field, and press Enter (Windows) or Return (Mac OS).

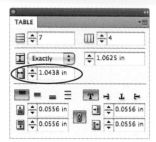

Use the Table panel to adjust the column width
for the column containing the pies' descriptions.

5   Click inside the topmost empty cell (the second from the left), and then press Shift+down arrow seven times to select the whole column.

6   Type **0.9715** in the Column Width text field in the Table panel, and press Enter (Windows) or Return (Mac OS).

7   Click the Apple Pie cell, and then press Shift+down arrow seven times to select the whole column.

8   Return to the Table panel and type **0.9382** in the Column Width text field. Press Enter (Windows) or Return (Mac OS). All row and column formatting is now complete for the Pies table.

9   Choose File > Save to save your file.

Using graphics in tables

Images can spice up any table and, perhaps, help sell a few more of Bella's pies and cakes. InDesign offers two ways to insert graphics into tables: select a cell with the Type tool and choose File > Place, or select the graphic with the Selection tool, cut or copy it, and then paste it into the table with the Type tool. When you add a graphic that is larger than the cell, the cell height increases to contain the graphic; the width of the cell doesn't change, but the image may extend beyond the right side of the cell. If you place a graphic in a cell of a row set to a fixed height and that image is taller than the row height, InDesign marks the cell as overset and adds a red circle, instead of the image, to the cell. You then need to correct either the height of the table row or the size of the image so the image appears in the cell.

Placing graphics in cells

In this exercise, you'll add images to the Bella's Bakery tables. To expedite the process, the document's pasteboard contains appropriately sized graphics that are ready to place. Instead of using the Selection tool to select them, changing to the Type tool, and then back to the Selection tool, you'll use a much more efficient shortcut to manage this task.

1 With the Selection tool (↖), click the cherry cheesecake picture in the top-left area of the pasteboard to select it. If you are still in Preview mode, you can't see your pasteboard. Press W on the keyboard to exit or enter Preview mode.

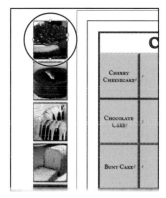

Choose the cherry cheesecake image on the pasteboard to the left of the document.

2 Choose Edit > Cut, or use the keyboard shortcut Ctrl+X (Windows) or Command+X (Mac OS) to cut the image to the clipboard. You will put all the graphics into the empty table cells in exactly the order they already appear on the pasteboard.

3 In the Cakes table, double-click the second-from-left cell in the second row. Double-clicking any cell that can contain text automatically turns the Selection tool into the Type tool (T).

4 Press Ctrl+V (Windows) or Command+V (Mac OS) to paste the picture into the selected cell.

5 Move back over the pasteboard, and then press and hold Ctrl (Windows) or Command (Mac OS) to change the Type tool to the Selection tool, and click the picture of a chocolate cake.

6 Press Ctrl+X (Windows) or Command+X (Mac OS) to cut the picture.

7 Click the second cell of the third row, and then press Ctrl+V (Windows) or Command+V (Mac OS) to paste the picture into the cell.

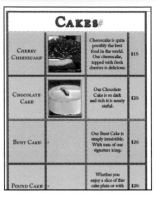

Cut and paste the cheesecake and cake images into the Cakes table.

8 Repeat steps 5 to 7 for the remaining cake pictures, and then repeat them again to paste the pie graphics from the right side of the pasteboard into the Pies table to fit in their respective rows.

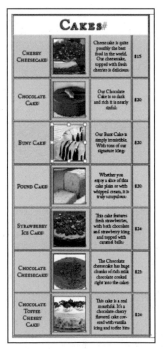

Keyboard shortcuts simplify cutting and pasting graphics into tables.

It is possible to make a photo fit entirely within a table cell; however, there are a few things to account for. Every cell has a text inset applied by default. To ensure that a photo fits within the cell, remove the cell inset so the photo can extend to the cell border. In addition, if you have any strokes applied to a cell, you need to reduce the size of the graphics frame by the value of those stroke values.

Cell styles and table styles

With InDesign CS5, you can use cell styles to format cells, and table styles to format tables, in the same way you use paragraph and character styles to format text. Beyond that, you can nest cell styles into a table style in the same way that you can nest character styles into paragraph styles. Cell styles contain such information as paragraph styles, cell insets, strokes, and fills, which means that you can apply all these attributes to a cell or range of cells with one click. When you make a cell style, however, it does not automatically include all the selected cell's formatting. From a collection of cell styles, you can build table styles. Table styles contain cell styles as well as Table Options settings, including table borders and row and column strokes. As with all InDesign styles, when you update a table or cell style, all elements to which the style is applied update automatically. These Table styles give you the ability to format an entire table with one click and implement changes throughout a document's tables.

By default, each new document contains a Basic Table style that you can customize to apply automatically to all new tables you create. In addition, each document contains a default cell style called None, which is a quick way to remove all cell attributes, as you discovered in the "Resetting the cell styles within a table" section. You cannot modify the None style.

When you use cell styles in a table style, you can specify which cell styles are applied to different sections of the table: header and footer rows, left and right columns, and body rows.

Cell styles

Because you have already formatted the table and cells and also created paragraph styles, you can now reap the rewards of setting up a table using the correct process. With all these elements in place, you can now easily create cell styles. In this exercise, you'll create four cell styles—Header, Name, Description, and Price—that contain the paragraph styles you made earlier.

1 Using the Type tool (T), click inside the Cherry Cheesecake cell, and then press Ctrl+/ (Windows) or Command+/ (Mac OS) to select it.

2 Choose Window > Styles > Cell Styles, to open the Cell Styles panel.

3 Choose New Cell Style from the Cell Styles panel menu (‑≡).

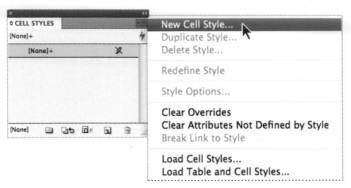

Choose New Cell Style from the Cell Styles panel menu.

4 In the New Cell Style dialog box that opens, type **Name** in the Style Name text field. Note that because the cell was selected when creating a new style, all of the attributes of the cell have been incorporated into the cell style definition. Choose Name from the Paragraph Style drop-down menu, and click OK to create the Name cell style. You have now created a cell style that contains a paragraph style. Remember that creating a style does not automatically apply it to the cell unless you choose this option in the dialog box when creating the style.

You will apply the style in the next exercise.

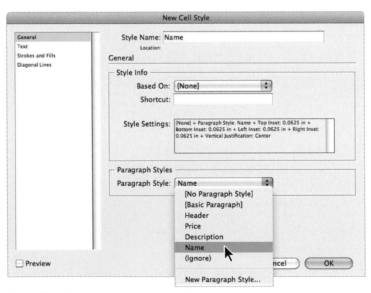

Choose Name from the Paragraph Style drop-down menu.

5 Click the Cakes header cell using the Type tool, and then press the Esc key to select it.

6 Choose New Cell Style from the Cell Styles panel menu, type **Header** in the Style Name field, choose Header from the Paragraph Styles drop-down menu, and click OK to create the Header cell style.

7 Click the first description cell (*Cheesecake is quite possibly the best…*), and then press the Esc key to select it.

8 Repeat step 6, naming the new cell style **Description** and choosing Description for the associated paragraph style.

9 Click the *$15* cell, and then press the Esc key to select it.

10 Repeat step 6, naming the final cell style **Price** and choosing Price for the associated paragraph style.

Applying cell styles

You can apply cell styles to cells with the usual point-and-click ease. Try it out by applying the styles you just created to the Cakes table.

1 Click inside the Cakes header cell using the Type tool (T), and then press the Esc key to select it.

2 Click the Header style in the Cell Styles panel to apply that style to the selected cell.

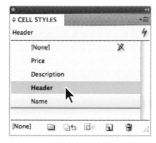

Click a name in the Cell Styles panel's list to select a cell style and apply it to a selected cell.

3 Click at the end of the Cherry Cheesecake text, press Shift+down arrow to select its cell, and then press Shift+down arrow six more times to select the rest of the column.

4 Click the Name style in the Cell Styles panel's list to apply that style to the selected cells.

5 Click in the first description cell (*Cheesecake is quite possibly the best…*) and drag down and to the left to select all the images and descriptions.

6 Click Description in the Cell Styles panel to apply the style. This centers the images in the cells for you as well.

Click and drag to select both the images and descriptions, and then apply the style.

7 Click in the $15 cell, and then drag down to select it and the rest of the price cells. You can also press Shift+down arrow eight times to select the remaining cells.

8 Click Price in the Cell Styles panel to apply the final style.

Creating table styles

Compared to setting up the initial attributes, making a table style from a group of cell styles is fast and easy. All you have to do is choose which cell styles you want to use and tell InDesign which style to use where. The action takes place in the New Table Style dialog box. Here you can specify which cell styles are applied to different sections of the table: header and footer rows, left and right columns, and body rows.

In this exercise, you'll compile the cell styles from your Cakes table into a table style for use on the Pies table.

1 Using the Type tool (T), select the entire Cakes table by clicking in the top-left corner of the table frame when you see a diagonal arrow.

2 If necessary, choose Window > Styles > Table Styles to open the Table Styles panel.

From the Table Styles panel, you can create and apply table styles.

3 Alt+click (Windows) or Option+click (Mac OS) the Create New Style button located at the bottom of the Table Styles panel. The New Table Style dialog box opens. Notice the Cell Styles section, which contains five drop-down menus. This is where you match the cell style to the location where it should be applied. Header and Body Rows are self-explanatory. The Left and Right Column menus, however, let you specify unique styles for the cells, so that you could have different paragraph styles within the cell style for each.

4 In the New Table Style dialog box, type **Bella's Bakery** in the Style Name text field.

5 In the Cell Styles section, choose Header from the Header Rows drop-down menu.

6 Choose Description from the Body Rows drop-down menu, choose Name from the Left Column drop-down menu, and choose Price from the Right Column drop-down menu. Click OK.

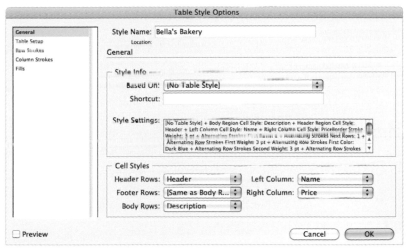

Assign the cell styles you want to use in the New Table Style dialog box.

7 With the table still selected, choose the Bella's Bakery style to apply it. Open the Cell Styles panel and click None to remove any manually applied Cell Styles as the Table Style is now doing all of the work. Choose File > Save.

Applying table styles

Here's where all that hard work pays off: you can format an entire table with one click. In this exercise, you'll style the Pies table and a new Cookies table.

1 Select the entire Pies table using the Type tool (T) by clicking in the top-left corner of the table's frame when you see the diagonal arrow.

2   Choose Bella's Bakery from the Table Styles panel to apply the style. If there are any plus signs to the right of the table style name, Alt+click (Windows) or Option+click (Mac OS) to clear the overrides. You may need to hold the Shift key and adjust the vertical size of the table with the Type tool. Now you can try it again.

 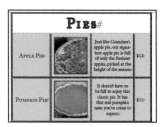

Choosing Bella's Bakery from the Table Styles panel formats the entire Pies table with one click.

3   Click the Layers button (⬡) in the panel dock to open the Layers panel, and then click on the left-hand gray box next to the Cookies layer. A table listing different types of cookies appears in the right-hand column of the document.

4   Select the entire Cookies table by clicking with the Type tool in the top-left corner of the table frame when you see a diagonal arrow.

5   From the Table Styles panel, choose Bella's Bakery from the list to apply the style to the Cookies table. You may need to adjust the height of the cells in the Cookies table so that they match the other tables.

6   Click the left-hand gray box next to the Background layer in the Layers panel. This shows you the intended background color that has been set to the bleed.

7   Choose Edit > Deselect All so that nothing in the layout is selected, and then press the **W** key on your keyboard to preview the finished layout. If necessary, choose Edit > Fit Spread in Window to view the project. Press W again when you are done previewing the project.

8   Select File > Save and you're done!

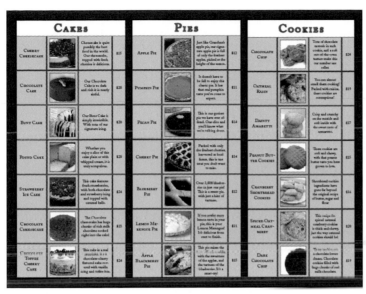

Take a look at the finished Bella's Bakery brochure.

Self study

Save another copy of your document as id0602_work.indd.

1   Because all three of your tables are designed with styles, you can make universal changes. Try changing the paragraph style Description, changing the font, and turning hyphenation off; click the Preview button to see all three tables change as you choose different options.

2   Select a cell and give the cell a stroke; then redefine the style in the drop-down menu of the Cell Styles panel to see the global change.

3   Change all the fonts and colors in the first table. Make new paragraph styles, and apply them. Change the attributes of the four sections of cells you used. Make a new set of cell styles, apply them to the first table, and then create a table style from that table. Apply your new table style to the other two tables.

Review

Questions

1 What are four ways to select a cell?

2 Can paragraph styles be included in cell styles?

3 In which five sections of a table style can you apply cell styles?

4 If you needed to remove all formatting to reduce a table down to its basic appearance, how would you make these changes?

5 If a plus sign (+) appears next to your table style name, it indicates that some change has occurred and there are overrides to some of the cells, tables, or text within the table. How do you clear these overrides?

Answers

1 Click and drag until the whole cell is highlighted; press Ctrl+/ (Windows) or Command+/ (Mac OS); click in a cell and press Shift+down arrow; press the Esc key.

2 Yes, but they are not chosen by default; you must select them in the Cell Style drop-down menu.

3 You can apply cell styles in a table style in these sections: header rows, footer rows, left columns, right columns, and body rows.

4 In the Table Styles panel, click on Basic Table.

5 Alt+click (Windows) or Option+click (Mac OS) the style name to clear overrides.

Lesson 7

What you'll learn in this lesson:

- Applying colors and strokes
- Using and saving spot colors
- Updating and editing colors
- Setting up color management

Using Color in Your Documents

Using color for text, frames, and paths is a basic task in InDesign. The more ways you know how to apply, change, and control color, the faster you can work. Color choices are not limited to picking from the small selection that appears in the Swatches panel. You can create your own colors, gradients, and tints, as well as choose from a number of swatch libraries, such as Pantone colors, that are supplied for you within InDesign.

Starting up

Before starting, make sure that your tools and panels are consistent by resetting your preferences. See "Resetting the InDesign workspace and preferences" on page 3.

You will work with several files from the id07lessons folder in this lesson. Make sure that you have copied the id07lessons folder onto your hard drive from the Digital Classroom DVD. See "Loading lesson files" on page 4. This lesson may be easier to follow if the id07lessons folder is on your desktop.

See Lesson 7 in action!

Use the accompanying video to gain a better understanding of how to use some of the features shown in this lesson. Visit digitalclassroombooks.com to view the sample tutorial for this lesson.

The project

To explore InDesign's color controls, you will add color to a fictional ad for FiFi's Face Cream. You'll use multiple types of colors, as well as tints and gradients, in the course of the lesson. If you want to see what the finished project will look like, open id0701_done.indd from the id07lessons folder now.

The finished project.

Applying colors to frames and text

There are several ways to assign color to an object with InDesign. You can assign color through the Tools panel, the Swatches panel, the Color panel, and the Color Picker. You can also assign color using the Eyedropper tool. No matter which method you choose, you must perform the same three steps: select the text or object that you want to color, specify which part of the object you want to color, and then choose the color to apply.

Applying color to text

Applying color is a quick, straightforward process. To practice, you will color the text in the FiFi's Face Cream ad.

1   Choose File > Open. Navigate to the id07lessons folder, select the file id0701.indd, and then click Open.

2   Choose File > Save As. In the Save As dialog box, navigate to the id07lessons folder and type **id0701_work.indd** in the Name text field. Click Save.

3   Select the Type tool (T) from the Tools panel and click inside the frame containing the text, *It leaves your skin feeling noticeably clean and absolutely radiant!*

4   Choose Edit > Select All to select all the text inside the frame.

5   Select Window > Swatches or click the Swatches button (■)in the dock on the right side of the workspace to open the Swatches panel.

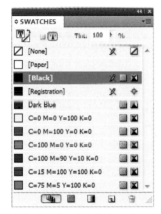

Color the object from the Swatches panel.

The first thing to consider is whether you want to color the border (stroke) or the inside (fill) of the selected text. In the upper-left corner of the Swatches panel are two icons overlapping one another. The icon with the outlined T and the red diagonal line running through it is the Stroke icon (□). The icon with the solid black T inside it is the Fill icon (□). In order to apply color, you must click the appropriate icon to bring it forward and make it active. In this case, you want to fill the text with the color Dark Blue. If necessary, bring the Fill icon forward.

You can also press the X key on your keyboard to toggle between Fill and Stroke in the Swatches panel, as long as you don't have the Type tool activated.

To quickly reset the default colors, click the icon in the lower-left area (⬚) near the Fill/Stroke box in the Tools panel. The default color for objects is no fill (None) with a black stroke; a black fill with no stroke (None) is the default color for text.

Choose the fill and stroke colors in the Swatches panel by bringing their respective icons forward.

6   In the Swatches panel, click on the Dark Blue option. The text turns blue. Choose Edit > Deselect All to view the change.

Applying color to frames

Next you will color the border, or stroke, of the frame around the text. Follow the same three basic steps that you went through to apply color to the text: Select the frame, specify fill or stroke, and choose the color.

1   Activate the Selection tool (↖) in the Tools panel. Notice that the Stroke and Fill icons no longer have a *T* (for Type), but now appear as a solid square for the Fill, and an outlined square for the Stroke. Make sure the text frame is selected.

2   Click the Stroke icon (◻) in the Swatches panel to bring it forward.

3   Select Dark Blue in the Swatches panel to apply the color to the frame.

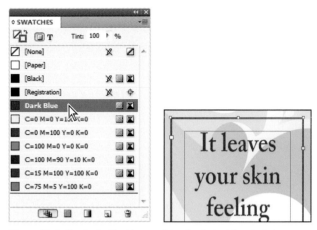

Choose Dark Blue in the Swatches panel to color the text frame's stroke.

Applying Live Corner Effects

InDesign provides a new feature called Live Corner Effects that enables you to adjust the radius and style of the corners of a frame visually without the need to open a separate dialog box. To give the frame a little more style, you will round its edges.

1   With the Selection tool (⬚) active, click on the text frame on the right side of the ad to select the frame.

2   You'll notice a yellow square in the upper-right corner of the frame. This square is the Live Corner Effects indicator. Click on the yellow square to enable Live Corner Effects, and you'll notice that a yellow diamond appears in each corner of the text frame, indicating that Live Corner Effects has been enabled.

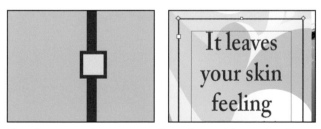

The yellow square is the Live Corner Effects indicator. Clicking on the yellow square enables Live Corner Effects and displays yellow diamonds in each corner of the frame.

3 Click on any of the yellow diamonds and drag toward the center of the frame to increase the corner radius for all corners of the frame. The further you drag, the higher the radius value will be. Drag until the smart guides display about .15 inches. Click anywhere in your document to deselect the frame.

Clicking on a yellow diamond and dragging toward the center of the frame adjusts the corner radius of the frame.

4 Choose File > Save.

Corner shape options

Although the rounded corner effect is the default when using the Live Corner Effects feature, it's not the only choice available. With a frame selected, you can quickly choose a different corner effect by clicking on the corner shape drop-down menu in the Control panel and choosing from a variety of shapes, including Fancy, Bevel, Inset, Inverse Rounded, and Rounded.

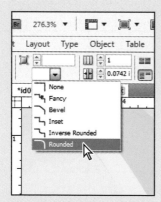

The corner shape drop-down menu.

Creating and saving a new swatch

You can create your own custom color swatches, or use those supplied by InDesign. When you create a color or gradient, InDesign automatically shows it in the Fill/Stroke box in the Tools panel, and also displays it in the Swatches panel and Color panel. Because InDesign also automatically applies the new color to whatever you have selected, you need to be very careful to select only the items you want colored before you begin. In the next exercises, you will create, name, and apply two new colors.

The Swatches panel can contain spot colors, process colors, mixed inks (combinations of multiple spot and process colors), RGB or Lab colors, gradients, or tints. This exercise concentrates on CMYK colors, Cyan, Magenta, Yellow, and Black, but you'll learn more about the specialized color options in later sections.

1 To make sure nothing on the pasteboard is selected, press Shift+Ctrl+A (Windows) or Shift+Command+A (Mac OS).

If you activate any of the InDesign drawing tools, such as the Rectangle tool, or any of the tools hidden beneath it—Line tool, Pen tool, Pencil tool, or the Type tool—and choose a color swatch, the default color is set for these tools, and every time the tool is used, it will be preset to this color. If you choose a color with one of these tools active and no objects selected, you will establish the new default color for this group of tools.

2 If necessary, click the Swatches button (▦) in the dock to open the Swatches panel. From the Swatches panel menu (◦≡), choose New Color Swatch.

3 In the resulting New Color Swatch dialog box, uncheck the *Name with Color Value* checkbox so you can name this color swatch as you create it. Type **Green** in the Swatch Name text field.

4   Increase the Cyan percentage to 80 percent by moving the slider bar to the right of Cyan or typing **80** into the % text field. Using the sliders or typing the percentages, set Magenta to **10** percent, Yellow to **100** percent, and Black to **0** percent. These percentage tints of the process inks combine to create the new color.

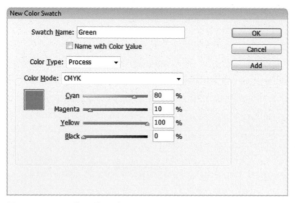

To create a new color, adjust the percentages in the New Color Swatch dialog box, and then click OK.

5   Click OK to create the new color. Green now appears at the very bottom of the Swatches panel. When you make a new color swatch, it always appears at the bottom of the list of swatches. You can change the order of the swatches by simply clicking and dragging them within the Swatches panel.

6   In the Swatches panel, click and drag the Green swatch upward so it is positioned just below Dark Blue, and then release it. You should see a black line indicating where the swatch will appear before you drop it. You may want to expand the size of the Swatches panel to minimize scrolling within the panel.

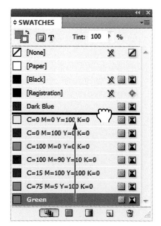

Click and drag to rearrange swatches in the Swatches panel.

7   Choose File > Save to save your work.

Applying strokes to text

In the next exercise, you will fill text with the new color, as well as create a contrasting color for the text's stroke. You'll also get your first look at the Stroke panel, which gives you control over the weight and appearance of an element's stroke or border.

1   With the Selection tool (𝕜) active, double-click the frame containing the words *Face Cream* in the lower-left corner of the document. This automatically converts the Selection tool to the Type tool (T). Alternately, you can also choose the Type tool and click inside the frame. Press Ctrl+A (Windows) or Command+A (Mac OS) to select all the text in the frame.

2   In the Swatches panel, click the Fill icon (□) to bring it forward, and click the Green swatch you made in the previous exercise. *Face Cream* is now green.

Turn the Face Cream *text green.*

You will now make a new color for the stroke.

3   Click the Stroke icon (□) to bring it forward. From the Swatches panel menu (◦≡), choose New Color Swatch.

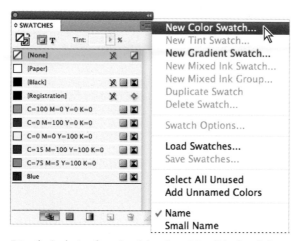

Bring the Stroke icon forward, and then choose New Color Swatch from the panel menu.

4   In the resulting New Color Swatch dialog box, uncheck the *Name with Color Value* checkbox, and type **Light Blue** in the Swatch Name text field.

5 Change the Cyan to 32 percent by moving its slider bar or typing **32** in the % text field. Using the sliders or typing in the percentages, set Magenta to **6** percent, Yellow to **3** percent, and Black to **0** percent.

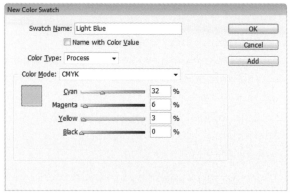

Create a light-blue color by adjusting the CMYK percentages.

6 Click OK. InDesign automatically applies Light Blue to the stroke of the text. The stroke doesn't quite stand out enough, however. In the next steps, you'll use the Stroke panel to increase the stroke's width.

Don't forget to reorganize the swatches for the best workflow. For example, because Green and Light Blue will be used in combination for text in the ad, click and drag the Light Blue swatch just below Green in the Swatches panel. A black line indicates where the swatch will appear before you drop it. Rearranging swatches into logical groups for your project is a good practice to follow.

7 Click the Stroke icon in the panel dock to open the Stroke panel.

8 Type **1.5** in the panel's Weight text field and press Enter (Windows) or Return (Mac OS) to increase the selected stroke's size.

Apply a stroke to the Face Cream *text and increase its size with the Stroke panel.*

9 Select File > Save to save your work.

Creating a tint reduction

A tint, sometimes called a screen, is a lighter shade of a color. Tinting is a great way to use colors at different intensities. Just as you can with regular colors, you can (and should) save tints in the Swatches panel to make editing tints fast and easy. Because colors and their tints maintain their relationship in the Swatches panel, a change to the original color swatch also updates any tints of that swatch that have been made. In this exercise, you will create a tint to use in the ad.

1 Using the Selection tool (⬆), click the frame that contains the word *FiFi's*. Use the Selection tool to select the frame as an object because it is no longer type. It was converted to outlines and is now a path, and therefore no longer editable as text.

2 Click the Swatches button (▦) in the dock to open the Swatches panel, and make sure the Fill icon is in the foreground. Select the Light Blue swatch to apply the color to the fill.

3 At the top of the Swatches panel, click the right-facing arrow to expose the Tint slider. Drag the slider to the left to reduce the fill's tint from 100 percent to 60 percent. Click the right-facing arrow again to accept the new value. The change is reflected in the selected object. Now that you have made the tint, you can save the modified version of the Light Blue swatch in the Swatches panel.

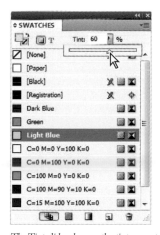

The Tint slider changes the tint percentage for the selected swatch.

4 In the Swatches panel, click and drag the Fill icon from the top of the Swatches panel into the list of swatches, and drop it below the Light Blue color swatch to add the tint Light Blue at 60 percent to the list.

The logo after applying the color tint.

5 Select File > Save to save your work.

Making a dashed stroke

You've practiced applying, coloring, and widening a basic stroke, but InDesign offers many more ways to customize strokes. To demonstrate, you will make a custom dash around the border of the FiFi's ad.

1 Using the Selection tool (✦), select the black frame running around the edge of the ad.

2 In the Swatches panel, click the Stroke icon (▫) to bring it forward.

3 Open the Stroke panel by clicking the Stroke button (≣) in the panel dock. Use the up arrow to the left of the Weight text field to increase the stroke thickness to 4 points. Notice that the frame, which was aligned to the size of the page, is now bigger than the page. This is because the default alignment of a stroke is centered on the frame. In this case, half the width of the stroke (two points) is now inside the frame and half the width of the stroke (two points) is outside the frame. You will change this stroke alignment next.

If every time you make a frame, you notice yourself changing the alignment to the inside so that the frame doesn't extend beyond the path, you can make yourself an Object Style with the stroke aligned to the inside. Or, better yet, change the settings right in the Object Styles panel by adjusting the Basic Text Frame and the Basic Graphics Frame options.

4 In the Stroke panel, click the Align Stroke to Inside button (▣). The border appears to jump inside the frame, because all stroke edges are now aligned to the inside of the frame.

5 Still in the Stroke panel, click the Type drop-down menu to reveal all the various styles of strokes you can make. Choose Dashed. Dash and Gap options appear at the bottom of the Stroke panel. The dash is the stroke segments, and the gap is the space between the dashes.

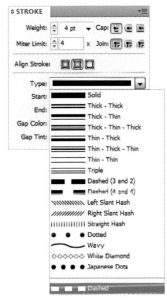

Choose Dashed for the ad's border.

6 Make sure the first dash text field shows 12 pt. This sets the length of the dash. In the first gap text field, type **3**, which sets the length of the gap between dashes. Type **11** in the third text field to set a second dash length. In the remaining gap and dash text fields, type **2** and **10**, respectively, leaving the final gap field empty. This sequence of dashes and gaps will repeat where this stroke is applied.

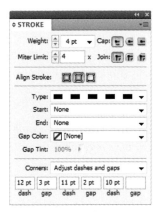

Set the color, dash, and gap options in the Stroke panel.

7 Press Enter (Windows) or Return (Mac OS) to apply the settings. You have created a custom dash.

Now you can change the color of both the dash (stroke) and gap.

8 In the Swatches panel, make sure the Stroke icon is forward, and choose Light Blue to apply it to the dash. Be sure to pick the original Light Blue swatch and not the tinted version.

9 In the Stroke panel, choose Dark Blue from the Stroke panel's Gap Color drop-down menu.

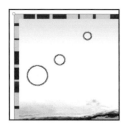

The finished border has light-blue dashes separated by dark-blue gaps.

10 Choose File > Save to save your work.

Creating and saving gradients

A *gradient* is a smooth and gradual transition between two or more colors. When you first apply a gradient, the default is set to two color stops. A *color stop* is the point at which a gradient changes from one color to the next. You can add as many stops as you want to a gradient, and also control how quickly or slowly the colors fade into each other. You can also change the direction of a gradient, and even choose whether it is a linear gradient, appearing as a straight-line transition, or a radial gradient, which appears in a circular form. In this series of exercises, you will make and save linear and radial gradients, as well as use the Gradient tool to change the direction of the gradient.

Linear gradients

You create gradients in the Gradient panel, and then add colors to the transition by dragging and dropping them as color stops on the gradient bar in the panel. You'll build a gradient next.

1 Using the Selection tool (⬑), click the frame containing the words, *It leaves your skin feeling noticeably clean and absolutely radiant.*

Always select an object before starting the gradient. It's easier to build a gradient when you have something selected because you can preview exactly how the color transitions will look.

2   Toward the bottom of the Tools panel are overlapping Fill and Stroke icons, just as in the Swatches panel. Select the Fill icon to bring it forward.

3   Choose Window > Color > Gradient to display it. From the Type drop-down menu in this panel, choose Linear. The frame now has a white-to-black linear gradient applied by default.

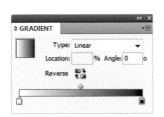 

Use the Gradient panel to apply a white-to-black gradient to the frame.

You will now add colors to the gradient. Make sure you can see both the Gradient and Swatches panels, as you will be dragging colors from the Swatches panel into the Gradient panel.

4   Click and hold the Light Blue swatch in the Swatches panel. Don't just click or you will simply apply the color to the selected frame. Drag the swatch to the right side of the gradient color bar until the cursor becomes a hand with a plus sign (⊞). The line cursor on the gradient bar disappears, indicating that it will replace the black color stop with the light blue one. Be careful to replace the original color rather than add another color next to it. Whether replacing or adding a color stop, the cursor displays a plus sign when you add a color stop to the gradient.

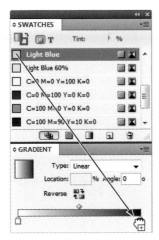

This cursor indicates that you are dragging a color from the Swatches panel to the Gradient panel. Drop the color over a color stop to apply it.

5 Release the mouse to drop the color. The gradient bar now has a white color stop on the left and a Light Blue color stop on the right. The frame in the ad should look the same way, with the color fading from white on the left to light blue on the right.

6 Choose File > Save to save your work.

Saving a gradient

You can save gradients in the Swatches panel to apply them later to other objects with a single click. You save a gradient by dragging its preview from the Gradient panel into the Swatches panel. Try it with the white-to–Light Blue gradient.

1 Click and hold the preview of the gradient in the top-left corner of the Gradient panel.

2 Drag the cursor to just below Light Blue 60% in the Swatches panel. A heavy black line appears, showing where the new gradient swatch will appear before you release it. The cursor changes to a white box with a plus sign (⊞) as you drag, indicating that you are about to add a gradient to the Swatches panel.

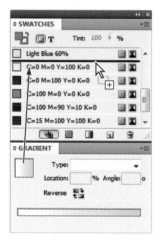

This cursor indicates that you are adding a gradient to the Swatches panel.

3 Release the mouse to drop the gradient into the Swatches panel. InDesign automatically names the gradient New Gradient Swatch. You will now change the name to something more recognizable.

4 Double-click the New Gradient Swatch. The Gradient Options dialog box appears.

5   In the Swatch Name text field, type **Light Blue Linear**, then click OK.

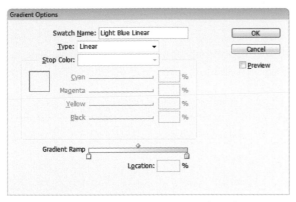

In the Gradient Options dialog box, you can name the gradient.

6   Drag the Gradient panel by its tab over the Swatches panel until a border appears. Release the Gradient panel, placing it into the dock.

7   Choose File > Save to save your work.

Adjusting fill opacity

As a preview of what's to come in Lesson 8, "Using Effects," you will now decrease the opacity of the fill so you can see through the frame. This effects feature lets you control fill, stroke, and text opacity separately.

1   Using the Selection tool (▶), select the text frame that you modified in the previous exercise and choose Window > Effects, or click the Effects button (*fx*) in the dock, to open the Effects panel.

2   Select Fill from the target list inside the Effects panel. Double-click inside the Opacity text field and type **70%**, or click the arrow to the right of the text field and move the slider to 70 percent. Press Enter (Windows) or Return (Mac OS) to apply the settings.

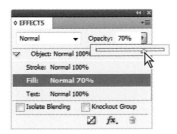

The Effects panel with the proper settings.

3   Choose File > Save. You have just changed the opacity of only the object's fill. You will learn more specifics of this and other effects in Lesson 8, "Using Effects."

Radial gradient

The last gradient you made was a linear gradient, which means it fades from one color to another along straight lines. This is the default in InDesign. You will now explore radial gradients, which are gradients that don't fade color in the form of lines, but as circles. If you wanted to make a sphere that looked like light was hitting the top of it, with the shadow at the bottom, you could use the radial gradient to accomplish this. You will use the radial gradient to make bubbles in this next exercise.

1 Using the Selection tool (🔨), click the far-left circle in the ad.

2 In the Swatches panel, click the Stroke icon (▢) to bring it forward. Select None for the stroke.

3 Bring the Fill icon forward. Select the Light Blue Linear gradient that you saved earlier.

4 If it is not already open, choose Window > Gradient, or click the Gradient button (▣) in the dock, to open the Gradient panel. Here you will change the type of gradient that is applied.

You can also double-click the Gradient Swatch tool in the Tools panel to open the Gradient panel.

5 Choose Radial from the Gradient panel's Type drop-down menu. The circle now has a radial gradient.

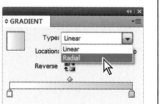

Choose Radial from the Type drop-down menu to change from a linear to a radial gradient.

6 Choose File > Save to save your work.

Adjusting the direction of a radial gradient

The Gradient Swatch tool in the Tools panel allows you to change the direction of both linear and radial gradients. In this case, the radial gradient appears with white in the middle of the circle and blends from the center outward to the Light Blue color. You will change that now using the Gradient Swatch tool.

1 Select the Gradient Swatch tool (▣) in the Tools panel. You will use this tool to set the span and direction of an applied gradient.

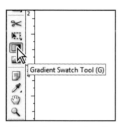

The Gradient Swatch tool enables you to change a gradient's span and angle.

2 Click and drag from the top-left to the bottom-right of the circle to give the sphere the look of a highlight in its top-left part. When you release the mouse, the top-left area appears white, and then fades radially into Light Blue.

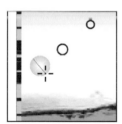

Drag with the Gradient Swatch tool in the direction you desire.

3 In the Gradient panel, right-click (Windows) or Ctrl+click (Mac OS) the gradient color swatch and select Add to Swatches to add the radial gradient to the Swatches panel. In the Swatches panel, move the New Gradient Swatch so that it is underneath the Light Blue Linear gradient.

4 Double-click the New Gradient Swatch in the Swatches panel to rename it.

5 In the resulting Gradient Options dialog box, type **Light Blue Radial** in the Swatch Name text field. Click OK.

One-click edits

InDesign makes it easy to share attributes among document elements, so that you can make global changes with minimal effort.

Using the Eyedropper tool to copy frame attributes

When you need to copy attributes from one element to another in a document, choose the Eyedropper tool. It can pick up both type and frame attributes, such as fill and stroke settings, and apply those characteristics to other types or frames. By default, the Eyedropper tool picks up all attributes, but you can choose to transfer only specific settings using the Eyedropper Options dialog box. You will use the Eyedropper tool to quickly copy the attributes from one frame to another.

1 Press Shift+Ctrl+A (Windows) or Shift+Command+A (Mac OS) to make sure nothing is selected.

2 In the Tools panel, select the Eyedropper tool (🖋).

3 Click on the circle that you previously filled with the radial gradient. The Eyedropper tool now appears filled; it contains all the formatting attributes of that circle.

When you click an object with the Eyedropper tool, the tool fills with formatting information.

4 Move the filled eyedropper cursor to the center of the nearest circle and click. The attributes are applied: the gradient fills the circle, and the existing stroke disappears.

5 Click a few more of the circles to apply the gradient attributes, but leave some circles, as they will be used in the next exercise.

6 Choose File > Save to save your work.

Applying colors to multiple objects

Although the Eyedropper tool is quite handy for copying multiple attributes to single objects, sometimes you want to apply changes to multiple objects at once. InDesign makes this simple. When you select a group of objects, you can apply a fill or stroke to all of them with one click. Practice this by adding gradients to the ad's remaining circles.

1 Choose the Selection tool (k) from the Tools panel, and then click a circle that still has a black stroke and no fill.

2 Shift+click every circle that does not have the gradient fill.

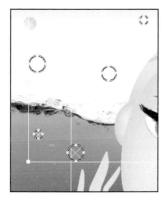

Shift+click to select all the unfilled circles.

3 In the Swatches panel, click the Fill icon to bring it forward, and then click the Light Blue Radial swatch for the fill color.

4 Select the Stroke icon (□) to bring it forward, and scroll up to select None for the stroke. All the selected circles now have the Light Blue Radial gradient and no stroke.

Apply the Light Blue Radial gradient to the selected circles.

5 Select File > Save.

Updating and editing colors

When you apply a swatch to multiple objects in InDesign, each of those objects is related to that color in the Swatches panel. If you then change the color of the swatch, all instances of the color throughout the document change. This makes it quick and easy to make global color changes. In this exercise, you will change the Light Blue swatch to experiment with a new look for the ad.

1 Press Shift+Ctrl+A (Windows) or Shift+Command+A (Mac OS) to make sure nothing is selected.

2 Double-click the Light Blue swatch in the Swatches panel to open the Swatch Options dialog box.

3 In the Swatch Options dialog box, click the *Preview* checkbox (below the OK and Cancel buttons) so that you can see the changes take effect as you apply them.

4 Drag the Magenta slider to the right so that Magenta appears at 38%. All the Light Blues you added to the ad now appear more purple.

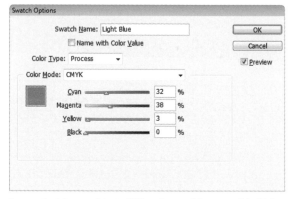

Increase the Magenta slider to 38% to change all instances of the Light Blue color in the ad to purple.

5 Click OK to implement the changes.

6 Choose File > Save As. In the Save As dialog box, navigate to the id07lessons folder, and then type **id0702.indd** in the Name text field. Click Save. You can use this file later for the Self study section.

Save the purple project to use later.

7 Choose File > Close, and then reopen id0701_work.indd. It should look as it did before you changed the light blue to purple.

Using and saving spot colors

Spot colors are premixed ink colors that provide very accurate and vibrant color when printed. They are often used to maintain brand identity when printing corporate logos or simply to add visual appeal to a job. Spot colors can produce colors that simply are not possible using process (CMYK) colors. Spot colors require their own printing plates on a printing press, which increases the cost of a commercial printing job; however, when critical color matching is required, spot colors are second to none.

For the most accurate representation of a spot color, certain things must be considered. First, you should pick the spot color from a color-matching system supported by your commercial printer. Several color-matching libraries ship with InDesign. You must also remember that a color's appearance depends on many variables such as the limits of your printer, and the paper stock it's printed on.

Fortunately, you can manipulate spot colors in InDesign just as you can ordinary CMYK colors. You can create your own spot colors in the Swatches panel, or place an image that contains a spot color to add that color automatically to the panel. You can adjust and apply spot colors in the Swatches panel, using them for fills, strokes, or gradients. In this exercise, you will create a spot color to apply to the ad.

1   Press Shift+Ctrl+A (Windows) or Shift+Command+A (Mac OS) to make sure nothing is selected.

2   In the Swatches panel, click the panel menu button (•≡) and choose New Color Swatch.

3   In the resulting New Color Swatch dialog box, choose Spot from the Color Type drop-down menu.

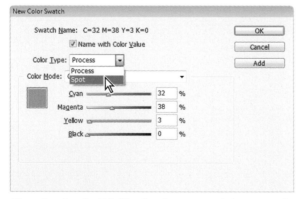

Choose Spot from the Color Type drop-down menu to designate a swatch as a spot color.

4   Choose PANTONE solid coated from the Color Mode drop-down menu to change it from CMYK. PANTONE solid coated and PANTONE solid uncoated are the two most common ink color libraries; coated is for a coated or glossy paper, while uncoated is for uncoated paper stock. Now you need to specify which spot color you want to work with.

5   In the Pantone text field, type **662**. This automatically brings you to that Pantone color, a dark blue.

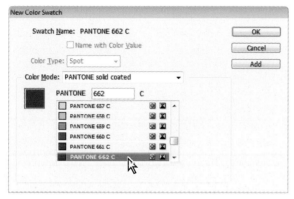

*Choose PANTONE solid coated from the Color Mode drop-down menu, and then enter color **662**.*

6   Click OK to close the dialog box and add the swatch named Pantone 662 C to the Swatches panel. The swatch is automatically named.

7   Drag the Pantone 662 C swatch up in the Swatches panel and drop it directly beneath the Light Blue Radial gradient swatch. You will apply the new spot color in the next exercise.

Colorizing a grayscale image

InDesign can colorize any grayscale image you import as long as it does not contain any spot colors or alpha channels. The two raindrops in the ad are grayscale images that had clipping paths applied. This format enables you to change the colors of black and gray into whatever color you would like. You will use the Pantone 662 C color created in the last exercise.

1   To color only the pixels of the image, choose the Direct Selection tool ( ) from the Tools panel. If you try to colorize the image when it is selected with the Selection tool instead, the fill of the whole box will be colored.

2   Select one of the raindrops. A path appears around the edge of the raindrop.

3   In the Swatches panel, make sure the Fill icon is forward. Select the Pantone 662 C swatch to apply the color to the raindrop.

4   Select the other raindrop with the Direct Selection tool ( ).

If the active tool changes from the Direct Selection tool to the Selection tool, just double-click to switch back to the Direct Selection tool.

5 In the Swatches panel, select Pantone 662 C to apply it to the second raindrop.

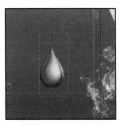

Apply color to the grayscale raindrops.

6 Choose File > Save to save your work.

Congratulations! You have completed the lesson.

Self study

Open the id0702.indd file you saved earlier in the id07lessons folder to practice some additional color variations:

- Try adjusting more colors in the Swatches panel to make universal changes across the ad.

- Create another spot color and recolor the grayscale raindrops again.

- Select the text frame with the linear gradient. Experiment by dragging more colors into the gradient, and use the Gradient Swatch tool to change the gradient's direction.

- Make a new color and put a stroke on the text, *It leaves your skin feeling noticeably clean and absolutely radiant.*

- Design a new radial gradient for the bubbles, and practice coloring some of them individually with the Eyedropper tool.

- Experiment with the Adobe Kuler panel to try different swatch groups and create new color combinations. Access the Kuler panel by choosing Window > Extensions > Kuler, and then create new color themes and add them to the Swatches panel or upload and share them.

Review

Questions

1 How do you change the fill of an object you are trying to color? How do you change the color of the stroke?

2 How do you save a gradient you have already made?

3 If you change a color in the Swatches panel, will it change the color wherever it is applied throughout the document?

4 Can you colorize any grayscale image?

5 True or False: You cannot change the direction of a linear gradient.

Answers

1 In either the Tools panel or the Swatches panel, click the Fill icon to bring it forward, and then click the color desired for the fill. To change the stroke, bring the Stroke icon forward, and then click a color.

2 Drag and drop it from the Gradient panel into the Swatches panel.

3 Yes. That is why the Swatches panel is especially handy for making universal changes to colors throughout your document.

4 Yes, as long as the image does not contain spot or alpha channels.

5 False— the Gradient Swatch tool lets you change the direction of any gradient.

What you'll learn in this lesson:

- Applying opacity to objects

- Singling out stroke and fill

- Adjusting effects for objects

- Combining object styles with effects

- Exploring blending modes

- Working with Imported files that use transparency

Using Effects

You can use Photoshop-like effects directly in your InDesign documents. You can apply effects such as Inner Shadow, Outer and Inner Glow, Bevel and Emboss, and Gradient Feather to objects in InDesign. In this lesson, you will discover how to apply changes to images, objects, and text using a sampling of the effects.

Starting up

Before starting, make sure that your tools and panels are consistent by resetting your preferences. See "Resetting the InDesign workspace and preferences" on page 3.

You will work with several files from the id08lessons folder in this lesson. Make sure that you have copied the id08lessons folder onto your hard drive from the Digital Classroom DVD. See "Loading lesson files" on page 4. This lesson may be easier to follow if the id08lessons folder is on your desktop.

See Lesson 8 in action!

Use the accompanying video to gain a better understanding of how to use some of the features shown in this lesson. Visit digitalclassroombooks.com to view the sample tutorial for this lesson.

The project

In this lesson, you will jazz up a two-page spread using the Effects panel in InDesign CS5. You can experiment with blending modes, opacity, and other effects without permanently changing the objects, and then you can save effects as an object style so that you can easily apply the effects to other objects. If you want to take a peek at what the finished project should look like, open the id0801_done.indd file located in the id08lessons folder.

The appearance of the final layout after you have completed the lesson.

Creative effects

InDesign's Effects panel offers a way to use Photoshop-like effects in InDesign documents. You can apply feathering and drop shadows, as well as control the opacity and blending modes of objects, text, and photos. Not only can you apply effects, but you can also apply them to either the whole object, or to just the fill, stroke, or text in a frame. Better yet, you can turn those effects on or off nondestructively, without permanently changing the objects.

Open the Effects panel by choosing Window > Effects, or by clicking the Effects button (*fx*) in the dock, and take a tour of where you'll be working.

The Effects panel has blending modes and opacity controls at the top, and the ability to target an effect to the stroke, fill, or text appears in the bottom portion of the panel. It's time to put these controls to work.

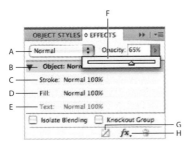

A. *Blending mode.* B. *Opacity and blend settings applied to the object.*
C. *Opacity and blend settings applied to the stroke.*
D. *Opacity and blend settings applied to the fill.*
E. *Opacity and blend settings applied to the text.* F. *Opacity level.*
G. *Clear all effects and make object opaque.* H. *Add an object effect to the selected target.*

Applying opacity to objects

Opacity settings make an object or text appear transparent; to varying degrees, you can see through the object to the objects that appear behind it. If the opacity is set to 0 percent, the object is completely invisible. By default, all objects are set to 100 percent, or completely opaque. Some people get confused about the difference between tint and opacity. Tint is a screened (lighter) version of a color and is not transparent, but opaque. Opacity is the way you control the transparency of an object. Adjusting the transparency allows objects below to show through the object that is transparent or semi-transparent.

Using these tools, you can apply many effects to images. For example, placing a red frame over a grayscale image and changing the opacity to 50 percent makes the image appear as if it has been colored. This is a task you might think is more suitable for Photoshop, but InDesign can give you that kind of control. Practice on a few objects now.

1   Choose Window > Mini Bridge to open the Mini Bridge panel. Click the Browse Files button and navigate to the id08lessons folder. Double-click the id0801.indd file to open the file and begin the lesson. Dock the Mini Bridge panel in the panel dock for quick access later.

2   Save a work version of this file before making any changes. Choose File > Save As. In the Save As dialog box, navigate to the id08lessons folder, type **id0801_work.indd** in the Name text field, then click Save.

3 Click the Pages button (⊞) in the dock on the right side of the workspace to open the Pages panel. Notice that the two pages are numbered 6 and 7. You will work on page 7 first. Double-click the page 7 icon in the Pages panel to center the page in the workspace.

4 Choose the Selection tool (↖) from the Tools panel, and select the blue rectangle in the lower-right corner of the page. Hidden underneath this blue frame is an image. You will change the opacity settings of the blue frame to see the image beneath.

5 If the Effects panel is not open, choose Window > Effects, or click the Effects button (*fx*) in the dock to display the Effects panel.

6 The opacity is set to 100 percent. Click on the right-facing triangle to the immediate right of the Opacity text field to access the Opacity slider.

7 Drag the slider to the left to change the opacity to 65 percent. You can now see the image—a pile of record albums—underneath the blue, but you still have the effect of the blue coloring. Click the triangle again to collapse the slider.

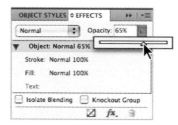

Set the Opacity slider to 65 percent to see the image beneath the blue frame.

8 Click the blue bar at the very bottom of the page using the Selection tool.

9 Highlight 100 percent in the Opacity field of the Effects panel and type **40**. This is yet another way to change the opacity of an object, without using the slider. Press Enter (Windows) or Return (Mac OS) to implement the change in opacity. The bar, with an opacity of 40 percent, is slightly more transparent than the frame, which has an opacity value of 65 percent.

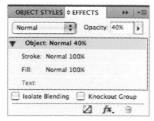

Adjust an object's opacity by entering the number directly in the Opacity text field.

10 Choose File > Save. Keep the file open, as you'll need it for the rest of the lesson.

Apply effects to stroke or fill only

In InDesign, an effect can be applied to an entire object, or to an object's stroke, fill, or text individually.

1   Use the Selection tool (⬉) to select the white box containing a quote in the upper-left corner of page 7.

2   In the Effects panel, click the right-facing triangle next to Opacity to reveal the slider, then drag the slider left to 50 percent. Click the triangle again to commit the change. Notice that both the text and the fill are now fairly transparent. Applying the effect to the entire object in this way makes the text difficult to read, which is something you don't want. The text needs to stand out and remain legible.

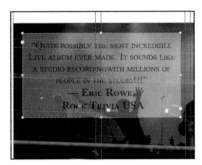

Apply the opacity change to both the fill and text.

3   Before you can apply the opacity change to the fill only, you must undo the last step. Either highlight 50 percent in the Opacity text field in the Effects panel and type **100** to return to the previous settings, or press Ctrl+Z (Windows) or Command+Z (Mac OS) to undo the previous action.

4   In the Effects panel, click to target the Fill listing. Selecting the Fill property ensures that the opacity applies only to the fill inside the frame and not to the text.

5   Click to reveal the Opacity slider, and drag it to the left to 50 percent. Commit the change by clicking the triangle again after setting the new value. The fill is transparent, but the text keeps an opacity value of 100 percent.

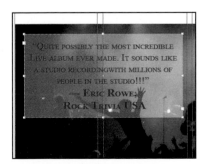

Adjust the opacity of the box's fill only.

Drop shadow

As with opacity, you can apply the drop shadow effect to a whole object or to just the stroke, fill, or text of the object. A drop shadow creates a three-dimensional shadow effect below whatever you have chosen in the document. You can also change such parameters as the drop shadow's color, offset, and blending mode, to name a few. This exercise demonstrates the effect and provides you with your first look inside the Effects dialog box.

1   Click the Pages button (⊞) in the dock on the right side of the workspace to reveal the Pages panel. Double-click the page 6 icon to center the page on screen. Press Ctrl+0 (Windows) or Command+0 (Mac OS) to fit page 6 on your screen.

2   With the Selection tool (⬧), click the box containing the words, *Johnny Guitar rocks again!* at the top of the page.

3   In the Effects panel, click the Add an object effect to the selected target button (*fx*) at the bottom of the panel. From the contextual menu that appears, choose Drop Shadow.

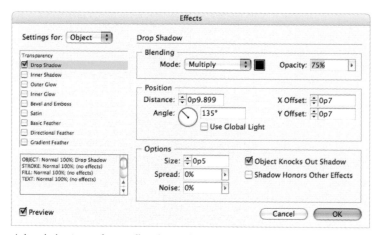

A drop shadow is one of many effects that can be applied in the Effects dialog box.

4   When the Effects dialog box opens, check the *Preview* checkbox in the bottom-left corner. Look at the change: InDesign applies a drop shadow to the frame because it has a fill of paper. If there were no fill color or stroke color, it would have applied a drop shadow to the text. Because InDesign lets you apply an effect to the fill, stroke, or text individually, you will adjust the settings in the Effects dialog box in the next step so that only the text gets the drop shadow.

5   Still in the Effects dialog box, click the *Drop Shadow* checkbox in the list on the left side of the dialog box to turn it off. A drop shadow is no longer applied to the whole object.

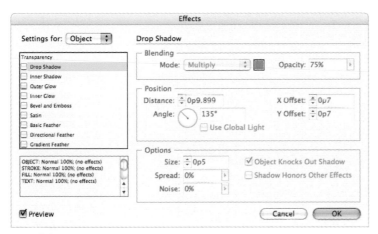

Turn off the drop shadow for the object

6   In the Settings for drop-down menu at the top of the dialog box, choose Text to affect only text with the effect.

7   Click the *Drop Shadow* checkbox to turn it on and apply the drop shadow to the text only. Click OK to close the dialog box and apply the effect.

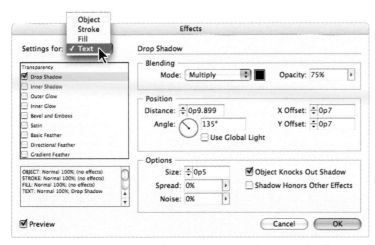

The Settings for drop-down menu specifies which portion of an object receives the effect.

8   Choose File > Save to save your work.

Adjusting effects for objects

All of InDesign's effects are nondestructive. In other words, when you implement an effect, you always have the option of turning it on or off, as well as re-editing it. You can, for example, change the Drop Shadow effect you applied to the text in the previous exercise. In this exercise, you will change the position of the drop shadow and add the Use Global Light effect, which makes any lighting effects consistent across the entire document. In other words, all drop shadows and other lighting effects appear as if they have the same light source. When the Use Global Light effect is on and you alter the drop shadow's position, all instances of the effect change. Think of a light shining in a room: if the light source changes position, all the shadows and highlights in the room also change accordingly.

1   Continuing from where you left off in the previous exercise, be sure that the box containing the words *Johnny Guitar rocks again!* is still selected. Double-click the effects symbol (*fx*) next to the Text listing inside the Effects panel, to open the Effects dialog box. Once you apply an effect, this symbol appears in the Effects panel next to the component of the document to which the effect was applied. This instance of the effects symbol appears because of the drop shadow you applied to text earlier. By double-clicking the symbol, you can edit the effects you applied.

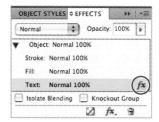

Double-click the fx *symbol next to the* Text *listing in the Effects panel to open the Effects dialog box.*

2   In the Position section of the Effects dialog box, click the *Use Global Light* checkbox to turn it on.

3   Type **0p7** (7 points) in the Distance text field. The Distance parameter controls how far from an object the drop shadow appears.

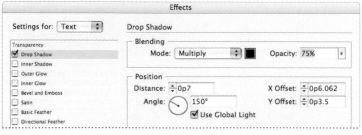

Turn on Use Global Light *and set the drop shadow's* Distance *parameter in the Effects panel.*

If you are not familiar with working in picas and would rather work in inches, simply right-click (Windows) or Ctrl+click (Mac OS) the ruler and change the unit of measurement. The Distance field should then be set to 0.0972 inches.

4 Click OK to apply the changes and close the Effects dialog box. The Drop Shadow changes from its former position to be consistent with other lighting effects in the document.

Global Light coordinates all transparency effects that use shading, such as Drop Shadow, Inner Shadow, or Bevel and Emboss. Effects that use Global Light will have the light source angle and altitude synchronized across the entire document. Angle represents the direction that the light source is coming from. The Altitude setting, used for Bevel and Emboss, indicates how close the light source is to the object. Change the direction of the light source on any object's effect, and all other effects controlled by Global Light will adjust accordingly. Using Global Light gives the appearance of a common light source shining on the objects, adding consistency and realism to the effects.

5 Choose File > Save to save your work.

Bevel and Emboss

The Bevel and Emboss effect, familiar from Photoshop, gives an object a three-dimensional look. In this exercise, you will apply Bevel and Emboss to one of the stars, and then apply this effect to another star more quickly by dragging and dropping the effect from the Effects panel.

1 Using the Selection tool (↖), select the leftmost star beneath the *Johnny Guitar rocks again!* article on page 6.

2 Click the Add an object effect to the selected target button (*fx*) at the bottom of the Effects panel. From the resulting contextual menu, choose Bevel and Emboss.

3   When the Effects dialog box appears, leave the settings at their defaults and click OK to apply a Bevel and Emboss lighting effect to the star. Press Ctrl+(plus sign) (Windows) or Command+(plus sign) (Mac OS) to zoom in on the stars and compare the changed star with the others. Now you'll apply the same effect to the second star, taking advantage of the ability to drag-and-drop.

Apply the Bevel and Emboss effect to one of the stars.

4   With the first star still selected, take a look at the Effects panel. To the right of the Objects entry is the same effects symbol (*fx*) that appeared next to the Text entry when you applied the drop shadow. Click and drag the symbol from the Effects panel into the layout and over the second-from-left star. When the cursor, which now looks like a hand with a plus sign over it ( ), is positioned over the star, release the mouse to apply the Bevel and Emboss effect. Dragging and dropping is an easy way to reapply an effect without having to work within the Effects dialog box. InDesign offers even more ways to apply effects. In the next exercise, you will apply Bevel and Emboss using object styles.

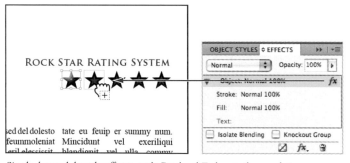

Simply drag and drop the effect to apply Bevel and Emboss to the second star.

5   Choose File > Save.

Object styles with effects

In Lesson 4, "Working with Styles," and Lesson 5, "Working with Graphics," you explored using object styles to record stroke, fill, and paragraph styles. With InDesign, you can also use object styles to record and apply effects. As with other style attributes, a change to an effect is reflected wherever you applied the style. In the next exercise, you will record an object style for the Bevel and Emboss effect and apply it to the rest of the stars.

1 On page 6, select the first star using the Selection tool (k).

2 Choose Window > Styles > Object Styles, or click the Object Styles button (⊡) in the dock, to open the Object Styles panel. From the Object Styles panel menu, choose New Object Style.

3 In the New Object Style dialog box, type **Embossed** in the Style Name text field to name the new style. Although the style automatically inherits all effects applied to the selected object, you can choose which of them you want to save with the style.

Notice the section in the bottom-left corner of the dialog box that details all the effects currently applied to the selected object, in this case Transparency and Bevel and Emboss. Before you save the style, you can turn these on and off individually by clicking the check box next to each attribute. For now, leave them as they are.

4 Check the *Apply Style to Selection* check box to automatically apply the new object style to the star. Click OK.

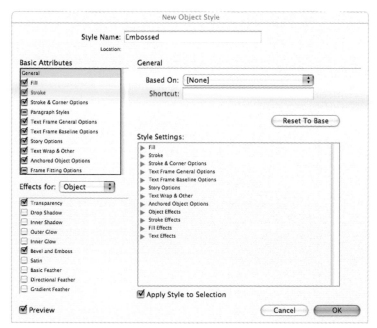

Note the listing of applied effects in the New Object Style dialog box when you create a new object style.

5   Using the Selection tool, Shift-click to select the remaining stars on the right side of page 6. Click the Embossed object style in the Object Styles panel to apply it to all the stars.

Using Find/Change to apply object styles

There are 13 more stars remaining on pages 6 and 7 that need the Embossed object style applied to them. Although the object style will make quick work of this, imagine if you had even more stars that needed the object style applied to them. Fortunately, InDesign provides an efficient method for you to do this.

1   Press Shift+Ctrl+A (Windows) or Shift+Command+A (Mac OS) to make sure that nothing is selected in the document.

2   Choose Edit > Find/Change to open the Find/Change dialog box. Click the Object button at the top of the dialog box.

3   In the Find Object Format section, click the Specify attributes to find button ($\mathcal{A}$). Click on the Fill category under the Basic Attributes section, and then click on the red swatch (C=15, M=100,Y=100, K=0) under the Fill category to tell InDesign to find objects with a red fill color. Click on the Stroke category under the Basic Attributes section, and then click on the Black swatch under the Stroke category. Click OK.

4   In the Change Object Format section, click on the Specify attributes to change button. Click on the Style Options category under the Basic Attributes section and choose Embossed from the Object Style drop-down menu. Click OK.

You've just told InDesign to search for any object with a red fill and black stroke and then apply the Embossed object style to the objects that it finds.

The Find/Change attributes are defined for the objects you want to find and change.

5 Click the Change All button. A dialog box appears, indicating that 18 objects have been changed. This is because it found the five original stars that had the object style already applied. InDesign simply applies the object style again, which is not a problem since an object style can only be applied to an object once. Click OK, and then click Done.

The object style applied to every star on the page.

Basic Feather

Feathering fades the transparency of an object's border from opaque to invisible over a distance along the edges. Instead of using Photoshop to feather an image's border, you can use InDesign. You can produce some pleasing effects by softening the edge of an image to make it appear as if the image fades into the page. Another feature is Directional Feathering, which allows you to control which side of an image or a colored frame receives the feather. The Basic Feather effect's settings include Corners, which determines how the corners of the feather appear; Noise, which sets how smooth or textured the feather transition appears; and Choke, which controls how much of the feather is opaque or transparent.

In this exercise, you will apply a Basic Feather effect to the image on page 6, and then use the Gradient Feather tool to apply a one-sided feather to the image on page 7.

1 If you didn't change the unit of measurement earlier, do so now by right-clicking (Windows) or Ctrl+clicking (Mac OS) the ruler guide and selecting inches. By placing the cursor in the upper-left corner where the ruler guides meet, you can change both horizontal and vertical measurement units at the same time.

2 In the Pages panel, double-click page 6 to activate it.

3 Use the Selection tool (⬉) to select the image of Tommy Acustomas in the lower-left area of the page.

4 If necessary, choose Window > Effects to open the Effects panel, then click the Add an object effect to the selected target button (*fx*). From the resulting contextual menu, choose Basic Feather.

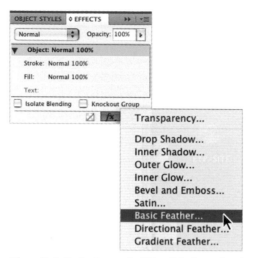

Choose Basic Feather to open the Effects dialog box and apply the Basic Feather effect to the photo.

5 Click the *Preview* checkbox to see what the feather looks like. All edges of the image are diffused and quickly blend into the background.

6 In the Effect dialog box's Options section, click in the Feather Width text field, which currently reads 0.125 inch.

7 To change the Feather Width, which is the distance the feather will be applied, press the Up Arrow key on the keyboard twice to increase the amount in the Feather Width text field to 0.25 inch.

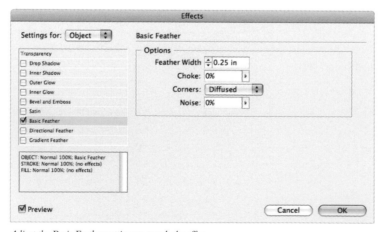

Adjust the Basic Feather settings to tweak the effect.

8 Click OK to close the Effects dialog box and apply the Basic Feather effect. Next, you will apply the same feather settings to the quote box on page 7.

This is how the image looks after Basic Feather is applied. Notice how the edges of the image appear to fade out.

9 Double-click the Hand tool (✋) in the Tools panel to fit the InDesign spread in the workspace.

10 Make sure you still have the lower-left image on page 6 selected; if not, do so using the Selection tool.

You will now apply the same effect to the quote box on page 7, using a different method.

11 From the Effects panel, drag the effects symbol (*fx*) that appears just to the right of *Object* and drop it over the quote box at the top of page 7. Now the quote box is also feathered; it is very easy to add and share effects this way.

12 Choose File > Save to save your work.

When dragging the fx symbol onto another object, watch for the cursor icon to change (⊕), indicating that the effect will be applied. You may need to aim for the edge of a frame (rather than the center) to get the effect to transfer.

The Gradient Feather tool

The Gradient Feather tool eases the transition of an object's opacity, from fully opaque to fully transparent. In this section, you will use the tool to fade the bottom of the Garage Band image on page 7 to transparency. In the previous exercise, Basic Feather applied the feather to all sides equally. InDesign also has a Directional Feather effect to adjust each feathered edge separately. You can use the Gradient Feather tool to dynamically fade one side of an image to transparency without affecting the other sides. You also have control over the angle at which the gradient effect is applied. By using this tool, you can click and drag as many times as you like, adjusting the gradient feather to whichever angle you want, without a dialog box.

1   Use the Selection tool (▸) to select the Garage Band image at the top of page 7.

2   Select the Gradient Feather tool (▨) from the Tools panel.

3   Click just below the baseline of the phrase *Summer of '88*, drag down so the cursor touches the bottom of the image, and then release the mouse. The bottom of the image fades to transparency. The longer you click and drag, the larger the area to which the fade is applied, and the more dramatic the effect. Try holding Shift as you drag to keep the gradient effect horizontally straight.

Drag down from the lower-middle area of the image.

The Gradient Feather effect fades the image to transparency along the direction you choose.

4   Choose File > Save to save your work.

Converting text to a path

Here you'll learn how to modify the text so that instead of filling it with a standard color, you fill it with a photo, producing a cool effect that's fairly simple to implement. You cannot place an image directly into text while it is still editable; you can only place an image into text after it is converted to outlines.

You can use the Type menu's Create Outlines command to convert the original font outline information into a set of compound paths. Compound paths are separate paths combined into a single object. In this exercise, you will convert the letters *GB* on page 7 to compound paths and place a photo inside them.

1   Using the Selection tool (▸), click the box on page 7 that contains *GB*.

Make sure you did not accidentally select the type with the Type tool; although you can still convert text to outlines this way, it will create an in-line graphic. Although this technique can be useful in some cases, it could make it hard to modify and position the outlined text.

2   Choose Type > Create Outlines to convert the font information to paths.

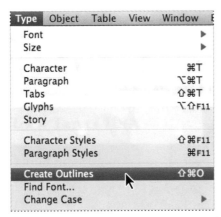

Choose Type > Create Outlines to convert text to paths.

3   Choose the Direct Selection tool (⊢) in the Tools panel to view the paths you created. Because these are compound paths, you can now place a picture inside them

View the new paths around the type.

4   Open the Mini Bridge panel and navigate to the Links folder inside the id08lessons folder, select id0807.psd, click the Tools button (⬛), and choose Place > In InDesign. The photo fills the GB compound paths.

Choose Place > In InDesign to position an image inside the paths.

5   With the Direct Selection tool still selected, click and drag the image to reposition it. You should see the image ghosted where it does not fall inside the path area. The photo you imported is the same as the image over which it appears, only cropped. Drag to fit the photo in the box however you like.

When repositioning an image inside a path, do not click and drag until you see the hand cursor. If you click and drag when it appears as the Direct Selection tool (⬉*), you could accidentally select and move a point on the path.*

Click and drag an image to see the ghosted portions of the image outside the path area.

6   Choose File > Save to save your work.

Applying blending modes to objects

If you have ever placed a black logo with a white background on a colored page, and then wondered how to get rid of the white background, you'll appreciate blending modes. While there are several ways you can resolve this using InDesign, in this exercise you will discover how to use blending modes to manipulate a logo.

Blending modes affect how color pixels on one level blend with color pixels on the levels and layers below it. The two most commonly used blending modes are Multiply and Screen. You can remember what they do in the following way: Multiply blends out the white; Screen blends out the black. In more detailed terms, Multiply looks at the color information for the items and multiplies the base color by the blend color. The outcome is always a darker color. Screen examines each item's color information and multiplies the inverse of the blend and base colors. The outcome is always a lighter color.

In the next two exercises, you will practice applying Screen and Multiply to examine how blending modes work.

The Screen blending mode

The Screen blending mode is useful for colorizing the black within an image. You will apply a Screen blending mode to the blue box that's part of the record albums image on page 7 to give the records below the box a blue tint.

1   With the Selection tool (k), click the blue box in the lower-right corner of page 7. This box is the one you altered in the first opacity exercise. Because InDesign effects are editable, you will remove the opacity.

2   Open the Effects panel from the dock, reveal the Opacity slider (click on the right-facing triangle next to the settings), and drag it to 100 percent. Click the triangle again to commit the value. The blue box covering the records image becomes solid blue.

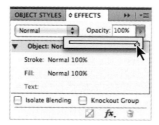

Return the box's opacity to 100 percent in the Effects panel.

3   To the left of the Opacity setting in the Effects panel is the Blending Mode drop-down menu. It is currently set to Normal. Click Normal to reveal the other options, and choose Screen. The color of the blue box is now blending with the image of the records.

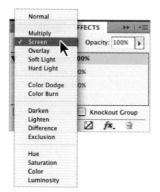

Once you change the blending mode to Screen, the records look blue where they were formerly black.

Remember that the Screen effect drops the black out of an image, so if you put a Screen blending mode on the blue box, the black parts of the image beneath the box appear blue.

The Multiply blending mode

You will now work with an image that has so far been hidden on a layer. You will use the Multiply blending mode to visually remove the logo's white area, while leaving the black areas unchanged.

1 Click the Layers button (◉) in the dock. There is a hidden layer called Johnny that you will need for this exercise and the next one.

2 Click in the leftmost box to the left of the Johnny layer to make that layer visible. An image of Johnny Guitar appears on page 6. On his T-shirt, in the upper-right corner of the image, is a swirly *J* and *G*—his signature and logo.

When the visibility icon is turned on next to a layer, the layer is visible.

3 Select the signature using the Selection tool (▸).

4 Open the Effects panel, if necessary, and from the Blending Mode drop-down menu at the top of the panel, choose Multiply. The white box around the logo disappears and the logo appears directly on Johnny's t-shirt.

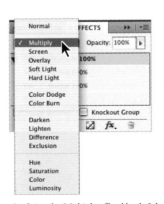

Applying the Multiply effect blends Johnny Guitar's logo with his shirt.

Because Multiply blends away the white, applying it is a handy trick to get rid of only the white in black-and-white images. This blending mode does not work with full-color images that have white around them, because it tries to blend white throughout the image, making it appear transparent or blended into the colors beneath.

As you'll learn in the next section, there are alternative ways to achieve this same effect, such as using a clipping path or alpha channel selection.

5   Choose File > Save to save your work.

Working with imported files that use transparency

If you have worked through the previous lessons in this book, you probably have noticed that incorporating images created or modified in Photoshop into InDesign is a well-established part of the print production workflow. In this exercise, you look at the ways that InDesign supports transparency in images edited in Photoshop.

Photoshop has a number of ways to define areas of transparency in an image. While Photoshop is not required for this lesson, there are concepts such as alpha channels, clipping paths, and selections that are worth investigating in Photoshop and that can help you get the most out of this lesson.

The choice of using alpha channels or clipping paths depends on which tools you are more comfortable using and the content of your image. As a rule, paths are cleaner because they are created using vectors, which give you nice, smooth curves, while an alpha channel selection is based on pixels and gives you an edge that is choppier yet more realistic in some cases. For example, if you were removing the background of a product such as a television or soda can, the pen tool would be the better choice. However if you are removing the background from a person, especially around their hair, an alpha channel might be the better choice. Know that regardless of which method you choose in the clipping options in InDesign, a vector edge will be created.

In this next exercise, you will place two images with different types of transparency. The first image simply has a transparent background, and the second has an alpha channel and a clipping path that were created in Photoshop. After learning how to control these transparent areas in InDesign, you will examine how transparency interacts with text wrap.

1   Press Shift+Ctrl+A (Windows) or Shift+Command+A (Mac OS) to deselect all objects in the document. In the Layers panel, select Layer 1, if necessary.

2   Open the Pages panel from the dock and double-click page 7 to select it. You will be placing a photo on this page. Double-click the Zoom tool (🔍), if necessary, to view the page at 100 percent.

3   Use the Mini Bridge to navigate to the Links folder within the id08lessons folder, select the id0802.psd file, click on the Tools button (■), and choose Place > In InDesign.

4   The cursor now contains a thumbnail image of the file being placed. In the second column of page 7's Allison Copper story, click in the white space to place the image. Using the Selection tool, click and drag to move the picture into position.

Use the Selection tool to position the image on page 7.

Move the image over some text; notice that it does not have a white background. Instead, the file has a transparent layer. InDesign automatically recognized the .psd file's transparency. Adjust the image position to match the example above.

Applying an alpha channel selection

The photo of the band members (id0802.psd) contains an alpha channel selection that was saved in Photoshop. An alpha channel is a way to save a selection you created in Photoshop so that you can later access it in InDesign for visibility and text wrap options. Alpha channels are stored, along with the color channels of an RGB or CMYK image, to capture a selection or indicate transparency. In this exercise, you will access an alpha channel using the Clipping Paths option. A clipping path is another term for the visibility edge that exists with this type of partially transparent image. Consider the outline of the two band members. This outline represents the clipping path; all areas inside the path are opaque, while all areas outside the path are transparent.

You could use InDesign's Detect Edges feature, which would build a path for you around the two band members based on the transparency or background contrast, but an even more accurate way is to access the saved alpha channel selection that is already made for you.

1   Make sure you still have the band photo selected. If it is not, select the image using the
Selection tool (⟋), and then choose Object > Clipping Path > Options.

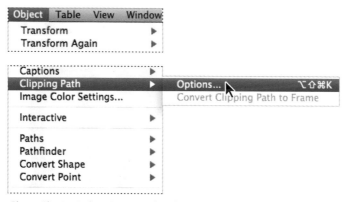

Choose Clipping Path > Options in the Object menu.

2   In the Clipping Path dialog box, choose Alpha Channel from the Type drop-down menu
and rockers from the Alpha drop-down menu. Notice that the Alpha setting default is
Transparency, based on the transparent pixels of the file. Click to turn on the *Preview*
checkbox to see the path you created from the alpha channel. This path is also helpful
when applying the text wrap.

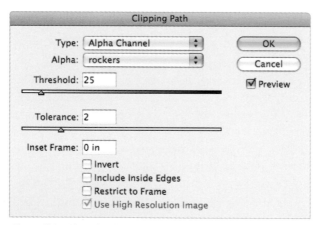

Choose Alpha Channel and rockers in the Clipping Path dialog box.

3   Click OK to accept the path shown in the preview and close the dialog box. Next you
will apply a text wrap around the alpha channel selection.

4   Choose Window > Text Wrap to access the Text Wrap panel.

5 In the panel, click on the Wrap around object shape button (⬚) to wrap the text around the image's shape rather than its bounding box. In the Text Wrap panel, enter an offset value of **10 pt (.1389 in.)** or experiment with different values, and then close the Text Wrap panel.

Notice that in the Contour Options section of the Text Wrap panel, the default Type setting is Same as Clipping. Although this is useful, it is possible to choose another contour method for the text wrap that is totally separate from what is used for the clipping. This opens up a world of possibilities to you as the designer.

Wrap the text around the object shape.

6 Choose the Selection tool (▶), and then click and drag the image slightly to the left to allow the text to wrap slightly around the guitarist's leg.

7 Choose File > Save to save your work.

Applying a path selection

A path selection is a selection made and saved in Photoshop using the Pen tool. You can access these selections in InDesign the same way you select a .psd file's alpha channel. Pen tool selections are cleaner than alpha channels in InDesign because they are vector paths. Alpha channel selections are based on pixels, and InDesign makes the path for you. You will now apply a pre-made path to Johnny Guitar and apply a text wrap again.

1 Open the Pages panel from the dock, and double-click page 6 to bring it into view.

2 Select the image of Johnny Guitar using the Selection tool.

3 Choose Object > Clipping Path > Options.

4 In the Clipping Path dialog box, check the *Preview* checkbox, and then choose Photoshop Path from the Type drop-down menu. *Guitarist* should automatically appear as the Path name.

5 Click OK. Notice how the black around the image disappears based on the saved Photoshop Pen tool path. Now you can apply the text wrap.

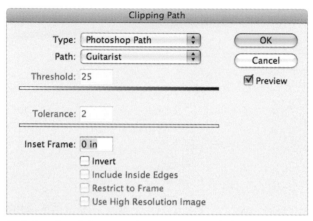

With the path applied, you're ready to wrap text around Johnny.

6 Choose Window > Text Wrap to open the Text Wrap panel, and then click the panel's Wrap around object shape button (⬛). Again, the text wraps around the object's shape and not its box, just as it did in the previous exercise with alpha channels. Set the offset value to **10 pt (.1389 in.)** or adjust it to a value you find acceptable.

Here is the final design with all the effects applied.

7 Choose File > Save to save your work. Take a look at the *rock 'n' roll journal* spread. You're finished working with imported files and transparency. Close this completed file by choosing File > Close.

Congratulations! You've finished the lesson.

Self study

Here are some projects you can create on your own:

- Apply a drop shadow to Johnny Guitar and choose Use Global Light to coordinate the effects throughout the document. Then adjust the direction of the Drop Shadow effect and watch the headline drop shadow update as well.

- Select the top photo on page 7, and remove the Gradient Feather effect. Try to accomplish the same effect with Directional Feathering.

- Apply more effects to Johnny Guitar, save the result as an object style, and then apply that style to the images of Johnny and Allison Copper. Change the object style so that both images update simultaneously.

- Experiment with blending modes by making a colored frame over Tommy Acustomas; then change the Blending modes and Opacity settings to get different effects.

Review

Questions

1 Can you alter an effect after you've applied it?

2 What is the difference between opacity and tint?

3 If you apply Create Outlines to type, can you still edit the text with the Type tool?

4 Can you feather only one edge of a photograph?

Answers

1 Yes, you can always return to the Effects panel, select the effect again, and double-click the effect to make adjustments.

2 Tint is a screened (lighter) version of a color, and is not transparent. Opacity achieves a similar result; however, it allows objects behind the transparent object to show through.

3 No, if Create Outlines is applied, the text is made into paths and is no longer related to the font information.

4 Yes, with the Directional Feather effect or the Gradient Feather tool, you can control the angle and direction of a feather to include only one of the image's edges.

What you'll learn in this lesson:

- Adding dynamic text variables to your document

- Managing multiple InDesign documents using the Book feature

- Generating a Table of Contents

- Generating an index

Advanced Document Features

Although the lessons so far have used single, small documents as examples, InDesign can manage complex, book-length documents, and maintain consistency across multiple files. The software's advanced document features enable you to add dynamic text, cross-reference and index information, and synchronize many files at once.

Starting up

Before starting, make sure that your tools and panels are consistent by resetting your preferences. See "Resetting the InDesign workspace and preferences" on page 3.

You will work with several files from the id09lessons folder in this lesson. Make sure that you have copied the id09lessons folder onto your hard drive from the Digital Classroom DVD. See "Loading lesson files" on page 4. This lesson may be easier to follow if the id09lessons folder is on your desktop.

The project

In this lesson, you will work with several chapters of a book to see for yourself the capabilities of InDesign's book feature. You will add chapters to a book file, and update the page number of each page based on its position in the book. Using text variables, you will automate the generation of elements on each page, which can save hours of manual work. You will then synchronize each chapter to give the book a consistent appearance.

Adding text variables

InDesign enables you to add dynamic text called *variables* to your documents. In a general sense, a variable is a way to store information that is not necessarily permanent. In InDesign, a variable is text-based content that dynamically changes when certain criteria are met or specific changes occur in the document. For example, you might want a running footer in the document that contains the title of the chapter. Traditionally, you would type the static text on a master page for the content to appear properly. Inserting a variable provides a more powerful option. In this case, using a variable would automatically update all footer text when the chapter title is modified.

When you place a text variable on a page, you must place it within a text frame, just like normal text. That frame can be in the live, printable area of the documents or in the non-printing portion. In this exercise, you will use text variables in a non-printing area to display the filename and modification date of the documents, which can be helpful in a collaborative environment.

1   Choose File > Open. Navigate to the id09lessons folder, choose TOC.indd, and click Open. Notice the light blue outline that extends beyond the edge of the page on the right side. This area is called the *slug*, and information entered here doesn't automatically print on the final page. You will use the slug area to house the filename and modification date variables, displaying the name of the file and the date it was modified. This is useful when viewing a printout of a document or when viewing it onscreen to determine when the most recent edit or modification was made.

About the trim and slug area

A slug is information placed outside of the final print area of the document. The final print area is known as the trim area, and the space immediately outside of where a document will be trimmed (cut) is the slug area. The slug may contain the job name, client name, a place for approval of the job, or colors used in the job. Slugs can be included when printing or generating PDF files from InDesign. The slug prints only when you choose Include Slug Area in the Marks and Bleed section of the Print dialog box or the Export Adobe PDF dialog box.

2 Select the Type tool (T) from the Tools panel, and then click and drag to create a text frame within the top of the slug area on the page. Be careful to keep the frame within the slug's bounds.

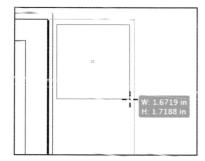

The slug area can hold information that will not show up in the final printed project.

3 Open the Paragraph Styles panel by choosing Window > Styles > Paragraph Styles or by clicking the Paragraph Styles button (⬛) in the dock on the right side of the workspace. Before inserting text or typing into this frame, choose the Variable Text style from the Paragraph Styles panel. This assigns the Variable Text style to text you type in the frame, and gives the text a standard appearance. Make sure the cursor is blinking in the text box before you choose this style.

4 With the cursor inside the text frame, choose Type > Text Variables > Insert Variable > File Name to insert the value of the File Name variable in the slug area's text frame. Because you're working in the file TOC.indd, InDesign inserts *TOC* in the frame. Choose File > Save.

5   Press the Enter key (Windows) or Return key (Mac OS) on your keyboard to move the cursor under the filename text you inserted in the previous step, then choose Type > Text Variables > Insert Variable > Modification Date. InDesign inserts the value of the second variable, Modification Date, beneath TOC in the text frame. The Modification Date's value reflects the time and date of the file's most recent save, and because you saved the document in the last step, the current date and time appear.

Later in the lesson, you will see how the File Name and Modification Date variables can be useful in a production environment. A quick look at the variable text tells which file you're working in and whether the file has been updated recently.

Text variables can provide dynamic information about the document.

6   Choose File > Save, and then close the document.

Creating a book from multiple files

Any project that contains numerous pages, whether it's a book, magazine, or other long document, can be large and cumbersome. Not only is file size an issue—especially if the project contains a lot of graphics—but the more pages the document contains, the more challenging it is to navigate through the document. InDesign's Book feature offers some help. The Book feature enables you to divide up a project into smaller, more manageable sections or chapters. It also boasts a number of document management capabilities that allow for easy navigation between sections and maintain consistency from one file to the next. You can also have different people work on different files, and use the Book feature to join the files together into one document.

To demonstrate the Book feature, you will work with five files that represent the different chapters of a work in progress. An important task in managing a large job like this is to create a book file.

1   Choose File > New > Book. When the New Book dialog box opens, navigate to the id09lessons folder, type **Book.indb** in the Name text field, then click Save. The Book panel appears and gives you access to the book file of the same name. If the welcome screen is displayed, you need to close it before accessing the Book panel.

2   Click the Add documents icon (⊕) at the bottom of the Book panel.

3 In the resulting Add Documents dialog box, Press Ctrl (Windows) or Command (Mac OS) to select the TOC.indd, 1_Trees.indd, 2_Flowers.indd, 3_Plants.indd, and Index.indd files located in the id09lessons folder. Click Open.

Because the files intentionally contain missing fonts, you may receive a warning that the pages will recompose using a substituted font and the resulting page numbers may not be accurate. Click the *Don't Show Again* checkbox to avoid viewing this dialog box in the future, and then click OK. You will fix the fonts later in this exercise. If requested, save the files. InDesign now lists the documents in the Book panel. Although the documents in the Book panel are still separate files, they are now being managed by the Book panel and are now related to each other.

Add the documents from the id09lessons folder to the Book panel.

Defining pagination and document order

When you choose files from the Add Document dialog box, InDesign adds them to the Book panel and adjusts the page numbers within each document so they are sequentially numbered. Unfortunately, this does not always match the logical sequence for your documents. For example, in this book, the TOC and Index files should be first and last, respectively, in the panel. Because InDesign adds files to the Book panel in numerical, then alphabetical order, based on each document's filename, they are currently fourth and fifth in the list. Rearranging the file order is a simple matter of clicking and dragging.

Once a book's pages are in order, you can turn your attention to the pagination within the files. Do you need the book documents to open on left pages, for example? InDesign's Book Page Numbering Options help you tweak the document flow.

In this exercise, you will resolve some typical pagination issues, rearrange files, and explore the Book Page Numbering Options dialog box.

1 Within the Book panel, click and drag the TOC document to the top of the list. A bold divider rule indicates the destination of the selected document. Release the mouse button.

The TOC file is now the first document of the book; the page numbers to the right of the list adjust to accommodate the change.

2 Rearrange the documents within the Book panel. After moving the files, put them in the following order: TOC, 1_Trees, 2_Flowers, 3_Plants, Index. Notice that when you rearrange the documents, the Book panel updates the page numbering based on the new page order.

The documents in the Book panel after arranging them in the correct order.

3 Double-click the 2_Flowers file in the Book panel. If any messages appear regarding modified links, click the Update button.

The document opens just like it would if you opened it from the Open dialog box. The Book panel performs several automated management tasks, such as pagination, which is only available when you use the Book feature. Look in the Pages panel and notice that the page numbering continues from the previous document in the book file. This book is designed so that each chapter begins with a photo on the left page and the chapter intro on the right page. Currently, the document is not set up that way, but you'll fix that in the following steps. Close the document.

4   Deselect all files in the Book panel by clicking in the empty area below the panel's list. Click the Book panel menu button (⸬≡), and from the resulting menu, choose Book Page Numbering Options.

Choose Book Page Numbering Options from the Book panel menu.

5   In the Book Page Numbering Options dialog box that appears, confirm the *Continue on next even page* option is selected. Also make sure that the *Insert Blank Page* check box is selected so that InDesign can insert a blank page when necessary.

6   Make sure that the *Automatically Update Page & Section Numbers* check box is selected. This tells InDesign to update pagination and section numbering automatically when pages are added, removed, or rearranged. For example, if new pages are added to documents at the start of the book, the pages in the following documents will be updated. Click OK. A progress bar may appear while InDesign rearranges and adds pages to the documents as needed. The page numbers in the Book panel adjust to reflect the changes.

```
Book Page Numbering Options

 Options                                                    ┌──────────────┐
    Page Order:  ○ Continue from previous document          │      OK      │
                 ○ Continue on next odd page                 └──────────────┘
                 ● Continue on next even page                ┌──────────────┐
                                                             │    Cancel    │
                 ☑ Insert Blank Page                         └──────────────┘
                 ☑ Automatically Update Page & Section Numbers
```

Control pagination within the Book Page Numbering Options dialog box, which is available in the Book panel.

7   If necessary, allow InDesign to automatically update any modified links. Scroll down the document and note that the pages are numbered consecutively at this point. The book numbering flows from one chapter to the next.

8   Double-click on the 2_Flowers document to open it, and notice that the document now begins on the left side (the even page). Close the document.

Synchronizing attributes across a book file

When multiple people collaborate on files for a large project, inconsistencies sometimes sneak in, no matter how well coworkers try to keep each other informed. Different colors may be used, styles may be defined differently, and fonts might even vary from one part of a document to another. The Book feature solves these hard-to-trace problems by synchronizing elements to maintain consistency across the documents within the book file. InDesign can synchronize the following items:

- Styles, including character, paragraph, object, table, cell, and TOC styles
- Swatches
- Numbered lists
- Text variables
- Conditional text settings
- Cross-reference formats
- Trap presets
- Master pages

In the design process, it isn't always feasible to start from a template with established master pages and styles. You can, however, create a base set of styles, such as body, subhead, and so on, and then synchronize all the related documents to these styles and any other attributes agreed upon later.

The book files in this lesson suffer from their own inconsistencies: The text and look of each document differs, which is the result of multiple designers using fonts unique to their system. This, in turn, creates conflicts in the chapters that need to be resolved. In this exercise, you will fix these discrepancies to establish cross-document consistency in the book.

1   Double-click the 1_Trees listing in the Book panel to open it. Update any modified links, if necessary. Notice the word *Chapter* at the top of page 3. You want the chapter number to appear next to the word for all the interior chapters in the book. To do this, you will use a variable.

2   Click the Pages button (⊞) in the dock to open the Pages panel. Double-click on the right page icon of the A-Chapter Intro master page in the Pages panel. This displays the contents of the right-hand master page for the chapter.

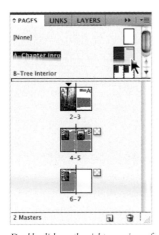

Double-click on the right page icon of the A-Chapter Intro master page.

3   Select the Type tool (T) from the Tools panel, and click to the immediate right of the word *Chapter* on the master page.

4 Type a space, then choose Type > Text Variables > Insert Variable > Chapter Number.

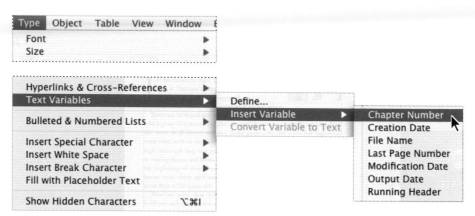

Add another variable so that each chapter's respective number appears.

The chapter number appears where you insert the variable text. Choose File > Save and then choose File > Close to close the document.

5 Now you're ready to synchronize attributes across multiple chapters. If necessary, click in the column to the left of the 1_Trees document name in the Book panel. This column selects the style source of your book. The style source is the document to which all other documents in the book synchronize.

The style source icon indicates the document to which all other documents synchronize.

6 Before you synchronize documents, you must specify the synchronize options. From the Book panel menu (⋅☰), choose Synchronize Options. In the resulting Synchronize Options dialog box, you can specify which styles or elements to synchronize. For this project, make sure all options are selected. Click OK.

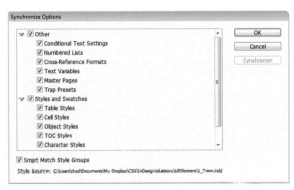

Choose synchronize options for the book.

7 In the Book panel, click 1_Trees, and then Shift+click 3_Plants to select all three of the interior chapters. You won't use Select All, because you don't want to synchronize the TOC or index.

8 Click the Synchronize styles and swatches using the Style Source icon (⚟) at the bottom of the Book panel to initiate the synchronization of the selected chapters.

Select the documents and click the Synchronize styles and swatches with the style source icon to begin synchronization.

You may receive messages during synchronization that indicate some text has become overset or non–overset. Overset means that the text no longer fits into the text frame that contains it. Accept these messages by clicking OK. When finished, InDesign displays a message to convey that synchronization completed successfully and that some documents may have changed. InDesign changes the styles, master pages, and so on, in the selected documents to match those of the style source document. Here synchronization changed the definition of the paragraph styles to match the style source.

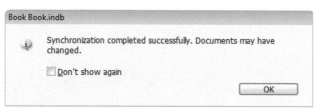

Book Book.indb

Synchronization completed successfully. Documents may have changed.

Don't show again

OK

Successful synchronization.

9 Click OK to accept the synchronization. To confirm the changes, click, then double-click to open the 2_Flowers document. If necessary, update any links. The chapter introductory pages now feature the appropriate chapter number because you included master pages in the synchronization options. The body text matches that of the style source document. Similar changes were applied to the 3_Plants file.

To add the finishing touches, you'll change the names of the chapters to reflect the actual name of each chapter, as each file had originally started from the same template file.

10 Go to page 9 of the 2_Flowers document and, using the Selection tool, press Shift+Ctrl (Windows) or Shift+Command (Mac OS) while you click the green title bar at the top of the page. This overrides the item from the master page so you can edit it. For information on master pages, refer to Lesson 2, "Building Documents with Master Pages."

11 Select the Type tool (T), highlight the word *Trees* in the green title bar, and type **Flowers**.

12 Choose File > Save to save your changes, and then choose File > Close to close the 2_Flowers file.

13 Double-click 3_Plants in the Book panel, then double-click on page 13 in the Pages panel, and repeat the process of using Shift+Ctrl (Windows) or Shift+Command (Mac OS) on the green title bar on the title page, changing the word *Trees* to *Plants*. Choose File > Save and then close the file.

14 Double-click to open 1_Trees, and Shift+Ctrl+click (Windows) or Shift+Command+click (Mac OS) on the green title bar at the top of the page to detach it from the master page. This is the Trees chapter, so don't change any of the text. The chapter title must be detached from the master page in preparation for the next exercise.

Now that the document has been synchronized, you have established consistency throughout the pages of the book. As the book grows, and documents are added, you can synchronize the book again to ensure consistency of styles and pages in those new documents.

15 Choose File > Save, and then choose File > Close to close the Trees chapter.

Creating a Table of Contents

A book needs a Table of Contents, and InDesign helps you build one by automating its creation and formatting. For the Table of Contents feature to work, however, you must prepare the files correctly. For example, you must use paragraph styles throughout the document or book, and you must also create styles to format the text in the Table of Contents itself. The TOC document in this lesson already contains these styles. In this exercise, you'll use these styles and the Table of Contents feature to generate and format a Table of Contents.

1 Double-click the TOC document in the Book panel to open it.

2 Choose Window > Styles > Paragraph Styles to open the Paragraph Styles panel. In the Paragraph Styles panel, notice that several styles begin with the prefix TOC. You will use these to style the Table of Contents text. The styles you used to style the text of the chapters have not yet been synchronized. To create a Table of Contents, you'll load those styles into the TOC document by performing another synchronization.

3 Click the Book panel menu button (-≡) and choose Synchronize Options to open the Synchronize Options dialog box.

4 Uncheck all the options except for *Paragraph Styles* and *Character Styles* to instruct InDesign to synchronize only these attributes. Click OK to close the dialog box.

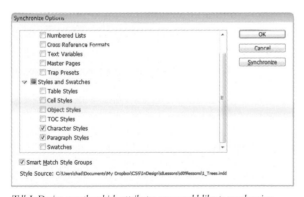

Tell InDesign exactly which attributes you would like to synchronize.

5 Make sure that the Style Source is set to the 1_Trees document in the Book panel (by clicking in the column to the left of the document name), and then Shift+click TOC and 1_Trees to select them for synchronizing.

6 Click the Synchronize styles and swatches with the Style Source button at the bottom of the Book panel. When the dialog box appears, announcing that the synchronization completed successfully, and that documents may have changed, click OK. Notice that several new styles have been imported into the TOC document during synchronization. Now you are ready to generate the Table of Contents for the book.

7 With the TOC.indd document open, choose Layout > Table of Contents. The Table of Contents dialog box appears.

8 In the area for Title in the dialog box, confirm the title is entered as *Contents*. If necessary, enter this as the title. This is the name that appears at the start of the Table of Contents.

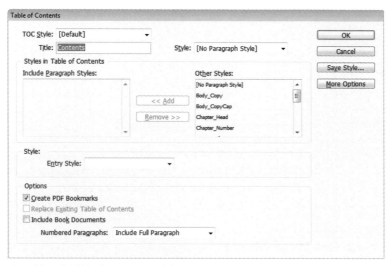

Control how the Table of Contents is styled and generated.

9 From the Style drop-down menu, choose TOC_Contents. This paragraph style defines how the title is formatted.

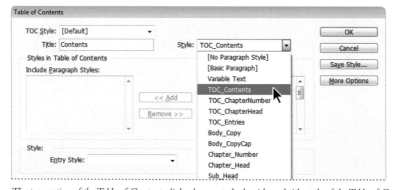

The top portion of the Table of Contents dialog box controls the title and title style of the Table of Contents.

10 The Styles in Table of Contents section is where you choose which styles in the document or book will appear in the Table of Contents. In the Other Styles list, click Chapter_Number to highlight it. Click the Add button to move the Chapter_Number style into the Include Paragraph Styles list. Highlight and click to add the Chapter_Head and Sub_Head styles as well, in that order.

In the Styles in Table of Contents section, specify which styles InDesign uses to pull content from the document or book.

11 Now you need to define the attributes of each style's appearance. Click the More Options button at the right side of the Table of Contents dialog box to expand the Style section. If you see a Fewer Options button, you don't need to do anything, as the additional options are already displayed.

12 Click the Chapter_Number style in the Include Paragraph Styles list. The Style section below it is now labeled as Style: Chapter_Number. From the Entry Style drop-down menu, choose TOC_ChapterNumber, and from the Page Number drop-down menu, choose No Page Number.

13 Click the Chapter_Head style in the Include Paragraph Styles list, and in the Style section, set Entry Style to TOC_ChapterHead. Leave all other fields in this section at their defaults. Click the Sub_Head style next, and set Entry Style to TOC_Entries. Leave all other settings at their defaults.

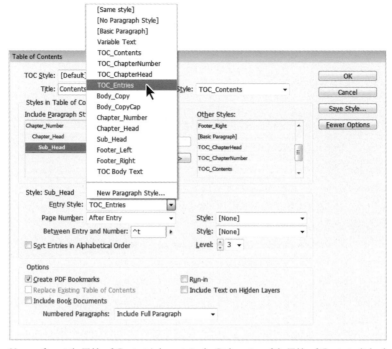

You can format the Table of Contents' elements in the Style section of the Table of Contents dialog box.

14 Click the *Include Book Documents* check box at the bottom of the dialog box to have all document files in the Book included when the Table of Contents is generated. InDesign locates text formatted with the specified styles you identified in the Include Paragraph Styles list, and the styled text is used for the Table of Contents.

15 Click the Save Style button in the upper-right corner of the dialog box. In the resulting Save Style dialog box, type **Book_TOC** in the Save Style text field, and click OK to save the settings that define how the Table of Contents is created. This saves time if you ever have to generate another Table of Contents with these settings in the future.

Clicking the Save Style button inside the Table of Contents dialog box captures the settings that you painstakingly configured for the Table of Contents. This can be useful if you have several versions of a document that each need their own Table of Contents, or if you made a mistake and later need to modify the settings.

16 Click OK in the Table of Contents dialog box to generate the Table of Contents for the book. A dialog box may appear, asking if you want to include items in overset text. Click OK. This ensures that if any of the text in the other documents is overset, it will still be included in the Table of Contents.

Overset text is text that appears in a frame that isn't big enough to display it. This can happen for several reasons; often when text is added or adjusted, it will make the text within a frame run longer than the actual frame. For this reason, you generally want to include items in overset text when creating a Table of Contents to make sure that any overset type styles to be listed as TOC entries are included.

17 The cursor changes to a loaded text cursor with a preview of the TOC text that is ready to be placed in the document. Click in the upper-left corner of the document where the margins meet. InDesign automatically creates a text frame within the boundaries of the margins and places the Table of Contents text within the frame.

Place the loaded cursor in the upper-left corner of the document, and then click to place the Table of Contents.

18 Choose File > Save and then choose File > Close to save and close the document.

Whether you add or delete pages and documents from the book while you work, you can easily update the Table of Contents to reflect these changes. Click the text frame that contains the Table of Contents text, and choose Layout > Update Table of Contents.

Building an index

Indexes are very complex components of a book. A good index is based on specific topics and can quickly direct you to the exact location of the information you need; a poorly created index is one that is confusing or unhelpful. InDesign doesn't know what you want indexed, so it can't automatically create an index for you. It can, however, make the process a lot easier. Using the Index panel, you can assemble an index with topics, references, and cross-references.

To demonstrate what's possible, two chapters of the example book have been indexed already. In this series of exercises, you'll tackle the third chapter, adding index topics to categorize the references, supplementing these with cross-references to help direct your reader to the correct topic, and finally, generating the index.

Adding topics

The most basic component of an index is its topics. Although InDesign can't help you with what to index, it makes adding the topics you choose a simple matter of pointing and clicking. Think of topics as categories into which entries will be sorted.

1   In the Book panel, double-click to open 3_Plants, the file you need to index.

2   Choose Window > Type & Tables > Index to open the Index panel.

3   Make sure the *Book* checkbox in the upper-right corner of the Index panel is checked. This tells InDesign to look in all the documents within a book for references when generating the index.

4   Click the *Topic* radio button at the top of the Index panel to switch to Topic view, and then click the Create a new index entry button (⌐ᵤ) at the bottom of the panel. The New Topic dialog box opens, allowing you to add the first topic.

Click the Topic button, and then click the Create a new index entry button to begin building a topic list.

5 In the New Topic dialog box, type **Plants** in text field 1 under Topic Levels and click the Add button on the right side of the dialog box to add *Plants* to the topic list. Each letter of the alphabet appears at the bottom of the New Topic dialog box, and there is now a triangle next to *P*. If you click the triangle, the list expands and you see the word *Plants* has been added to the list of topics. In text field 1 under Topic Levels, type **Genus**, and then click Add. Click the OK or Done button. You have now added *Plants* and *Genus* to the topic list of the index.

The new topics are added to the topic list of the index.

6 Click the *Reference* radio button at the top of the Index panel to switch to the Reference view, which shows each entry's page number and any cross-references that you add.

7 If the Pages panel isn't open, click on the Pages button in the dock to open it. Double-click on page 14 in the Pages panel to display page 14 and, using the Type tool (T), select the phrase *Fountain Grass* at the top of the page.

8 Click the Create a new index entry button at the bottom of the Index panel. The New Page Reference dialog box appears with *Fountain Grass* entered in the Topic Level 1 text field. Click the Add button to add the reference to Fountain Grass to the index. In order to accommodate a range of searching styles, you will add Fountain Grass as a subtopic beneath the Plants entry.

9   With the New Page Reference dialog box still open, click the down arrow icon to move Fountain Grass to the Topic Level 2 text field. Click to insert the cursor in the Topic Level 1 text field, then scroll down to the P topics in the list at the bottom of the New Page Reference dialog box. Click on the triangle next to P to expand its entries, and then double-click Plants to insert it in the Topic Level 1 text field. Click the Add button, and click OK or Done to close the New Page Reference dialog box.

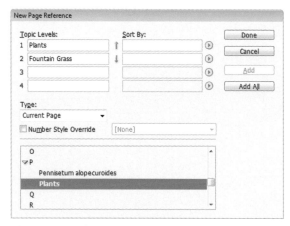

The New Page Reference dialog box allows you to add index references for topics and subtopics within the text.

10 Repeat steps 7 to 9 for the word *Aloe* on page 15 and the phrase *Golden Ball Cacti* on page 16.

Now, in addition to the plant's name, you need to add each plant's scientific name to its Genus topic.

11 Double-click on page 14 in the Pages panel to go to that page. Highlight the scientific name *Pennisetum alopecuroides* and click the Create a new index entry button at the bottom of the Index panel. Click the down arrow icon to move the entry to the Topic Level 2 text field. Click to select the Topic Level 1 text field, then scroll down to the G topics in the list at the bottom of the New Page Reference dialog box. Click on the triangle next to G to expand its entries, then double-click Genus to insert it in the Topic Level 1 text field. Click the Add button, and click OK or Done.

12 Repeat step 11 to highlight the scientific name for each of the remaining plant names on pages 15 and 16, then add their references to the topic Genus. Click OK or Done to close the New Page Reference dialog box. Save the 3_Plants.indd document and keep the file open for the next exercise.

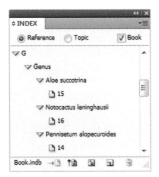

The Index Reference list shows what page each entry appears on in the documents.

Adding cross-references

Now that you've added all the necessary references to the index for the 3_Plants document, it's time to think about adding cross-references to the index. Cross references refer a reader to a similar topic if there are no entries for the topic being looked up. For example, someone may look up the topic *grass* in the index. It does not contain a topic for grass, but the index can refer the reader to the closest thing, which would be Fountain Grass. Try adding the cross-reference now.

1 With the 3_Plants.indd document still open, choose New Cross-reference from the Index panel menu. If you see New Page Reference instead, deselect any text on the page by pressing Shift+Ctrl+A (Windows) or Shift+Command+A (Mac OS), and then choose New Cross-reference from the Index panel menu. The New Cross-reference dialog box appears.

2 In the list at the bottom of the New Cross-reference panel, scroll to the letter F and expand the topic by clicking on the triangle to its left. Double-click *Fountain Grass* to add it to the Topic Level 1 text field.

3 In the Referenced text field, type **Grass**. This tells InDesign to direct the reader to the Fountain Grass topic when the word *grass* is referenced. This places an entry in the index under the topic *Fountain Grass* that says, *See also* Grass.

4 Click the Add button to add the cross-reference to the index, and click OK or Done to close the New Cross-reference dialog box.

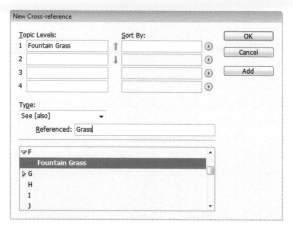

Enter the referenced word, as well as the related topic to which you will direct the reader.

5 Choose File > Save to save your work, and then close the file by choosing File > Close.

Generating the index

With all the pieces in place, you're ready to generate the index and place it within the book.

1 Open the Index.indd file from the Book panel.

2 If the Index panel is not open, choose Window > Type & Tables > Index to open it.

3 Make sure that the *Book* checkbox in the upper-right corner of the panel is checked.

4 Choose Generate Index from the Index panel menu.

5 In the resulting Generate Index dialog box, leave the settings at their defaults. It's important that the *Include Book Documents* option is checked. Click OK to close the dialog box and generate the index.

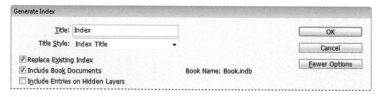

In the Generate Index dialog box, you can name the index and format it with a paragraph style.

6 The cursor changes to a loaded text cursor containing all the text that makes up the index. Click in the upper-left corner of page 18 of the Index document to place the text. InDesign creates a text frame on the page with the index text inside it.

If the entire index does not fit on the page you choose, simply flow the extra text onto the second page of the document. For more on flowing text from one frame to another, see Lesson 3, "Working with Text and Type."

7   Save and close the Index.indd file.

When you make changes to an index and need to update the existing index with new content, simply choose the Generate Index option from the Index panel menu to display the Generate Index dialog box. Within that dialog box is a check box called Replace Existing Index. When that check box is turned on, InDesign replaces the current index with the new index content.

Creating PDFs and printing from the Book panel

Now that you are finished working on your book, you may want to send the files to a coworker or client as proof of progress or for review. Because not everyone has InDesign, you can convert the InDesign documents to a file type that can be easily shared. InDesign's Book panel simplifies the process of creating PDF files and printing so you can easily share the project.

Creating PDFs

Creating a PDF from a book file is quick and easy in InDesign, and the results can be read by anyone with Adobe Reader, a free download is available at *get.adobe.com/reader*. InDesign CS5 allows you to create PDF files for print output or for interactive output. You will now export the InDesign book as a PDF.

1   Click in the open area below the list of documents in the Book panel to ensure that no documents are selected. From the Book panel menu, choose Export Book to PDF.

2   In the resulting Export dialog box, name the file **id09_book.pdf**, navigate to your desktop, choose Adobe PDF (Print) from the Save as type drop-down menu, and click Save.

3   In the Export Adobe PDF dialog box, choose High Quality Print from the Adobe PDF Preset drop-down menu. Click Export. A Generating PDF dialog box appears with status bars showing the progress of the PDF file creation.

The High Quality Print preset generates a PDF file of approximately 12MB. If you need a smaller PDF, choose the Smallest File Size setting from the Adobe PDF Preset drop-down menu. This setting presents an additional dialog box indicating that the transparency blend space is different from the document's blend space. Simply click OK and proceed as usual.

Printing

The Book panel also simplifies the process of printing the book, should you want a hard copy. Although the steps are few, keep in mind that printing the entire book—six files—will take some time.

1   Click in the open area below the list of documents in the Book panel to ensure that no documents are selected.

2   From the Book panel menu, choose Print Book. InDesign opens the standard print dialog box from which you can print all the pages from all documents of the book simultaneously.

For more on printing from InDesign CS5, see Lesson 10, "Document Delivery: Printing, PDFs, and XHTML."

3   Click Cancel to close the Print dialog box.

4   From the Book panel menu (-≡), choose Save Book, then from the Book panel menu again, choose Close Book to close the project.

Congratulations! You've just finished working in your first InDesign book file.

Self study

Work with other text variables available in InDesign to find out other ways in which they can be used. The Running Header variable, for instance, allows you to define a paragraph style within the document, whose content will appear where the Running Header variable is placed. This can save considerable time when working with long documents.

Create your own paragraph styles for the Table of Contents to change its appearance. Get creative by changing the fonts and paragraph spacing, and then choose Update Table of Contents to see the changes.

Add additional references to the index. Practice creating index references and cross-references and then regenerate the index to apply the recent entries. With index copy, you can customize the appearance of the text by using paragraph styles. You can change these settings by clicking on the More Options button in the Generate Index dialog box.

Experiment with Conditional Text to add more ways to reference text within your InDesign layouts.

Review

Questions

1 What feature in InDesign allows you to ensure that paragraph and character styles have a consistent appearance across multiple files?

2 What is the key requirement for creating a Table of Contents in InDesign?

3 How do you update an existing index within InDesign?

4 How can you make a PDF file of all pages within a Book file?

Answers

1 The synchronize options feature in a Book ensures consistent styles and appearance.

2 Paragraph styles must be used to format text throughout the document.

3 Choose Generate Index from the Index panel menu and make sure that the *Replace Existing Index* checkbox is checked.

4 Choose Export Book to PDF from the Book panel menu.

What you'll learn in this lesson:

- Preflighting your document
- Collecting for distribution
- Creating and customizing a PDF file
- Exporting an XHTML file
- Printing a proof

Document Delivery: Printing, PDFs, and XHTML

Designing your document is only half the job. You still need to deliver it, whether to a commercial printer, the Web, or just your coworkers for review. To help you, InDesign offers multiple methods for proofing and packaging your files, as well as flexible export controls for a variety of formats, including PDF and HTML.

Starting up

Before starting, make sure that your tools and panels are consistent by resetting your preferences. See "Resetting the InDesign workspace and preferences" on page 3.

You will work with several files from the id10lessons folder in this lesson. Make sure that you have copied the id10lessons folder onto your hard drive from the Digital Classroom DVD. See "Loading lesson files" on page 4. This lesson may be easier to follow if the id10lessons folder is on your desktop.

For this lesson, you need either Adobe Acrobat or Adobe Reader to view the PDF files you will create. If necessary, you can download the free Adobe Reader at *get.adobe.com/reader*.

See Lesson 10 in action!

Use the accompanying video to gain a better understanding of how to use some of the features shown in this lesson. The video tutorial for this lesson can be found on the included DVD.

The project

To sample the PDF, XHTML, and print-related controls offered by InDesign, you will prepare a car ad for delivery to multiple customers. You'll package it using the InDesign Preflight and Package feature, match it to a printer's specifications, and convert it to XHTML for posting to a web site using the Export for Dreamweaver feature.

Package inventory

Before you send your files to a printer or other service provider, in order to print your job professionally, it's important that you check the file for common errors that can occur during the design phase of your project. If your files aren't prepared to the required specifications, your job could be delayed or, even worse, reproduced incorrectly. The InDesign CS5 Live Preflight feature enables you to check all the mechanics of your file to ensure that everything is in working order. You can even define custom Preflight profiles in CS5 that will preflight your document to your specific needs.

For example, say you're planning to submit an ad for the new IDCS5 sports car to a newspaper. In this exercise, you'll use Package to see the Package Inventory of the file, and then you'll define a Preflight setting to see how well your ad complies with the newspaper's specifications.

1   Choose File > Open, navigate to the id10lessons folder, and select CarAd.indd. Click Open.

2   Choose File > Package. InDesign analyzes the document, and displays a summary of its findings in the Package Inventory dialog box. For more information on a specific category, click its name in the list on the left side of the dialog box.

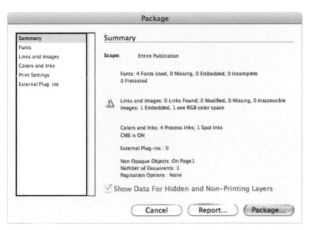

The Package Inventory dialog box displays detailed information about your file, and flags potential errors that could cause problems.

3   From the list on the left side of the dialog box, choose Fonts. The right side of the dialog box now lists all the fonts used in your document as well as their format and status. If the status is OK, the font is loaded onto your system and recognized by InDesign. A status of Missing indicates that the font cannot be found. Because this lesson file was created using fonts that load with InDesign, all your fonts should say OK.

4   Choose Links and Images from the list on the left side of the dialog box. This section displays information about the images that are used within your document. At the top of this dialog box is a caution icon (⚠), indicating that InDesign found a potential problem, specifically that one of the images uses the RGB color space. Most printing companies require images to be submitted in the CMYK color space; ask your printer for their specifications prior to sending your files.

Because you won't be printing this document, you don't need to worry about this message. If you were working on a piece for printing, however, and this warning appeared, you would open the RGB file in Adobe Photoshop and convert it to CMYK or carefully check the color conversion options set within InDesign.

The Links and Images section also indicates the state of your images, linked or unlinked, as well as the actual versus effective resolutions of your images.

Actual versus effective resolution

The resolution of an image is indicated by the number of pixels per inch (ppi) that make up the image—a seemingly simple concept that can be a bit complicated. As a general rule, the higher the resolution of an image, the higher its quality. Most images that you see when browsing the Internet are 72 ppi or 96 ppi, which is the standard screen resolution of most monitors. For high-quality printing, however, image resolution should generally be around 300 ppi.

To further complicate things, the Package window's Links and Images section lists two different numbers at the bottom: actual ppi and effective ppi. Actual ppi is the actual resolution of the file that you are placing into InDesign. The effective ppi is the resolution of the image after it has been scaled in InDesign. For example, if you place a 300-ppi image in your document and then scale it 200 percent, the effective resolution becomes 150 ppi. As you increase the size of images in InDesign, the effective resolution decreases. The effective resolution is the number that you should pay most careful attention to, as it determines the quality at which the image is output.

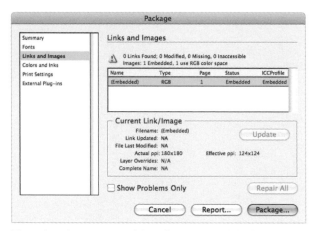

The Links and Images section of the Package Inventory dialog box.

5   Select Colors and Inks in the Package list to see which ink colors the document uses. This file uses a color called Pantone 187 C. Any color besides cyan, magenta, yellow, or black is considered a spot color or plate. You'll learn more about these later in the "Separation Preview" section. Click the Cancel button to close the Package dialog box.

For more information on Pantone colors, see Lesson 7, "Using Color in Your Documents."

Keep the file open, as you'll need it for the next part of the lesson. Now you're ready to package it to send to the newspaper that is running the ad.

6   Choose File > Save As. Navigate to the id10lessons folder and type **CarAd_work.indd** in the Name text field. Click Save.

Preflight checks

Like a pilot checking over his plane prior to takeoff, Preflight assesses your document, then reports potential problems—missing fonts, missing images, RGB (Red, Green, Blue) images, and more—that could prevent a printer from outputting your job properly, or hinder a customer's ability to view your file accurately. You can set up different profiles for all the intended destinations of your documents. For example, you could define a Preflight profile for all the documents you create that will end up as just PDFs on the Web, which are not intended for high-end output. You could define the profile to look for images with a resolution over 100 ppi. Whenever a photo was placed that had a higher resolution than 100 ppi, an error would appear in the Preflight panel. You can also see the Preflight status in the bottom-left area of your document window. In this exercise, you will define a new profile in the InDesign CS5 Preflight panel, and then check your document against the profile.

1 Choose Window > Output > Preflight. The Preflight panel opens. Right now, the Preflight profile is set to Basic, which looks only for broken links to images, missing fonts in the document, or overset text. You will now define a new profile that will look for RGB images in the document.

The new Preflight panel in InDesign CS5.

2 From the Preflight panel menu (▾≡), choose Define Profiles.

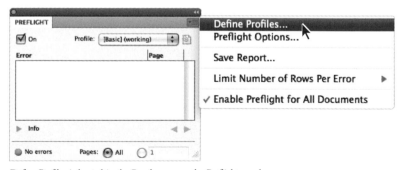

Define Profiles is located in the Panel menu on the Preflight panel.

3 The Preflight Profiles dialog box opens. You cannot change the default Basic profile, so you will define a new one that looks for RGB color in your document. In the Profiles section on the left, click on the plus sign (⊕) at the bottom to create a new profile.

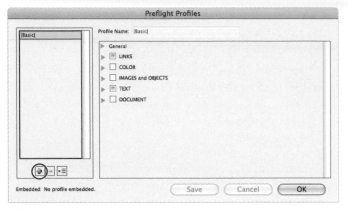

Make a new profile by clicking on the plus sign.

4 In the Profile Name text field at the top, select the text New Preflight Profile, then type **CMYK**.

5 In the Profile definition area, open the triangle next to Color by clicking on it. Now open the triangle next to Color Spaces and Modes Not Allowed. Check the box next to *Color Spaces and Modes Not Allowed*. Now check *RGB*.

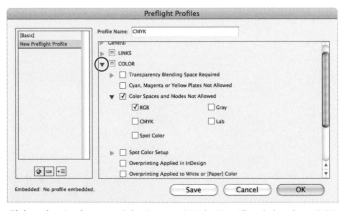

Click on the triangle next to Color Spaces and Modes Not Allowed, then choose RGB.

6 Click Save, then click OK. You have now defined a new color profile.

7 Change the profile in the Preflight panel from Basic to the new CMYK profile you have just made. Notice that the bottom-left area of your document and the Preflight panel now state that there is one error.

8 Expand the triangles to see the error that InDesign has found from within the Preflight Error window. Click on the triangle next to Color, and then click on the triangle next to *Color space not allowed.* The Preflight profile you have just built will now give you an error message for any RGB color that might find its way into your document. To fix this issue, you would need to open the problem image in Photoshop and change the color space to CMYK. But that is only if you are sending a Package to a printer. Certain PDF settings would automatically change the color space of the RGB images to CMYK.

The Preflight panel showing you that the red car has a color that is not allowed in this document.

9 Switch the profile back to Basic and close the Preflight panel.

10 Choose File > Save.

Packaging your document

When you need to send your InDesign document out for review, alterations, or printing, you must be sure you're sending all the necessary pieces. Without the font and image files used by the document, your coworkers or service provider can't accurately see and reproduce the file as you intended. To avoid this frustrating scenario, turn to the InDesign Package feature. Package gathers all the document elements the recipient needs into one folder and even enables you to include an instruction file. In this exercise, you will use Package to collect the car ad's fonts and graphics.

1 Choose File > Package. InDesign automatically runs Package Inventory and displays a warning if it finds problems. Click Package because the Package Inventory dialog box would display the same information you reviewed in the previous exercise.

2 For this exercise, click Continue when the Printing Instructions dialog box opens. For a real project, you would enter your contact information as well as any detailed instructions that the printer might need to output your file properly.

3 The Package Publication (Windows) or Create Package Folder (Mac OS) dialog box opens; here you choose what to include in the file Package, what to call it, and where to save it. Make sure the first three options are checked: *Copy Fonts*, *Copy Linked Graphics*, and *Update Graphic Links in Package*. All others should be unchecked. Type **CarAd Folder** in the Folder Name (Windows) or Save As (Mac OS) text field, choose Desktop from the Save in (Windows) or Where (Mac OS) drop-down menu, and click the Package button.

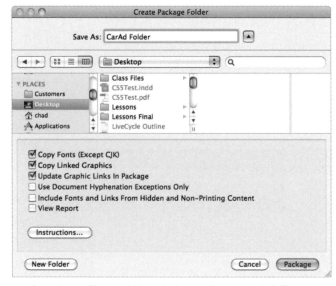

Use the Package Publication Folder dialog box to tell InDesign which files to gather and where to save them.

4 In response to the Font Alert dialog box that details the legalities of giving your fonts to a printer or service provider, click OK to begin packaging the files. If you don't want to see this alert in the future, click the *Don't show again* checkbox before you click OK.

5 When the dialog box closes, a small progress window appears, displaying the status of the packaging process. Once it has finished, close your CarAd_work.indd file.

6   In the Windows Explorer or Finder, navigate to the desktop, and double-click the CarAd folder. Inside, you'll find a copy of the document file, an instructions file, a Fonts folder with all the fonts used in the job, and a Links folder that contains all the graphics—all in one easy-to-send Package. In this Package folder, there is no Links folder because the graphic has been embedded only for the purposes of this lesson. Click Cancel to close the dialog box.

When the Package process is complete, all the project's elements are grouped together in the CarAd folder.

Now that all the files required to reproduce your job have been copied to the location you specified and are contained within their own folder, you can send this folder to another person to review, or to your printer or service provider to output your job. To ensure the integrity of the files and speed the transfer, compress the packaged folder before sending the files through e-mail or uploading them to an FTP server.

Creating an Adobe PDF

The Package feature collects all your data files, but the recipients still must have InDesign to read the document. But what if they don't?

The answer is to send a PDF file. PDF (Portable Document Format) is a common format that can be viewed and printed from any computer platform—Mac, Windows, Linux, and others—that has the free Adobe Reader program installed. A PDF file is an excellent way to make your project available for a wide range of users, and InDesign CS5 makes the process of creating a PDF file of your project very easy. In the following steps, you will create a PDF file of your CarAd_work.indd file so that other people can see your progress and provide feedback on changes that might need to be made before this project is sent to a printer for production.

PDFs can also be used for presentation purposes. PDFs generated in InDesign can contain sound, movies, and hyperlinks. To find out more about this, see Lesson 12, "Creating Interactive Documents."

1   Choose File > Open Recent > CarAd_work.indd to open your work file.

2   Choose File > Export. In the resulting Export dialog box, name the file **CarAd.pdf**, choose Desktop from the Save in (Windows) or Where (Mac OS) drop-down menu, and select Adobe PDF (Print) from the Save as type (Windows) or Format (Mac OS) drop-down menu. Click Save.

Choose the destination for your PDF file in the Export dialog box.

3   The Export Adobe PDF dialog box appears. From the Adobe PDF Preset drop-down menu at the top of the dialog box, you can choose settings that control the PDF file's size and quality, among other options. Because you will send the car ad to several people for general review, choose the [*Smallest File Size*] option from the Adobe PDF Preset drop-down menu.

PDF presets are a way of saving favorite settings for the final generated PDF file. If you own Adobe Acrobat 7.0 or a more recent version, InDesign CS5 shares these settings with Acrobat Distiller, which is included with Acrobat. Likewise, if you create a custom setting within Distiller, you'll see those settings in the Adobe PDF Preset drop-down menu when you export a PDF file from within InDesign CS5.

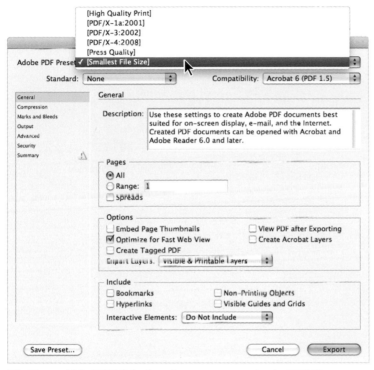

The Export Adobe PDF dialog box allows you to customize the PDF file you create from your InDesign file.

4   Click the Hyperlinks checkbox near the bottom of the Export Adobe PDF dialog box. Activating the Hyperlinks option makes any hyperlinks created in the InDesign document clickable hyperlinks in the resulting PDF document. Also click the *View PDF after Exporting* checkbox so that the resulting PDF file opens in Acrobat after the export.

5   Click the Export button. InDesign displays a warning that your document's transparency blend space doesn't match the destination color space. Because your PDF file is for viewing purposes only, this is not a concern. Click OK to begin generating the PDF file.

6 When the PDF export is finished, it should automatically open in Adobe Acrobat or Reader. If not, double-click the CarAd.pdf file on your desktop to open it. Hover your cursor over the *www.idcs5.com* link, and the cursor changes to a hand. Click on the link to go to the web site specified in the ad. If you receive a message warning you that the document is trying to connect to a web site, choose Allow.

The exported PDF file can contain interactive elements that are included in your InDesign file.

7 Choose File > Close to close the PDF file.

Generating XHTML

That takes care of the print and general viewing aspects of the ad campaign, but what about the Web? Your client wants all the used cars listed in the ad to be published on the company Web site. Although InDesign is a page-layout program, it can help you generate XHTML files from your document. XHTML is a markup language used for formatting pages on the Web. In this exercise, you'll use the Export for Dreamweaver controls to publish your content in XHTML format. Greatly improved from previous versions of InDesign, the InDesign CS5 Export for Dreamweaver function allows you to repurpose the content of your document to an XHTML file that is easily opened in an XHTML editor such as Adobe Dreamweaver. In several of the Adobe Creative Suite packages, Dreamweaver is included, making it easier to move content from print to the Web.

HTML versus XHTML

HTML (HyperText Markup Language) has been the standard markup language on the Web since the inception of the World Wide Web as you know it today. HTML allows you to describe how a page is formatted and displayed in a Web browser. XHTML (Extensible HyperText Markup Language) expands on traditional HTML by separating the presentation of a page from its structure, allowing you to describe the content of a page in addition to its formatting. XHTML incorporates the power of XML in HTML, so basically an XHTML document is both a hypertext document and an XML document, making pages easier to maintain and more flexible at the same time. Some very powerful tools developed for use with XML can now also be utilized on an XHTML document. For more on XML, see Lesson 11, "Using XML with InDesign."

1   With the CarAd_work.indd file open, choose File > Export for > Dreamweaver.

2   In the Save As dialog box, name the file **CarAd.html**, choose the desktop for its location, and click Save.

 When using the Export for Dreamweaver feature, make sure that you don't have any objects or text selected in your document. If an element is selected, InDesign exports only that text or object.

3   In the XHTML Export Options dialog box that opens, leave the General settings at their defaults, as there aren't any bulleted or numbered lists in the ad.

4   Select Images in the list on the left side of the dialog box. In the image-related settings that appear to the right, choose Optimized from the Copy Images drop-down menu. For Image Conversion, choose JPEG, and for Image Quality, choose High. This generates a separate folder called CarAdFormat-web-images containing all the images formatted for the Web.

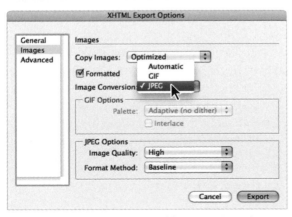

Control the quality of the images exported from your InDesign layout.

5   Select Advanced in the list on the left side of the dialog box. In the Advanced setting on the right side, click the Embedded CSS radio button and click the Include Style Definitions checkbox. This option inserts cascading style sheet (CSS) selectors in the resulting XHTML file so that you can later add CSS definitions to format the copy. See the next section for more information about CSS. Make sure that all other options are unselected, then click Export to save the XHTML file.

Customize the formatting of the exported XHTML file to change the appearance of the resulting file.

6   On the desktop, double-click on the CarAd.html file to view it in your default web browser. Or, if your browser is already open, choose File > Open in the browser to view the file.

Adding CSS formatting

The web page you exported has fairly rudimentary formatting, because formatting in XHTML isn't nearly as flexible as in a page-layout application such as InDesign CS5. You can, however, improve the formatting of your web page by using cascading style sheets (CSS). Just as styles control element formatting in InDesign, cascading style sheets specify which elements of an XHTML file should be formatted in which way. By linking your exported XHTML file to an external CSS file, you can mimic the formatting of your InDesign styles with cascading style sheets. For your text to be properly identified in the resulting XHTML file, however, you must use Character and Paragraph Styles to format the text and code (or have someone else code) a separate CSS file. If you format your copy manually (without styles), the CSS file cannot interpret what needs to be formatted. Try exporting the car ad again, this time linking it to a ready-made CSS file.

1   Close the CarAd.html file and return to InDesign. Choose File > Export for > Dreamweaver and name the file **CarAdFormat.html**. Save it to your desktop.

2   In the XHTML Export Options dialog box, leave the General settings at their defaults.

3   Click Images in the list to the left, and choose *Optimized* for Copy Images, *JPEG* for Image Conversion, and *High* for Image Quality.

4   Select Advanced, and then click the External CSS radio button and type **CarAd.css** in the text field, if it's not already entered. This is the CSS file that contains the document's formatting instructions. Now you need to reorganize a few files so that the XHTML file can find the CSS file.

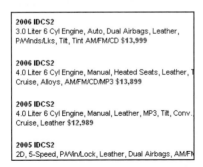

Select the External CSS radio button, then type in the name of the CSS file in the text field.

5   Click Export. Once the process is completed, navigate to the desktop. On the desktop, create a folder called XHTML. Move the CarAdFormat.html file and the CarAdFormat-web-images folder from your desktop into the XHTML folder. Copy the CarAd.css file from your id10lessons folder to the XHTML folder.

6   Open the XHTML folder and double-click the CarAdFormat.html file. You should see that the text for the used cars is now formatted similarly to the text in the print ad design. Close the file when you are done reviewing it.

> **2006 IDCS2**
> 3.0 Liter 6 Cyl Engine, Auto, Dual Airbags, Leather,
> P/Winds/Lks, Tilt, Tint AM/FM/CD **$13,999**
>
> **2006 IDCS2**
> 4.0 Liter 6 Cyl Engine, Manual, Heated Seats, Leather,
> Cruise, Alloys, AM/FM/CD/MP3 **$13,899**
>
> **2005 IDCS2**
> 4.0 Liter 6 Cyl Engine, Manual, Leather, MP3, Tilt, Conv.
> Cruise, Leather **$12,989**
>
> **2005 IDCS2**
> 2D, 5-Speed, P/Win/Lock, Leather, Dual Airbags, AM/FM

This is what the generated HTML looks like.

CSS and XHTML

Traditionally, formatting in HTML was limited to a predefined list of tags that changed the appearance of text and objects on a web page. These tags provided general formatting and were often inconsistent because different browsers' preference settings made it difficult for a designer to ensure the accurate appearance of a web page. CSS (cascading style sheets), as the name implies, are similar to Styles in InDesign CS5. This feature allows you to be more specific when formatting text, images, and layout in an XHTML file and streamlines the process of applying formatting to a page. CSS can be used to apply consistent formatting to a number of pages because multiple pages can be linked to a single CSS file. This also makes formatting adjustments quick and easy, because modifications to a CSS file are automatically translated to all pages that are linked to that CSS file.

Separation preview

Designed primarily to produce print layouts, InDesign supports both traditional methods of printing color: the four-color process (CMYK) model and spot colors. In the four-color process model, cyan, magenta, yellow, and black inks (C, M, and Y, with black as the K) combine in various values to reproduce numerous colors. A printing press uses a separate plate for each of these four colors, laying the ink down on the substrate in separate layers. Spot colors are pre-mixed inks that match standard color values. To ensure the green in your company's logo matches across all your print jobs, for example, you could choose a specific green spot color to use consistently.

Probably the most widely used spot color system is the Pantone Matching System, which is also called PMS, or simply Pantone colors. As a companion to the system it developed, Pantone Inc. also offers a swatch book so you can see how the colors reproduce on paper. All the Creative Suite applications have the Pantone library built in, so you can add spot colors to your document easily. Spot colors each require their own plates as well.

All Pantone colors have CMYK equivalents that enable you to reproduce the color using the standard process colors as well, should you need to conform to CMYK-only printing requirements, or reduce the number of plates.

Printing a Pantone color as a CMYK color may cause it to look different from the spot version of that Pantone color. This is because of the limited gamut, or color range, that process colors are able to reproduce. Pantone offers a Process Color Simulator guide that compares the printed spot color against the printed process color and is indispensable when you reproduce spot colors as four-color process.

In the printing industry, printers charge customers for each plate that has to be produced for the printing job. You want to be sure that unnecessary colors aren't mistakenly sent to the printer, as extra colors increase your cost and can cause confusion. To prevent this added expense and frustration, the InDesign Separations Preview panel lets you view the separate plates, or separations, as the printer would see them before you send your file. Take a tour of the panel as you check the car ad's separations.

1   Choose Window > Output > Separations Preview, or press Shift+F6, to open the Separations Preview panel.

2   Click on the Separations Preview panel menu button (·≡) and choose *Show Single Plates in Black* to turn off that option and see each plate in its actual color.

3   Choose Separations from the View drop-down menu in the Separations Preview panel.

4   Click the visibility icon (👁) to the left of the CMYK entry to turn off the visibility of the Cyan, Magenta, Yellow, and Black plates in your document. InDesign now displays only the elements in Pantone 187 C.

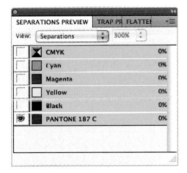

See where certain colors are used in your document.

You can tell that Pantone 187 C is a spot color because it is still visible after all the other separations have been hidden. Another way to identify a spot color in your document is to look at your Swatches panel. If any color has this icon (◙) to the right of the color name, it indicates that the color is a spot color and outputs on its own plate. Because the newspaper's specifications forbid spot colors, you must replace them in the car ad.

5   Click on the panel menu button in your Separations Preview panel, and choose Ink Manager from the list. The Ink Manager lists all the plates or inks that are currently in your document.

6   In the Ink Manager, click the spot icon to the left of the Pantone 187 C plate to change it from a spot color to a process color. You now see a process color icon (✖) to the left of the Pantone 187 C plate, indicating that the color will output as process instead of spot. Click OK. Because you mapped the Pantone 187 C plate to process and you turned off display of your process colors in step 4, no colors are currently visible.

7 Click on the visibility icon to the left of CMYK to see all the colors in your document again. The red color that was Pantone 187 C is now a red made of the four process colors. If you hover your cursor over different areas of your document, you can see the ink percentages to the right of each color in the Separations Preview panel.

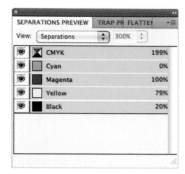

Hover your cursor over areas of your document to see the ink percentages.

8 Toggle the visibility of various separations in your Separations Preview panel to see how the colors in your document are combined to achieve other colors, called *builds*.

9 Choose Off from the View drop-down menu in the Separations Preview panel to get back to your normal viewing mode, and close the Separations Preview panel. Now your ad is properly prepared for printing in the newspaper.

Printing a proof

The best way to avoid surprises at press time is to print a proof of your document on your desktop printer. Seeing your project on paper sometimes reveals design flaws or mistakes you missed when viewing your document on screen. Printing out a version of your document on a printer is referred to as printing a proof. The term proof is used to describe any type of output that is generated prior to making plates for a printing press. In this exercise, you'll use InDesign to print a proof to your desktop printer.

1 With CarAd_work.indd open, choose File > Print to open the Print dialog box.

2 From the Printer drop-down menu at the top of the Print dialog box, choose a printer that is available to your computer.

3 Because there is only one page in your CarAd_work.indd file, leave Pages set to *All*. For multi-page documents, however, you could specify a limited range of pages to print.

4   Click Setup in the list on the left. On the right side, choose US Letter [8.5 x 11] from the Paper Size drop-down menu and click on the Landscape Orientation icon (🖳) to print your document in landscape orientation on standard letter-sized paper. The preview in the lower-left corner shows your page orientation and selected printer.

5   Your ad is larger than the letter-sized paper you specified in step 4, so click on the *Scale to Fit* radio button to scale your document to fit the available space. This automatically centers your document on the printed page. (If you have a large-format printer, of course, you can adjust the paper size as needed and print at full scale.)

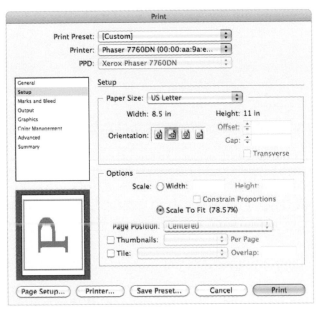

The Print dialog box enables you to control all aspects of how your page is oriented to the paper and printer.

6 In the list on the left, click Marks and Bleed. Click the *All Printer's Marks* checkbox to tell InDesign to add the appropriate trim, bleed, and color marks to your page as you would see on a printer's proof. Leave the other settings at their defaults.

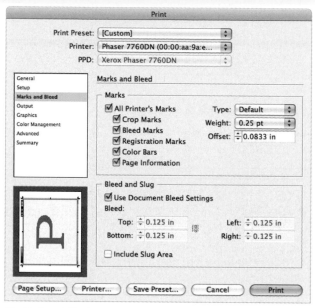

The Marks and Bleed section allows you to control the marks that are placed on your page when it is printed.

7 Click Output in the list on the left. If you are printing to a color printer that prints CMYK colors, choose Composite CMYK (or Composite RGB, if your printer doesn't print CMYK colors) from the Color drop-down menu on the right. If you are printing to a black-and-white printer, choose Composite Gray instead.

8 Click Graphics in the list on the left. In the Send Data drop-down menu of the Images section, choose the output quality of the graphics. Choose All for the best quality possible; choose Optimized Subsampling to let InDesign reduce the quality of your images slightly so the document prints faster. The higher the quality of the graphics, the more data InDesign needs to send to the printer and the longer it takes.

9 Click Print.

10 Choose File > Save to save your file, and then choose File > Close to close it.

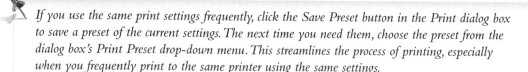

If you use the same print settings frequently, click the Save Preset button in the Print dialog box to save a preset of the current settings. The next time you need them, choose the preset from the dialog box's Print Preset drop-down menu. This streamlines the process of printing, especially when you frequently print to the same printer using the same settings.

Congratulations! You have completed this lesson.

Self study

Try the Find Font feature by choosing Type > Find Font to replace the fonts that Preflight or Package identifies as missing, with fonts you have loaded on your computer. Likewise, use the Links panel by choosing Window > Links to fix images that are missing or modified in your document. To find out more about what it means when fonts are missing, go to the Help file.

Investigate the numerous tools in InDesign CS5 that enable you to add interactivity to a PDF document when it is exported. For example, you can use the Button tool to add navigation to your exported PDF document, or you can add hyperlinks that are clickable links in the final PDF file. InDesign CS5 now offers two PDF output methods, Print and Interactive. The interactive choice allows you to output a PDF file with interactive components like page transitions and animation. Practice modifying the PDF settings to achieve different results in file size and other properties. When you create a configuration that you like, save it as a PDF Preset so you can easily use it again in the future.

Using the Separation Preview panel's Ink Manager, you can create an Ink Alias that maps one spot color to another. For instance, if you have two spot plates, you can map one ink to output on the same plate as the other ink. This feature is great when you realize at the last minute that you have too many spot colors in your document and need to minimize them. Practice this by creating a new document and adding at least two spot colors to your document. For more information on spot colors, check out Lesson 7, "Using Color in Your Documents."

Review

Questions

1   What command groups the active document and all the fonts and graphics used in the document into a single folder on your computer?

2   When creating a PDF file from InDesign, what's the easiest way to make sure that the settings for the PDF file are consistent every time?

3   What Web technology is used to automatically format text in an XHTML file exported from InDesign?

4   The Package dialog box tells you that there is a spot color used in your InDesign document. What's the easiest way to see where that spot color is used?

Answers

1   The Package command.

2   You can save the settings as a PDF Preset.

3   You use CSS (cascading style sheets) to create automatic formatting.

4   You can use the Separations Preview panel to see where the spot color is used. InDesign shows only the spot color plate.

Lesson 11

What you'll learn in this lesson:

- Importing and exporting XML

- Applying tags to your InDesign Layout

- Validating XML

- Understanding the XML structure

- Using data merge to automatically generate documents

Using XML with InDesign

You can use XML to repurpose your InDesign documents. You can apply tags to an existing print layout and export its content, including text and images, as an XML file for reuse in another document, on the Web, or another computer application. InDesign can also import XML from a database or the Web into a layout and you can automatically format the layout after importing the XML.

Starting up

Before starting, make sure that your tools and panels are consistent by resetting your preferences. See "Resetting the InDesign workspace and preferences" on page 3.

You will work with several files from the id11lessons folder in this lesson. Make sure that you have copied the id11lessons folder onto your hard drive from the Digital Classroom DVD. See "Loading lesson files" on page 4. This lesson may be easier to follow if the id11lessons folder is on your desktop.

See Lesson 11 in action!

Use the accompanying video to gain a better understanding of how to use some of the features shown in this lesson. Visit digitalclassroombooks.com to view the sample tutorial for this lesson.

The project

In this lesson, you'll work with content for a fictitious ski resort called Feather Ridge. Beginning with a flyer that has already been created, you will tag the content of the flyer using XML tags and a variety of XML tools, then repurpose that content for a large poster for display in local stores and other venues. To finish up, you will use the Data Merge feature in InDesign CS5 to generate business cards for employees of Feather Ridge to hand out to potential clients. This lesson is intended for users with some previous InDesign experience. If you just started with InDesign, you may want to use the program to gain some experience before working on this lesson.

XML basics

Before you can effectively work with XML in InDesign, you should understand a bit about the language itself. XML, which stands for Extensible Markup Language, allows for the repurposing and distribution of content to multiple destinations. XML does nothing to describe how its content is formatted—that is left to the destination program where the XML will be used. XML does, however, describe data. Because XML encloses content in tags, other programs can interpret the tagged data in a variety of ways. Consider this simple example of tagged and structured information:

```
<application>

    <name>Adobe InDesign</name>

    <version>7.0</version>

    <vendor>Adobe Systems, Inc.</vendor>

</application>
```

In this example, you can see that the tags or elements define and describe the content. Each tag resides within opening (<) and closing (>) angle brackets, and elements appear in opening and closing pairs (*<name>* and *</name>*, for example) that tell any program reading the file when the element starts and stops. In this example, the *<application>* element (open at the start, closed at the end) is called the root, or document, element because it contains all other elements. Every XML file must have a root element, but it doesn't necessarily need to be named as such. By looking at the example, you can determine that the application is Adobe InDesign version 7.0 and is manufactured by Adobe Systems, Inc.

You don't need an XML-specific program to write XML; a basic text editor suffices. In fact, to work with XML in InDesign, you don't even need to know how to write XML code; just select and click to tag the text or image.

XML tags in InDesign

Tags in InDesign are used to represent and specify the occurrences of elements within an InDesign layout. InDesign uses the Tags panel and a list of tags to specify the type of content that is, or will be, contained within a frame. A frame can be tagged as text or an image, and the text within a frame can be tagged as well. These tags are used whenever you import or export XML in InDesign.

1 If necessary, start InDesign CS5. Choose Window > Mini Bridge to open the Mini Bridge panel.

Mini Bridge is a panel driven by the main Bridge application but provides the same features within the InDesign application. Mini Bridge is an excellent tool for browsing through files on your computer, allowing you to preview files before opening them.

2 In the Mini Bridge panel, click the Home Page button (⌂) at the top of the panel, and then click the Browse Files button to begin browsing the files on your computer.

3 Navigate to your desktop on the right side of the Navigation section, and then navigate to the id11lessons folder to display the items within that folder.

Notice that when you view items using Mini Bridge, you can preview many different file types at once. There is a slider at the bottom of the Mini Bridge panel that allows you to change the size of the thumbnails within Mini Bridge. As a result, Mini Bridge is extremely useful when you are searching through a folder with many kinds of documents or images.

The Mini Bridge panel makes it easy to view files that can be opened and placed in InDesign.

4 Double-click the file named id1101.indd to open it in InDesign. If prompted, click Update Links to update the links.

5 Save a work version of this file before making any changes. Choose File > Save As. In the Save As dialog box, navigate to the id11lessons folder, type **id1101_work.indd** in the Name text field, then click Save.

6 Choose Window > Utilities > Tags to open the Tags panel, which displays an alphabetical list of the tags available in the document. Currently, the panel lists two: Root and slopename. Root is always in the Tags panel because every XML file needs a root element. The slopename tag was added to the document manually.

The Tags panel displays all the tags available in the active document.

The root element doesn't need to be named Root. You can rename it whatever you like by double-clicking on that tag within the Tags panel to bring up the Tag Options. In fact, any element can be renamed this way, provided you follow the rules for naming XML elements. To learn more about the rules of XML, visit w3schools.com/xml.

Basic rules for naming XML elements

- XML tag names can't start with "xml", numbers, or punctuation. Tag names must start with an alphabet letter or underscore (_).

- XML tag names cannot contain white space, thus spaces cannot be used.

- XML tag names are case-sensitive, so use consistent capitalization (Tag, TAG, tag, and tAg are all considered to be different XML names).

- There are several characters that are reserved for other uses in XML, so don't use less-than characters (<), greater-than characters (>), ampersands (&), apostrophes ('), or quotation marks (") in XML tag names.

7 Choose View > Structure > Show Tag Markers, and then choose View > Structure > Show Tagged Frames. Turning on these options enables you to see tagged items in the document while working in Normal viewing mode.

If Tag Markers and Tagged Frames are already displaying, the menu will provide the option to hide these items. Do not hide them, as you need them to display for this lesson.

8 Activate the Selection tool (k) from the Tools panel, and then select the frame that contains the phrase *Feather Ridge* to make the frame active.

9   Click on the slopename tag in the Tags panel to apply the slopename tag to the Feather Ridge frame. Notice that the frame changes color to indicate it was tagged, and that the associated tag is highlighted in the Tags panel. Because the Tags panel assigned orange to the slopename tag, the frame turns orange. The color of each tag is simply a visual aid and does not affect the actual XML content. If you don't like the tag preview color, you can easily change it.

A tagged frame takes on the color assigned to its tag.

10   Double-click the slopename tag in the Tags panel to open the Tag Options dialog box. Choose Magenta from the Color drop-down menu, and click OK. The Feather Ridge frame and its tag are now magenta.

You may need to scroll up through the list of colors when choosing the color magenta.

11   Choose File > Save.

If you don't see the color on the frame after you've tagged it, you may not have turned on the Show Tag Markers and Show Tagged Frames options in the View > Structure menu. If those options are on and you still don't see the markers, you may be in Preview mode. Turn this off by clicking the View button (▣) at the bottom of the Tools panel and making sure Normal is selected from the view options.

Importing and applying XML Tags

You can create XML tags directly within InDesign CS5, but most often you are given a list of tags to use. For instance, if you're repurposing the content of a print layout for the Web, your client or IT department may supply an XML document containing all the tags required in the final XML output. Import it into InDesign, and then click to apply the tags as necessary. If at any time you are not provided with tags and need to create them directly in InDesign, you can do so by simply clicking the New Tag button (⬏) at the bottom of the Tags panel.

1 From the Tags panel menu (-≡), choose Load Tags. In the Open a File dialog box, navigate to the id11lessons folder, select the file named id1101tags.xml, and then click Open. The tags contained in the XML file now appear in the Tags panel; it's that simple.

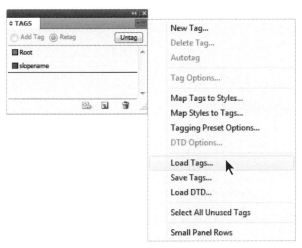

Import tag names from an external file into InDesign.

2 If the tagged frames are not activated from the beginning of the lesson, choose View > Structure > Show Tagged Frames so that you can see the tags you're about to apply.

3 Using the Selection tool (✸), click the image of the snowboarder in the page's lower-right corner, and then click the image tag in the Tags panel. The image is highlighted with a color, indicating that it is tagged.

4 Select the Type tool (I) from the Tools panel and triple-click on the phrase *A Seasonal Paradise!* to select the entire line. Click on the subhead tag in the Tags panel. Three things happen: pale-blue brackets appear around the selected phrase, showing that it is tagged; InDesign automatically adds the Story tag to the Tags panel and applies it to the frame that contains the tagged phrase and the untagged text below it; and that frame changes to the Story tag's color. When different tags are applied to selections of text within a frame, instead of using the same tag for the frame's entire text contents, InDesign tags that frame using the Story tag. InDesign does this to create an element that contains the various tagged and untagged sections within the text, giving them a logical structure. Story is the default element that InDesign uses, but this can be changed in the Tagging Preset Options found in the Tags panel menu.

To more easily see what is tagged, you may prefer to turn off the visibility for guides and frame edges. Choose View > Extras > Hide Frame Edges and also View > Grids & Guides > Hide Guides. You can also hide tagged frames by choosing View > Structure > Hide Tagged Frames.

A Seasonal Paradise!
Located in the heart of Histogram Mountain, you'll find a seasonal paradise waiting for you! You'll find a variety of skiing, snowboarding, and snow tubing that provides fun for the whole family.

In the off-season, we also provide mountain biking, swimming and

The tagged frames.

A Seasonal Paradise!
Located in the heart of Histogram Mountain, you'll find a seasonal paradise waiting for you! You'll find a variety of skiing, snowboarding, and snow tubing that provides fun for the whole family.

In the off-season, we also provide mountain biking, swimming and

Guides, frame edges, and tagged frames are hidden to reveal the text that was tagged.

5 Highlight the two paragraphs below the subhead using the Type tool; take care to include the paragraph return after the second paragraph. Click the body tag in the Tags panel to tag the paragraphs.

To be sure you include a paragraph return in a selection, turn on Show Hidden Characters by pressing Ctrl+Alt+I (Windows) or Command+Option+I (Mac OS).

To get another view of the applied text tags, have an active cursor in the text frame and choose Edit > Edit in Story Editor, or press Ctrl+Y (Windows) or Command+Y (Mac OS), to open a Story Editor window. This is another view of the document; you can edit and tag here or in the layout.

```
[X] subhead >A Seasonal Paradise!
</subhead [X] [X] body >Located in the heart of
Histogram Mountain, you'll find a seas
paradise waiting for you! You'll find
variety of skiing, snowboarding, and s
tubing that provides fun for the whole
family.
In the off-season, we also provide mou
biking, swimming and an alpine slide s
you'll keep coming back for more!
</body [X] A Snowboarder's Dream!
```

The tags in the Story Editor.

6 Highlight the next subhead, *A Snowboarder's Dream!,* and apply the subhead tag to it. Apply the body tag to the remainder of the text in the current frame and the threaded frame to the right.

7 Close the Story Editor window.

You have finished tagging this InDesign document. Now every item that you want to export as XML has been tagged so that it's included in the final XML file. In the Exporting XML section later in this chapter, you'll export all the tagged elements in the InDesign file to an XML file and reuse the content in another project. Remember that untagged content in the InDesign document does not appear in the final XML file, and it is therefore very important to be thorough during the tagging process to ensure that all the text and image information you want to repurpose is tagged.

Using a DTD

XML is incredibly flexible; you can create a language that meets your needs by customizing element names to match what you are trying to accomplish. Unlike other markup languages, such as HTML, XML doesn't have standard, predefined elements that are required for proper interpretation of the file. In XML, you can create your own element names or tags to apply to content within the XML file.

Although XML is flexible, there is the potential for errors and miscommunication. One safety net is the DTD, or Document Type Definition. A DTD is basically a set of rules that dictates how an XML file can be structured. For instance, a DTD could specify that the *<person>* element can have *<firstname>* and *<lastname>* child elements but not a *<middlename>* element. The DTD's job is to govern the structure of any XML file that is validated against it.

More than likely, you will receive a DTD from the same source that supplies the tags to be used. Validating the structure of a document to a DTD is not required, but it is often helpful. In this exercise, you'll validate the newly tagged file with a DTD to check compliance.

1 Choose View > Structure > Show Structure, or press Ctrl+Alt+1 (Windows) or Command+Option+1 (Mac OS), to open the Structure pane.

2 Click the triangle to the left of the word *Root* in the Structure panel. The Root element expands to display the elements contained within it.

3 Click the Story and Image elements' triangles to expand them.

Alt+clicking (Windows) or Option+clicking (Mac OS) on the triangle to the left of the Root element expands it and every other element with it.

Press Alt/Option+click on the triangle next to Root to expand all elements.

4 Click the panel menu button (-≡) in the upper-right corner of the Structure pane. Choose Load DTD from the menu. In the Load DTD dialog box, navigate to the id11lessons folder, select the id1101.dtd file, and then click Open to load the associated DTD into the document.

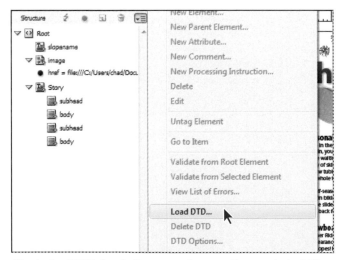

Choosing Load DTD from the Structure panel menu enables you to load a DTD file to validate the XML structure.

5 Simply loading the DTD file doesn't do anything by itself. You still need to perform a validation to see if the XML structure of the InDesign document complies with the DTD. Click the Validate structure using current DTD button (⚡) in the top bar of the Structure panel to validate the XML structure to the DTD. Several elements in the Structure panel turn red; these elements did not validate to the DTD. In the next exercise, you will fix those problems.

Items that fail to validate to the DTD show up red with error icons.

Viewing and organizing structure

As you tag elements in a layout, InDesign lists each tag in the Structure panel in the order that you use it. As a matter of fact, when you tag elements in InDesign manually, they are added to the Structure pane in the order in which you tagged the items. The tagging process, however, doesn't always happen in a logical order that matches what a DTD might be expecting. Fortunately, InDesign CS5 provides a means of fixing these structural problems.

1 Continuing from where you left off in the previous exercise, click on the image element in the Structure panel. A window at the bottom of the panel displays possible solutions to eliminate the error for the selected element. Two of the three suggestions in this case are unacceptable: retagging the element would incorrectly identify the content, and deleting the element would remove it from the XML output. The remaining option is to insert the Story element before the image element. You'll try that in the next step.

2   Click the Story element to highlight it, and then drag straight up in the Structure panel until the black dragging bar appears above the image element.

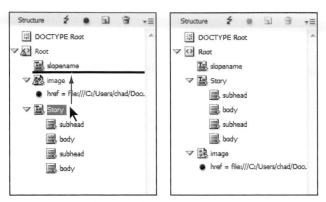

Reposition the Story element to validate the DTD.

3   Click the Validate structure using current DTD button (⚡) again to refresh the DTD validation.

Now there are no reported errors during the validation process, and the existing XML structure of the InDesign layout validates to the current DTD loaded into the document.

Viewing and applying attributes

Another component of an XML file is the attribute. An attribute defines a property of an element and comprises two parts: a name and a value. Attributes do not show up as content of an element; rather, they can add descriptive information about the element itself and are generally interpreted by other programs. A DTD often dictates that an attribute is applied to an element to more accurately describe information about the content of that element. For example, when an image is tagged in InDesign, the program automatically creates an attribute that points to the location of the image file on a server or hard drive. That pointer information doesn't show up in the content of the element, but it is necessary for the interpreting program to display or locate the image. InDesign CS5 makes it easy to both view and apply attributes within the current layout.

1   In the Structure pane, make sure that the image element is still expanded. Notice the entry within the image element that has a bullet in front of it followed by *href = file://...* This bulleted entry is an attribute.

Use attributes to add additional information about a tag.

2   Double-click the image element's bulleted attribute to open the Edit Attribute dialog box. Here the components of the attribute are shown, including the Name and Value. By default, when you tag an image in InDesign, an attribute named href (or Hypertext Reference) is automatically applied; its value is the path to the image location on your computer. The attribute does not need to change at the moment, so click Cancel.

3   In this layout, you want to add some attributes that indicate the location of the ski resort. In the Structure pane, click on the slopename element to select it.

4   Click the Add an attribute button (•) in the Structure pane to open the New Attribute dialog box.

5   In the Name text field, type **slopecity**, and in the Value text field, type **Killington**. Click OK.

Add an attribute with information about the slope's location to the slopename element.

6   Repeat steps 3 to 5, typing **slopestate** in the Name text field, and **Vermont** in the Value text field.

7   Now that you have the attributes applied, click the Validate structure using current DTD button (⚡) to determine if the document structure validates to the DTD. There shouldn't be any problems.

If the document structure doesn't validate to the DTD, verify that the attribute names are spelled exactly as shown in steps 5 and 6. Attribute names, just like element names, are case-sensitive and cannot contain spaces. The value, however, can contain any characters you desire. In the exercise, the attributes validated to the DTD because you used the names given to you. When you are creating your own projects, you can find out which attributes are valid by asking your IT department or by opening the DTD file in a text editor.

8   Choose File > Save to save your work.

Exporting XML

The document is tagged, the structure validates to a DTD, and you added attributes about key elements in the document—you're now ready to export the XML to a separate .xml file. From there, the content can be repurposed to a web site, intranet, RSS feed, content aggregator, or another InDesign document. You are now beginning to experience the power of XML. The fact that it only describes content and not formatting makes it extremely versatile. Give it a try.

1   Choose File > Export. In the Export dialog box, choose XML from the Save as type (Windows) or Format (Mac OS) drop-down menu.

2   In the Name text field, type **id1101_done.xml**, and in the Save in text field at the top of the dialog box, navigate to the id11lessons folder. Click the Save button to save the XML file and open the Export XML dialog box.

Use the Export XML dialog box to control how the XML file is exported.

3 Leave the settings at their defaults, and click the Export button. InDesign exports all the tagged content in the layout as an .xml file. Choose File > Close, and choose Save, if necessary.

4 Launch any text or XML editor on your computer. For Windows users, common text editors are Notepad and WordPad. Mac OS users can open a text editor like TextEdit or BBEdit and open the id1101_done.xml file to see what the finished XML file looks like. When you are finished, close the document.

Importing XML

Because XML describes content as opposed to formatting, you can easily repurpose XML content in multiple ways. For example, imagine you need to create an advertising poster for the Feather Ridge ski resort. Why start from scratch when you have the content in XML format? Simply set up a poster template and import the XML content into it. XML also gives you the flexibility to reproduce the same poster design quickly with details from different resorts.

Preparing the document template

In this exercise, you will prepare the poster template to receive the content, and in the next exercise, you will import the XML content that you exported from the first project to create the advertising poster.

1 Using File > Open or Mini Bridge, open id1102.indd from the id11lessons folder. If necessary, update the links in this file.

2 This file is a poster that you will populate with XML data. Currently, it is simply an InDesign document with frames placed where content should go. If you were to import XML data now, you would end up with elements in the Structure pane but no content on the page. The document must first be tagged so that the XML flows into the tagged frames when the file is imported.

Save a work version of this file before making any changes. Choose File > Save As. In the Save As dialog box, navigate to the id11lessons folder, type **id1102_work.indd** in the Name text field, then click Save.

3 If the Tags panel is not open, choose Window > Utilities > Tags to open it. By default, the only tag available in the document is the Root tag. You need to load more tags, and your client supplied you with an XML file of the necessary poster tags, as well as usage instructions to make it easier for you to tag the layout.

4 From the Tags panel menu (-≡), choose Load Tags. Navigate to the id11lessons folder, choose id1102tags.xml, and click Open. The Tags panel should now list a few more choices.

5 Using the Selection tool (⬉), click on the empty frame that partially overlaps the image of the snowboarder at the top of the document. Click the facility tag in the Tags panel to apply it to the selected frame. If the frames are not changing color after tagging them, make sure that the tagged frames and tag markers are visible by choosing View > Structure > Show tag markers and View > Structure > Show tagged frames.

6 Click the empty frame in the middle of the poster, then click the article tag in the Tags panel.

7 Click the empty frame at the bottom of the document, and apply the photo tag.

8 If the Structure panel is no longer open, choose View > Structure > Show Structure to open it. Click the Root element in the Structure panel to select it, then click poster in the Tags panel to change the Root element's name to poster, as required by the client's usage instructions.

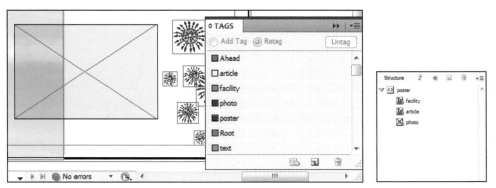

Tag the poster's empty frames and rename the Root element in the Structure panel. Notice the icon representing the empty tagged image frame.

9 Choose File > Save.

Applying an XSLT on import

You have now prepared the empty poster layout to receive XML data, but you have run into a common dilemma: the tag names in the template file are different from those used in the XML file you're about to import. The solution is to apply an XSLT to the XML file to transform it into the format necessary for the poster layout. An XSLT (eXtensible Stylesheet Language Transformation) transforms an input XML file into an output XML file that is formatted or altered in some way. In this lesson, you'll apply the XSLT to the XML file you created in the previous exercise. The XSLT looks for any image element, for example, in the input XML file, and changes it to a photo element in the output XML file, keeping its attributes while applying other transformations.

XSLT is extremely powerful because it can do so much more than a text editor's basic find and change feature. It can reorganize the structure of the incoming XML file in any way that is necessary: renaming elements, making some elements children (sub-elements) of others, and so on. An XSLT is written in the same format that an XML file is written, which makes it easier for someone familiar with XML to write. Now it's time to put this theory into practice.

1 Choose File > Import XML to open the Import XML dialog box.

2 In the resulting Import XML dialog box, navigate to the id11lessons folder and choose the id1101_done.xml file. Click the *Show XML Import Options* checkbox at the bottom of the dialog box to turn it on (if it's checked already, don't click it). Click Open.

3 In the XML Import Options dialog box, click to turn on the *Apply XSLT* option. From the Apply XSLT drop-down menu, select Browse (Windows) or Choose (Mac OS), and open id1102.xsl from the id11lessons folder. You should now see the file path to the XSL file in the field next to Apply XSLT. Leave all other settings at their defaults, and click OK.

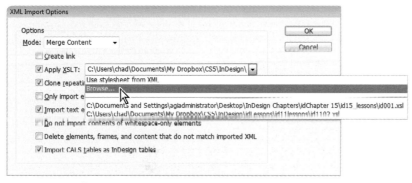

Choose an XSLT file to transform the incoming XML data into a format that you need.

4 After you import the XML file, several things happen:

- InDesign applies the XSLT to transform the incoming XML, which changes the names of the elements in the original XML file to the names of the elements that the poster layout was expecting.

- The XML file imports into the InDesign layout.

- Because the structure of the incoming XML data matches the structure of the pre-tagged poster layout, the text and images automatically flow into their respective pre-tagged frames.

5 Choose File > Save to save your work.

Where to get an XSLT

An XSLT can be created directly on your computer using a basic text editor. It uses an XML-like structure that makes it fairly easy for somebody with a basic programming background to get up-and-running quickly. Writing XSLT is beyond the scope of this book, and some people may find that they do not have the background or the desire to learn XSLT. A quick search on the Internet provides you with many resources that can create an XSLT quickly and affordably for your project.

Mapping tags to styles

Importing the XML file did a considerable amount of the work for you, but the poster isn't quite finished. When InDesign imports XML data into tagged frames, it formats the text in the receiving document's default font and formatting. You need to map the tags to InDesign styles in order to automatically format the text to match the poster's design concept. This exercise explores how to do just that and puts the finishing touches on the poster.

1 Click on the Paragraph Styles button (¶) in the dock on the right side of the workspace, or choose Type > Paragraph Styles to open the Paragraph Styles panel. Notice that it contains several styles with the same names as the elements in the Structure panel. These are used in the next steps to apply tags to the text.

2 From the Structure panel menu (-≡) or the Tags panel menu, choose Map Tags to Styles.

The Map Styles to Tags option automates the XML tagging process by tagging elements based on the applied paragraph styles in a pre-styled layout.

3 In the resulting Map Tags to Styles dialog box, make sure the *Preview* checkbox is checked and click the Map by Name button at the bottom of the dialog box. This tells InDesign to map paragraph styles to their matching tag names.

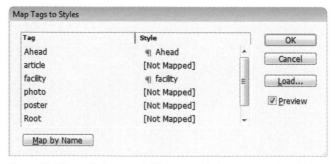

Choose Map Tags to Styles to match XML tags with the paragraph styles of the same name, which automates formatting of tagged text.

You can see that three paragraph styles match the tag names exactly. Content whose tag matches the name of a paragraph style now has that style applied, automatically formatting that copy in the layout. If the paragraph style names do not match the tag names, you can map them manually in the Map Tags to Styles dialog box by choosing which style you want mapped to which tag. Whichever way you approach this process, it is generally much faster than manually formatting the copy within the layout. In this case, you leave the unmapped styles as they are. Click OK.

4 Choose File > Save to save your work, and then choose File > Close to close the file.

Using data merge

Data merge automates the creation of multiple versions of a project and populates areas of the layout with different content for each version. Data merge pulls variable content from a source file. The data source file might contain a list of names, for instance, so that you could easily populate the poster project with the names of Feather Ridge ski trails first, then the names of Loon Mountain ski trails, followed by a version with the name of Snowmass trails.

In this exercise, you use data merge to create business cards for all Feather Ridge employees, quickly creating many versions of the same layout.

1 Choose Window > Mini Bridge, navigate to the id1103.indd file from the id11lessons folder, and double-click on it to open it.

2 Save a work version of this file before making any changes. Choose File > Save As. In the Save As dialog box, navigate to the id11lessons folder and type **id1103_work.indd** in the Name text field. Click Save.

This file contains the general layout for the business cards. You need to add a graphic to the business card and then prepare the layout for the data merge.

3 In the Mini Bridge panel, navigate to the id11lessons folder on the desktop, and then click and drag the Snowflakes_Snippet.idms file from Bridge into the InDesign document. A loaded graphic cursor appears.

4 Click on the left side of the business card to place the Snippet onto the business card.

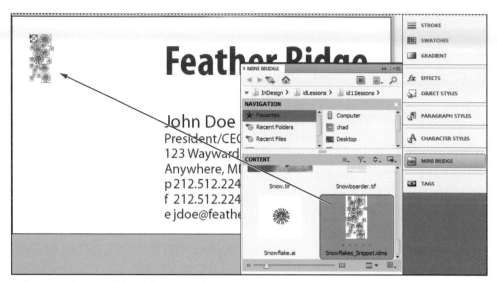

In the Mini Bridge panel, click and drag the snowflakes Snippet item directly into the InDesign document.

Snippets can be placed as freely positioned objects or inline graphics. Be careful if you have an active text cursor while dragging a Snippet into the layout, as it may be placed inline in the text.

XML Snippets

The file that you dragged into InDesign in step 3 of this exercise is called a Snippet. A *Snippet* is a single file that is a collection of objects that originated from InDesign. Snippets are extremely versatile because everything that you need is located within that one single file. Notice that the elements created by the Snippet are a group of items. There are multiple frames containing images created by the Snippet. This can't be done by simply placing a graphic.

An XML Snippet is simply an XML file that describes the objects it contains, such as size, shape, location on the page, and link locations. Snippets aren't the only places that InDesign uses XML behind the scenes. In addition to the tagging process that you used in the beginning of this lesson, when you add an item to a Library in InDesign CS5, an XML Snippet is created in the process. Saving an InDesign CS5 file as an .idml (InDesign Markup Language) document saves the file in XML format so that previous versions of InDesign can interpret the file and open it. XML is what makes all these things possible.

5 Activate the Selection tool (♦) from the Tools panel and use it to position the snowflakes contained in the Snippet file on the left side of the business card.

6 Choose Window > Utilities > Data Merge to open the Data Merge panel.

7 From the Data Merge panel menu (-≡), choose Select Data Source. In the resulting Select Data Source dialog box, open buscardlist.csv from the id11lessons folder. The Data Merge panel now contains a list of fields that indicate all the available groups of specific information that can be merged into the document. Data merge can use either a .csv (comma-separated value) or a .txt or .tab (tab-delimited) text file; the difference between the formats is in the type of delimiters used to separate the data.

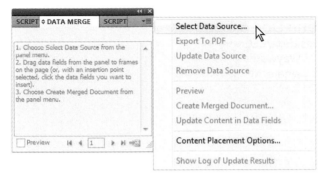

The Select Data Source option allows you to choose the source file that contains the data to merge into the layout.

Both .csv and .tab files can be exported from a spreadsheet using programs such as Microsoft Excel, or from databases created with applications such as FileMaker Pro.

To assist you in properly positioning the data fields, display the hidden characters in the document by pressing Ctrl+Alt+I (Windows) or Command+Option+I (Mac OS). If you can't see the hidden characters, make sure that you are not in Preview mode by clicking on the Normal Mode button at the bottom of the Tools panel.

8 Add some data fields to the document to prepare it for the data merge. Using the Type tool (T), highlight the word *John*, and click once on Fname in the Data Merge panel.

9 Highlight the word *Doe*, and click once on Lname in the Data Merge panel.

Do not include spaces or returns when you highlight text to replace with a data field. Spaces and returns generally should be static, meaning that they aren't pulled into the layout from the data source. Turning on the hidden characters in the document makes it easier to avoid selecting unwanted whitespace characters.

10 Select the title *President/CEO*, and click the Title field in the Data Merge panel. Select the line below the title, and click the Data Merge panel's Address field.

11 For the next line, highlight the word *Anywhere*, leaving out the comma, and click on the City field. Highlight *MD* (no spaces), and click on the State field. Finally, highlight the five-digit Zip code, 00001, and click on Zip in the Data Merge panel.

12 Repeat this process for the phone, fax, and e-mail copy, taking care not to include the tab at the beginning or the return at the end of each line. You're almost finished. Don't be too concerned if some of the placeholder copy runs into the graphic on the right side of the business card or even if some of the text becomes overset. This happens sometimes if the field names in the data file are particularly long. The double-angle brackets at the beginning (<<) and end (>>) of each field take up additional space.

This is what the card should look like with placeholder text after you have added all the data fields.

13 The work document now contains placeholders and links to the data source file. Save your work by choosing File > Save.

14 Click the Create Merged Document button (⇥) in the lower-right corner of the Data Merge panel to open the Create Merged Document dialog box. This process creates either an InDesign or a PDF document. Leave the settings at their defaults, and click OK to generate a new InDesign document with the merged results. You should receive a warning message that indicates that no overset text was generated. Click OK. InDesign displays the new merged document.

15 Open the Pages panel by clicking the Pages button (⬚) in the dock or by choosing Window > Pages, and navigate through all the pages created in the merged document. Each one has the same basic components, but wherever you designated a merge field, new data appears on each respective business card.

16 Choose File > Save As. In the Save As dialog box, navigate to the id11lessons folder, type **id1103_final.indd** in the Name text field, then click Save. Close this completed merged file by choosing File > Close.

By using data merge, you automated what would have been a time-consuming and tedious process had you created each card yourself. Using data merge furthermore eliminates typos and other mistakes (at least on your end) that could be costly if missed. Data merge in InDesign is not limited to text; you could have also defined an image field that would populate each card with a different image.

Congratulations! You have completed the lesson.

Self study

Practice tagging one of your existing documents and export the XML to repurpose in another document. Pre-tag a layout in a different orientation and then import the XML file to see the different possibilities that XML can create.

In this lesson, you used the Map Tags to Styles command to map tagged information to paragraph styles to automate the formatting of content on your page. There is also a Map Styles to Tags option that does just the opposite. It takes a pre-styled layout that utilizes paragraph styles to format the copy, and automates the tagging process by tagging elements based on the name of the paragraph style.

Create some InDesign Snippets. For example, you could select one or more items in the InDesign layout and drag them to the desktop of your computer. E-mail the newly created Snippet file to a colleague, who can then drag it from the desktop onto a blank document to see how InDesign recreates every element from the original document. One item to note: If you make a Snippet out of InDesign elements that include an image, InDesign still looks at the original file path from where that placed image was linked, unless you embed the image.

InDesign Snippets

An InDesign Snippet is an XML file generated from within InDesign that allows you to repurpose commonly used elements throughout multiple documents in InDesign. If you are familiar with InDesign Libraries, Snippets work the same way but don't have to live inside of a Library. Snippets can be created in one of two ways:

1 Select an element(s) within an InDesign document and drag the item onto your desktop. You may need to adjust the document window prior to doing this so that you can see the desktop behind the document. An InDesign Snippet file is created.

2 Select an element(s) within an InDesign document and choose File > Export. In the resulting Export dialog box, choose InDesign Snippet from the Format drop-down menu and give the Snippet file a name. Click Save.

Once you've created some Snippets, you can reuse them by dragging them from an Explorer (Windows) or Finder (Mac OS) window and dropping them onto an open InDesign document. You can also place them as you would any other graphic file in InDesign. One of the great benefits of Snippets over an InDesign Library is that you can browse them using Adobe Bridge. This allows you to save the Snippet files to a central location on a server where several people can browse them at the same time.

Automate the placement of images as well as text during a data merge. You simply need to have the path to the image for each record within the source data file to make it work.

Review

Questions

1   What does XML stand for?

2   How can you tell if an InDesign file contains tagged content?

3   Which XML component can be added to an XML element to provide additional information about the element, but does not show up in the content of an element?

4   Which type of file can change the structure of an XML file on import or export?

5   Where in InDesign CS5 can you adjust the XML structure of a document?

6   Which document formats can be used as a source for a data merge?

Answers

1   It stands for Extensible Markup Language.

2   Choose Show Tag Markers and Show Tagged Frames from the View > Structure menu.

3   An attribute can be added, but does not show up in the content of an element.

4   An XSLT (eXtensible Stylesheet Language Transformation).

5   You can adjust the XML structure in the Structure panel.

6   You can use .csv (comma-separated), .tab (tab-separated), or .txt (plain text) format.

What you'll learn in this lesson:

- Importing multimedia content

- Creating page transitions and buttons

- Creating and viewing a Flash file

- Creating an interactive PDF

Creating Interactive Documents

You can use InDesign to create documents for print or on-line distribution. Your InDesign documents can be enhanced for on-line distribution using movies, buttons, and animations. You can distribute your interactive document as a PDF or Flash file on the Web. You can also create Flash documents that can be edited using the Adobe Flash Professional application.

Starting up

Before starting, make sure that your tools and panels are consistent by resetting your workspace. See "Resetting the InDesign workspace and preferences" on page 3.

You will work with several files from the id12lessons folder in this lesson. Make sure that you have copied the id12lessons folder onto your hard drive from the Digital Classroom DVD. See "Loading lesson files" on page 4. This lesson may be easier to follow if the id12lessons folder is on your desktop.

In this lesson, you will create a multimedia brochure promoting a blueberry farm. You will add video and export the content to a multimedia PDF (Portable Document Format) file, and also export the content to the Flash format.

See Lesson 12 in action!

Use the accompanying video to gain a better understanding of how to use some of the features shown in this lesson. Visit digitalclassroombooks.com to view the sample tutorial for this lesson.

InDesign relies upon the free QuickTime Player to import video file formats. If you work on a Mac OS computer, you probably have QuickTime. If you work on a Windows computer, be certain to download and install QuickTime at www.apple.com/quicktime/download.

Interactive design considerations

It's not enough simply to convert your document to PDF or SWF format and place it online. You must recognize that readers use online content differently, and that you'll need to make your content fit within their computer display and be clearly readable. Some simple considerations with the type and layout can be very helpful. Sans-serif fonts, such as Myriad Pro, Arial, and Helvetica, are easier to read on-screen. Additionally, you need to adjust the layout to fit the medium. Print layouts are often designed to be tall and narrow in a portrait orientation, which does not translate well to a computer display. Online layouts work better in landscape (wide) orientation so that they can be viewed completely without scrolling.

While InDesign supports the ability to create multimedia content, it's not the best authoring tool for Flash documents. Flash files created using InDesign will likely need significant editing in the Flash authoring program, and it's often easier to build Flash documents from scratch rather than trying to repurpose InDesign content into a Flash file. InDesign documents exported to the Flash file format have limitations. While InDesign lets you import video content into a file, the movies and animations do not export to the Flash file format. Additionally, text created using InDesign is broken into individual, disconnected lines. This makes the text extremely difficult to edit.

The finished online layout.

Importing multimedia content

You can use InDesign to import a variety of media types into your layout, including FLV, F4V, MP4, SWF, MOV, AVI, and MPEG for video and MP3 for audio. However, only files exported as interactive PDFs will support MOV, AVI, and MPEG; an exported SWF file will not. InDesign does *not* support the common Windows Media file format (WMV), which is used with Windows Media Player and the Silverlight platform. You will start by importing a movie file into an existing frame.

1 Choose File > Open. In the Open dialog box, navigate to the id12lessons folder, select the id1201.indd file, and click Open. If necessary, update the links in this file.

2 Make certain that page 1 is visible, or, if necessary, use the page drop-down menu in the lower-left corner of the document window to navigate to page 1. Choose the Selection tool (⬚) from the Tools panel and select the yellow frame in the lower-right corner.

3 Choose File > Place. In the Place dialog box, confirm that *Replace Selected Item* is selected and *Show Import Options* is not selected. Navigate to the Links folder within the id12lessons folder and select the file 1202.f4v; then click Open. The multimedia file is placed into the layout.

4 InDesign does not provide a preview of the placed video file because no poster is chosen. Choose Window > Interactive > Media to open the Media panel, which provides options for you to control the selected media. Choose Window > Interactive > Media if the Media button isn't visible.

5 Click the Play button to preview the video, or manually drag (scrub) the playhead to preview different parts of the video. When the video displays a frame that you'd like to use for the poster, choose From Current Frame from the Poster drop-down menu.

The Media panel provides a way to preview the video file and choose a poster frame.

6 Using the Selection tool, right-click (Windows) or Ctrl+click (Mac OS) on the frame containing the imported .f4v file, and from the contextual menu, choose Fitting > Fit Content Proportionally. The preview fits within the frame.

For the Fitting options to work correctly, the frame must be selected with the Selection tool. If the content is selected, the multimedia may not resize correctly.

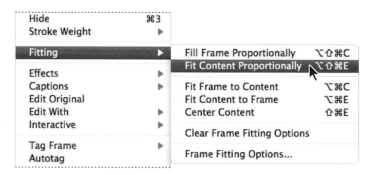

Fitting multimedia content into the frame.

As you can see, adding multimedia content to an InDesign layout is similar to adding still images and graphics. Next you'll add buttons to control the playback of this video file.

7 Choose File > Save As. In the Save As dialog box, navigate to the id12lessons folder and type **id1201_work.indd** in the Name text field. Click Save.

Creating buttons to control multimedia content

You can add buttons to your InDesign document for controlling placed multimedia content, or to help the user navigate to other pages or even an external web site.

1 Using the Selection tool (k), double-click the green frame located below and to the left of the multimedia file you imported in the previous exercise. The cursor changes to an insertion point, and the Type tool (T) is selected.

2 Type **Play Movie** in the text frame.

3 Choose the Selection tool from the Tools panel, then right-click (Windows) or Ctrl+click (Mac OS) on the text frame and choose Interactive > Convert to Button from the contextual menu that appears.

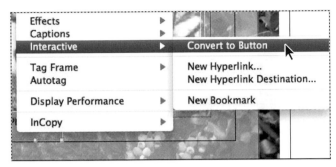

Converting an object to a button.

The Buttons panel appears. The button does not yet have any actions applied to it. You will assign actions to the button to control the movie.

4 In the Buttons panel, type **Play** in the Name text field to name the button. Leave the Event drop-down menu set to its default of On Release, which causes the action to occur after the mouse has been clicked and then released.

5 Click the Add new action for selected event button (✛) under Actions and choose Video for the button to control a movie. After choosing the Video action, the Video drop-down menu appears.

6 From the Video drop-down menu, choose the 1202.f4v movie, and then ensure that the Options drop-down menu is set to Play. You have applied an action to a button, causing it to control the movie clip you imported earlier.

Adding an action to a button.

Button actions control the file after it has been exported to PDF or SWF (Flash) format. The buttons do not control any actions within InDesign.

Adding more buttons

You will add buttons to both play and stop another video.

1   In the lower-left corner of the document window, click the pages drop-down menu and navigate to page 2.

2   Using the Selection tool (▸), click the text frame containing the words *Play Movie*. Right-click (Windows) or Ctrl+click (Mac OS) and choose Interactive > Convert to Button from the contextual menu that appears.

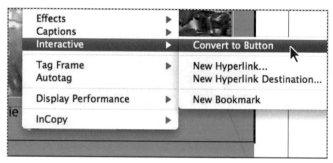

Converting another object to a button.

3   In the Buttons panel, type **Play** in the Name text field to name the button. Leave the Event drop-down menu set to its default of On Release, which causes the action to occur after the mouse has been clicked and then released.

4   Click the Add new action for selected event button (⊕) under Actions and choose Video for the button to control a video. After choosing the Video action, the Video drop-down menu appears.

5   From the Video drop-down menu, choose the 1203.f4v video, and then ensure that the Options drop-down menu is set to Play.

Selecting a movie for the button to control.

6   Using the Selection tool (⬈), select the text frame containing the words *Stop Movie*. Right-click (Windows) or Ctrl+click (Mac OS) and choose Interactive > Convert to Button from the contextual menu that appears.

7   In the Buttons panel, type **Stop** to name the button. For Event, keep the drop-down menu set to the default setting of On Release.

8   Click the Add new action for selected event button (⊕) next to Actions and choose Video for the button to control a video. After choosing the Video action, the Video drop-down menu appears.

9   From the Video drop-down menu, choose the 1203.f4v movie, and then ensure that the Options drop-down menu is set to Stop.

Creating a button to stop the movie.

Previewing your document

InDesign CS5 has added a Preview panel that allows you to preview your interactive elements without the need to actually export the document. In the next steps you'll use the Preview panel to see the interactive elements in your document.

1 Double-click on page 2 in the Pages panel to make page 2 the active page.

2 Click on the Preview button (⊡) to display the Preview panel. If you don't see the Preview button, choose Window > Interactive > Preview to display it. Feel free to detach the Preview panel from the panel dock and make it larger to make it easier to view.

3 Click the Play Preview button (▶) in the lower-left corner of the Preview panel to preview the active page.

4 Move your cursor over the Play Movie button below the video that you inserted onto page 2 earlier in this lesson. Your cursor becomes a pointer finger (⌐). Click on the Play Movie button to begin playing the video on page 2. Click the Stop Movie button when you are finished.

5 Collapse the Preview panel or dock it in the panel dock.

The Preview panel allows you to preview and test your interactive document without exporting the file to a .swf or .jpg format.

The buttons to play and stop this movie should be working as expected. Next you'll add some transitions to change how the page appears as you navigate from one page to the next when viewing the on-line version of the document.

Sample buttons can be used to apply pre-created buttons to your page. Access the Sample Buttons panel by clicking the panel menu option in the Buttons panel and choosing Sample Buttons. The Sample Buttons panel is actually a library of many buttons that have been created for you. Click and drag the sample buttons onto the page, and then apply the appropriate actions to them.

Creating animations

InDesign CS5 introduces the ability to apply animation to objects within your document that will animate when exported to the .swf format. This provides numerous opportunities for enhancing what can be done with interactive documents in InDesign.

Double-click on page 1 in the Pages panel to center page 1 in the workspace.

1   Using the Selection tool (↖), click on the frame at the top of the page that says Blueberry Picking Guide. Right-click (Windows) or Ctrl+click (Mac OS) on the frame and choose Fitting > Fit Frame to Content. This reduces the size of the frame, making it easier to work with.

2   With the Blueberry Picking Guide frame still selected, click on the Animation button to display the Animation panel. If the Animation button isn't available, choose Window > Interactive > Animation to display the Animation panel.

3   From the Preset drop-down menu, choose Fly in from Top. The preview area at the top of the Animation panel displays a proxy of how the animation will appear, and a motion path appears above the selected frame on the page indicating how the animation will appear.

The Animation panel allows you to specify how the selected object will be animated on the page.

The motion path indicates the length and direction that the frame will be animated.

4   Set the duration to **1.5 seconds** and leave the remaining choices at their defaults.

5   Open the Preview panel and click the Play Preview button to see how the animation appears.

6   Collapse the Preview and Animation panels and save the document.

Creating page transitions

You can make the on-line viewing experience more interesting by adding transitions that cause the pages to change appearance when you navigate from one page to another in an interactive document.

1 Click the Pages button (⊞) in the dock on the right side of the workspace to open the Pages panel. Double-click on page 1 to center page 1 in the workspace. Make certain that page 1 remains selected in the Pages panel.

2 Choose Window > Interactive > Page Transitions to open the Page Transitions panel, or click the Page Transitions button (⊞) if it's available in the panel dock.

3 In the Page Transitions panel, choose Comb for Transition, Horizontal for Direction, and for Speed, choose Medium. Note the icon that appears next to the page icon in the Pages panel, indicating that the page has a transition applied to it.

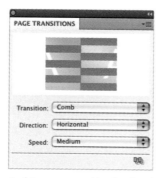

Applying a page transition for when the document is viewed on-line as a PDF or SWF file.

4 In the Pages panel, double-click on page 2 to return to it.

5 In the Page Transitions panel, choose Push for Transition, choose Down for Direction, and for Speed, choose Medium.

Once again, you can save a lot of time by previewing these page transitions directly with the Preview panel.

6 Open the Preview panel and click the Play Preview button (▶) to preview the animation.

7 In the bottom of the preview panel, click the Set Preview Document Mode button to preview the entire document. To see the page transitions, click the Go to Next Page and Go to Previous Page buttons (▸) in the lower-left corner of the Preview panel. The page transitions appear within the Preview panel.

Previewing the page transitions in the Preview panel.

8 Collapse or dock the Preview panel and Choose File > Save.

Creating an interactive PDF

To create an interactive PDF file, you will export the InDesign document.

1 Choose File > Export. The Export dialog box opens.

2 In the Export dialog box, choose Adobe PDF (Interactive) from the Save as type drop-down menu, and type **blueberries.pdf** in the Name text field to name the PDF file. Choose a location to save the file, such as the current lesson folder. Click the Save button, and the Export to Interactive PDF dialog box appears.

3 In the Pages section, click All, if necessary, to export all pages to PDF. Also make sure that both *View After Exporting* and *Embed Page Thumbnails* checkboxes are checked.

4 In the Page Transitions drop-down menu, choose From Document to use the page transitions that you specified in the Page Transitions panel within InDesign.

5 In the Buttons and Media section, be sure that the *Include All* radio button is selected so that all of the interactive elements defined in the InDesign document are included in the final PDF file.

6 In the Image Handling section, Choose JPEG (Lossy) for compression, Medium for JPEG Quality, and 72 for Resolution (ppi).

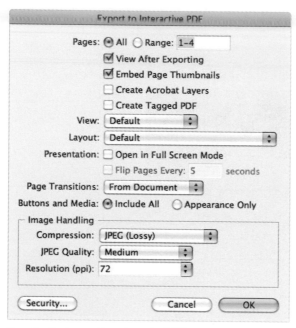

Exporting the document to an interactive PDF.

7 Click OK to create the PDF file. If you receive a warning message relating to the transparency blend space, or that some interactive elements have been clipped in ways that a PDF cannot produce, click OK to proceed and create the PDF file. This will not impact your PDF in a negative way. The PDF will open in Adobe Acrobat or the free Adobe Reader.

If you use another PDF viewing utility, you should open the file using Adobe Acrobat or Adobe Reader. Start the Adobe Acrobat or Adobe Reader program, choose File > Open, navigate to the location where you saved the blueberries.pdf file, and then open it.

Viewing an interactive PDF

Once the interactive PDF document is open using Acrobat, you can view the multimedia elements and review the page transitions you created.

1 In Acrobat, move the cursor over the Play Movie button in the lower-right corner of page 1, and click it to play the movie. The movie plays and then stops when it is completed. You may need to approve playing the video in a Manage Trust dialog box, depending upon the version of Acrobat or Adobe Reader you are using.

2 Continuing to work in Acrobat, choose View > Full Screen Mode. The document displays in a presentation format, without any menus or tools. Press the right arrow key on the keyboard to advance to the next page. Notice that the page transitions are displayed as you navigate from one page to the next. Use the left arrow key to return to the start of the document. Press the Escape (or Esc) key to return to the normal viewing mode.

Viewing the interactive PDF using the Full Screen mode in Acrobat or Adobe Reader.

3 In Acrobat, Choose File > Quit (Windows) or Acrobat > Quit Acrobat (Mac OS) to leave Acrobat and return to InDesign.

Creating a Flash SWF file

Now you'll return to Adobe InDesign and generate an interactive Flash file from your PDF content. Like the PDF, the completed Flash file can be posted on-line or sent through e-mail and viewed by the recipient. Flash files are designed primarily for on-line viewing, while the PDF document you created earlier can be viewed on-line or in print.

1 In InDesign, choose File > Export. The Export dialog box opens.

2 In the Export dialog box, choose Flash Player (SWF) from the Save as type drop-down menu, and type **blueberries.swf** in the Name text field to name the file. Choose a location to save the file, such as the current lesson folder. Click Save, and the Export SWF dialog box opens.

Be certain to not choose Adobe Flash CS4 Pro (XFL), as the XFL format creates a file for editing using the Adobe Flash software program. For more information, see the sidebar, "Editing Flash content created using InDesign."

3 In the Export SWF dialog box, click on the General button at the top of the dialog box and make sure that Pages is set to All and that Scale is set to 100 percent. Also make sure that *Generate HTML File, View SWF after Exporting,* and *Include Interactive Page Curl* are selected. Keep all other settings unchanged. The Interactive Page Curl option is described in the next exercise.

The General and Advanced windows of the Export SWF dialog box control how the final SWF file is generated.

4 Click OK to generate the SWF Flash file and the accompanying HTML file.

You may receive a warning dialog box, indicating that the CMYK color space used in the document is designed for print, but is being output using RGB, which is used for on-screen viewing. Click OK to dismiss the warning.

Viewing a Flash file

Now you'll review the SWF Flash file you created using InDesign. The SWF file should open within your default Web browser provided that the *View SWF after Exporting* checkbox was enabled when you exported the SWF file. If you use Internet Explorer, you may need to click the security warning, choose the *Allow Blocked Content* option to see the page, and then click Yes to allow the page to display.

1 Notice that the Blueberry Picking Guide text animates in from the top. If you missed it, simply click the refresh button in your browser to reload the page, causing the animation to occur again.

2 Click the Play Movie button to see the movie play.

3 Move the cursor over the lower-right corner of the first page. Notice the page curl that appears as you move the cursor in this area of the document. Click once to navigate to the second page. Note that the page transition defined in the InDesign document is used. To use the interactive page curl, click and drag to the left as if you're flipping the pages of a book or magazine.

SWF files created from InDesign can include an interactive page curl for changing pages.

4 On the second page of the document, position the cursor over the picture of the hand picking the blueberry. With the cursor positioned over the image, right-click (Windows) or Ctrl+click (Mac OS) and choose Zoom-in. Repeat this a second time to zoom in to the location where the cursor is positioned.

5 Right-click (Windows) or Ctrl+click (Mac OS) and choose Show All to display the entire page.

6 Position the cursor in the upper-left corner of page 2. As the interactive page curl displays, click and drag to the right. Notice that the interactive page curl is used as you change pages.

7 Close the browser.

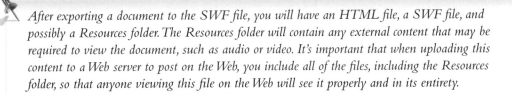

After exporting a document to the SWF file, you will have an HTML file, a SWF file, and possibly a Resources folder. The Resources folder will contain any external content that may be required to view the document, such as audio or video. It's important that when uploading this content to a Web server to post on the Web, you include all of the files, including the Resources folder, so that anyone viewing this file on the Web will see it properly and in its entirety.

Congratulations! You have finished the lesson.

Editing Flash content created using InDesign

You can edit some of the Flash content that is created using InDesign, to make the content more useful. To do this, export the file using the XFL format, then open the file using Flash Professional.

For this exercise, you could add new interactive elements or edit some of the text—however, the text only edits one line at a time. If you need to make major edits to your files using Flash Professional, you may be better off developing the entire file within Flash, which provides an authoring environment dedicated to the needs of creating interactive files.

Self study

1 Use the Buttons panel to add additional buttons and apply interactivity to the buttons after adding them to your page.

2 Add buttons to go forward and backward through the pages.

3 Experiment with the Animation panel to see the various animations that can be applied in InDesign CS5.

Review

Questions

1 What type of interactive content can you add to PDF files? Are there any unsupported formats?

2 What items can be converted to a button?

3 How does interactive document design differ from print design?

4 Is it necessary to export a file to PDF or SWF in order to see interactive elements that have been applied to the document?

Answers

1 You can import FLV, F4V, MP4, SWF, MOV, AVI, and MPEG for video and MP3 for audio formats. However, only PDF will support MOV, AVI, and MPEG, whereas Flash will not.

2 Buttons can be created from almost any text or graphic element by selecting the object and using the contextual menu or by choosing Object > Interactive.

3 Interactive documents are viewed on-screen, and so they need to reflect the wider layout of a computer display. Additionally, they need to use typefaces that are easily read on-screen, such as sans-serif typefaces.

4 No, InDesign CS5 provides the Preview panel, which allows you to easily see the interactive elements and how they will appear in your final SWF or PDF file.

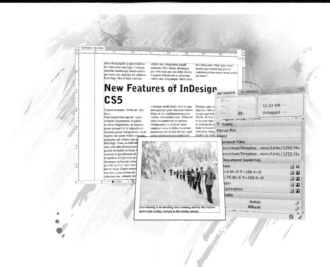

What you'll learn in this lesson:

- Using the Mini Bridge panel

- Implementing Metadata captions

- Drawing multiple frames in a grid

- Exploring the Animation features

What's New in Adobe InDesign CS5?

Adobe InDesign CS5 introduces some significant changes to an already amazing page layout application. This chapter shows you what's new in InDesign CS5 so you can benefit from these changes immediately.

Starting up

This lesson provides an overview of the new or modified features in InDesign CS5 and does not require any lesson files.

See Lesson 13 in action!

Use the accompanying video to gain a better understanding of how to use some of the features shown in this lesson. The video tutorial for this lesson can be found on the included DVD.

Design and Layout

Some great new options have been introduced in InDesign CS5 that make it much easier to layout your document and design more freely.

Mini Bridge

Since Adobe Bridge was introduced back in the original release of the Creative Suite, it has become a powerful tool for searching, navigating, and placing content into other Adobe and non-Adobe applications. InDesign CS5 introduces the Mini Bridge. Instead of switching to a completely separate application to browse and view files, a separate panel called Mini Bridge has been added that alleviates the need to exit InDesign to view and place files.

Mini Bridge allows you to view and place files directly from a panel within InDesign CS5.

Mini Bridge allows you to control the size of the image thumbnails and also allows you to place files directly from the Mini Bridge panel as illustrated in the figure above. Both the Bridge and Mini Bridge also allow you to see multiple pages of an InDesign file as well.

Bridge Enhancements

Bridge now can preview the first several pages of an InDesign document. In prior versions of InDesign, only an InDesign template provided page previews within Bridge, but now normal InDesign documents can be previewed. By default, InDesign writes previews for the first two pages of a document. By going to the File Handling section of the Preferences dialog box, you can increase the number of pages that a preview is generated for within InDesign.

Another very useful feature that has been added is the ability to view files that are linked to the selected InDesign document with the Adobe Bridge. This allows you to quickly see any files that are linked to the selected file in the Metadata panel under the Linked files category. Note, this section will not display for older versions of InDesign or for a document that contains no linked images.

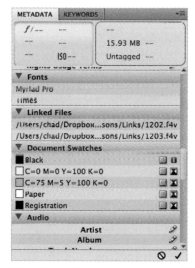

The Bridge provides a convenient way to see files that are linked in an InDesign CS5 document.

Metadata Captions

InDesign CS5 takes full advantage of the ability to view and utilize metadata that is embedded within a graphic file. When a graphic is placed in an InDesign CS5 document, you can right-click (Windows) or Ctrl+click (Mac OS) and choose Captions > Generate Live Caption or Generate Static Caption. A Live Caption will update when the metadata of the file updates, where a Static Caption will pull the current content of the caption for one-time use. You can determine which metadata field that InDesign uses as well as other options by right-clicking (Windows) or Ctrl+clicking (Mac OS) and choosing Captions > Caption Setup.

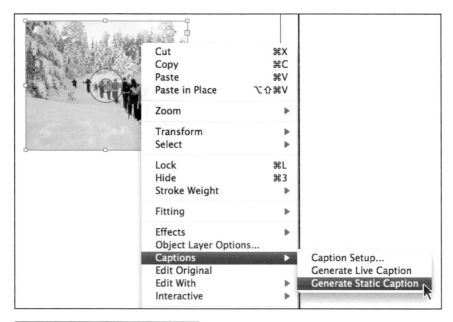

Choosing Static Caption from the contextual menu. The resulting caption extracted from the Description field of the image's metadata.

Draw multiple frames in a grid

When drawing with any of the frame-based tools, you can divide a frame up into a grid of frames easily using the new gridified tools. For example, click and drag with the text tool to begin drawing a frame, while dragging with the mouse, press the left and right arrow keys on the keyboard to add or remove the number of columns that are being drawn. Furthermore, press the up and down arrow keys to add or remove rows from the number of rows being drawn. This works with the Rectangle and Rectangle Frame tools as well.

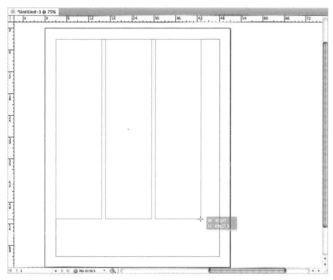

The new gridified tools allow you to draw multiple frames with a single drag of the mouse.

The new Super step-and-repeat works in a similar fashion as the gridified tools. With an object (frame) selected, press the Alt (Windows) or Option (Mac OS) key and begin dragging the object. Release the modifier key and press the right arrow key on your keyboard to add to the number of columns that are created and use the up arrow key to add to the number of rows that are created.

Super step-and-repeat allows you to visually step and repeat objects in a layout.

Live Corner Effects

InDesign has always been able to apply corner effects to a frame. However, InDesign CS5 provides a new method of applying corner effects to a frame called Live Corner Effects. With Live Corner Effects, you can visually adjust all corners of a frame or selected corners without the need to enter a dialog box. What's more is that you can apply different Effects to each corner independently of one another.

With any rectangular frame selected, click on the yellow box in the upper-right corner of the frame. Diamonds appear in each corner of the frame. Click on any diamond and drag left to right to change the radius of the default rounded corner effect of the frame. Alt+click (Windows) or Option+click (Mac OS) on any of the diamonds to toggle through the available effects that can be applied to the frame. Shift+Alt+Ctrl click (Windows) or Shift+Option+Command+click (Mac OS) on any diamond to change the effect for only a single corner at a time.

This is a fantastic improvement from prior versions of InDesign! In addition, note that after applying these effects, the radii of the corners remain accurate and do not distort when changing the size of the frame.

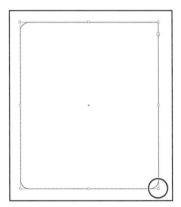

The Live Corner Effects diamonds.

Multiple Page Sizes

For the first time, InDesign CS5 allows multiple size pages with a single document. The possibilities of this feature are endless. In the figure on the next page, you can see that there are three pages in the document positioned side-by-side, however, the first and third pages are smaller than the second page. This type of document is commonly referred to as a gatefold and can be challenging to create, and to convey to a printer who will be producing this type of a job. Thankfully, InDesign CS5 makes this extremely easy.

InDesign CS5 provides a new tool called the Page tool (📄) who's sole purpose is adjusting the size and position of the selected page. Click on any page in your document with the Page tool to select the page. With the page selected, you'll see size and position information in the Control panel at the top of the screen. Adjust the size as necessary, and then click and drag on the page with the page tool to adjust it's location or type in coordinates for the page in the Control panel.

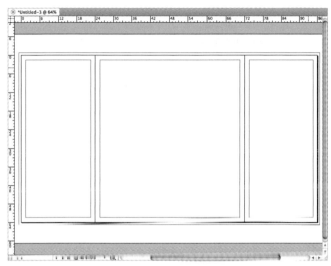

An InDesign document with multiple page sizes applied to various pages.

The Gap tool

Another tool that is a new addition to InDesign CS5 is the Gap tool (↔). The job of the Gap tool is to make adjustments to the space between objects or between an object and the margin of the page. The Gap tool is very useful for modifying a layout without needing to recalculate the space between objects.

With the Gap tool selected, hover the cursor over the space between two objects or between an object and it's margin. You'll notice that space becomes highlighted with a gap indicator displayed within the gap. Click and drag left to right or top to bottom, depending on the orientation of your objects, and you'll notice that the gap is maintained, but the frame of the objects next to the gap are adjusted accordingly to the distance that you drag.

In addition, hold down the Ctrl (Windows) or Command (Mac OS) keys to resize the gap instead of the objects. Hold down Alt (Windows) or Option (Mac OS) to move the gap and related objects at the same time.

The new Gap tool.

Content Grabber

Adobe InDesign has always given the user great control over positioning graphics within a frame. However, it could often become frustrating having to constantly switch between the Selection tool (▶) and the Direct Selection tool (▷). InDesign CS5 changes that by introducing the Content Grabber. The Content Grabber is displayed whenever you hover the Selection tool over an existing frame that contains a graphic. Clicking the Content Grabber will immediately select the frames content (the graphic) without the need to switch to the Direct Selection tool. What's more is that with the Selection tool still selected, you can click and drag to reposition the graphic within the frame as well as resize the graphic within the frame. This feature is bound to be a favorite for all InDesign users!

The Content Grabber allows you to reposition a graphic within a frame without the need to switch tools.

Improved Transformations

InDesign CS5 provides a number of improvements when transforming objects. First of all, all the transformation tools have been consolidated to one button. Now the Rotate, Scale, and Shear tools can be found directly within the Free transform tool button (⌖). Simply click and hold on the Free Transform tool to display all of the Transformation tools. That being said, they've also made it easier to transform objects without the need to select some of the transformation tools. With the Selection tool active, click on a frame to select it. Move the cursor outside of one of the frame's corners and a rotate indicator is displayed. Simply click and drag to rotate the object. Scaling an object can still be accomplished with the Selection tool active by simply holding down Shift+Ctrl (Windows) or Shift+Command (Mac OS) and dragging one of the corner handles of the frame. InDesign CS5 also allows you to transform multiple selected objects very easily in the same way without having to group the items first.

You can also easily distribute multiple selected items on the page by selecting all of them with the Selection tool (▸) and then dragging one of the handles of the selected group of items while holding down the Spacebar on the keyboard.

*Easily distribute multiple items on a page by selecting the items
and then dragging a handle while holding down the spacebar.*

Spanning and Splitting paragraphs

When working in a text frame defined as a multi-column frame, you can specify that a paragraph can span more than one column of that multi-column text frame. With the text cursor clicked within the paragraph that should span multiple columns, choose an option from the Span Columns drop-down menu in the Control panel. If you don't see this option, make sure that you are viewing the Paragraph formatting controls in the Control panel.

InDesign CS5 also allows you to split a column for instances where you want multiple columns within a single column of a text frame or within a single column text frame. Simply select the text that you'd like to split, then from the Span Columns drop-down menu, choose Split and the number of columns that you'd like to split the selected text into.

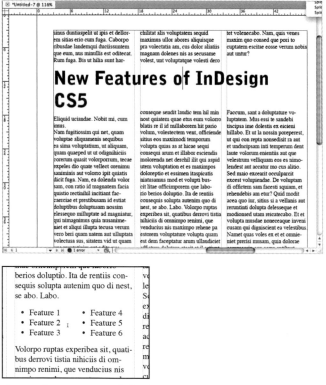

A paragraph can now span multiple columns in a multi-column text frame or split selected text into multiple columns.

Interactive Elements

Animation

InDesign adds some significant improvements to interactive documents generated from an InDesign application. One such improvement is the ability to add motion to an object on an InDesign document. Using the new Animation panel, you can add motion paths to objects and control how they are animated in an exported .swf file. The new Preview panel makes the process of viewing how an animation will appear quick and easy.

To help with adding animation to a document in InDesign, there is a new pixel measurement available to make the dimensions more relevant to the final output destination.

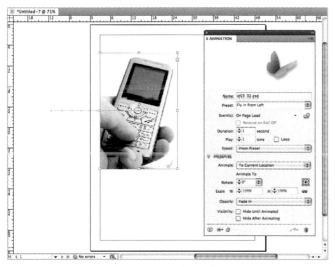

The animation panel controls how a selected object will be animated in the final .swf file.

File Distribution

Document Fonts

An age old problem in print applications is that when you send a file to another user, all of the fonts must be sent along with the InDesign application file so that the document will appear to the other user as expected. Although InDesign has always made the process of collecting the fonts an easy one, the fonts still need to be manually loaded on the other users computer in order for the fonts to be available to the InDesign document.

InDesign CS5 offers an amazing solution to this problem called Document Fonts. When sending an InDesign document to another user, simply create a folder called Document Fonts in the same folder where the InDesign document resides. Place all of the necessary fonts into that Document Fonts folder. When the InDesign document is opened, it will automatically load those fonts on launch so that they are immediately available to that document. These fonts are available to this one InDesign document only and not to all open InDesign documents.

Buzzword Integration

As part of Adobe's *acrobat.com* service, you can create Buzzword documents, a way of creating online word processing, spreadsheet, and presentation documents. InDesign CS5 takes advantage of this service by allowing you to place Buzzword documents directly from your *acrobat.com* account into any InDesign document. Simply choose File > Place from Buzzword, and sign in to your *acrobat.com* account. From there you can select the Buzzword document that you'd like to place and then flow it into your InDesign CS5 document. This is great for users who work in a collaborative workflow where writers and editors need to see the original text story and make changes to it before it goes into layout. Once finalized, you can flow the file directly into InDesign CS5. One major benefit of this workflow is that all you need to open and edit a Buzzword document is a web browser!

Self study

1   Go to Window > Workspace > New in CS5 so that all the new features in InDesign CS5 will be highlighted throughout the menus.

2   Experiment with the Gap tool to see the different options available for modifying objects within a layout.

3   Use the Mini Bridge to practice placing files into your InDesign layout.

4   Build a file with page transitions and animations. Export the file to PDF, and then also export it to SWF.

Review

Questions

1 Can InDesign generate Flash content?

2 Can InDesign automatically generate captions for graphics and images?

3 True or False: you can't make a button in InDesign because the Button tool is gone.

4 Have the Rotate, Scale, and Shear tools been removed from InDesign CS5?

5 What is that circle that appears in the middle of an image when I hover over it?

Answers

1 Yes, InDesign can output directly to the SWF format or to the XFL format, which can be used to edit the files in the Flash Professional editing application.

2 Yes, using the new Live Captions and Static Captions feature, InDesign can automatically add captions to graphics and images based on their metadata.

3 False, you can still make a button using Object > Interactive > Convert to Button.

4 No, they've just been relocated. Simply click and hold on the Free Transform tool (⬚) and choose them from the resulting list.

5 That's the new Content Grabber in InDesign CS5. It allows you to easily reposition a graphic within it's frame without having to switch to another tool.

Index

F

favorite settings, 305

Favorites tab, 151

feathering
- Gradient Feather tool, 255–256
- overview, 253–255

features
- advanced document
  - books, creating from multiple files, 272–276
    - indexes, building, 286–291
    - overview, 269–270
    - PDFs, 291–292
    - review, 293
    - self study, 292
    - slug area, 270–271
    - synchronizing attributes across book files, 276–281
    - Tables of Contents, creating, 281–285
    - text variables, adding, 270–272
    - trim area, 271
- new
  - animation, 349, 367
  - answers, review, 369
  - Buzzword documents, 368
  - Content Grabber, 364
  - Content Indicator, 31, 33, 147
  - design and layout, 358–366
  - Document Fonts, 367–368
  - drawing multiple frames in a grid, 361
  - file distribution, 367–368
  - Gap tool, 8, 363–364
  - GREP. *see* GREP
  - interactive elements, 367
  - Live Corner Effects, 217–218, 362
  - metadata captions, 360
  - Mini Bridge. *see* Mini Bridge
  - multiple page sizes, 362
  - overview, 357–358
  - Page tool, 363
  - previewing your interactive document, 348
  - review, 369
  - self-study, 368
  - spanning and splitting paragraphs, 366
  - Track Changes, 90–92
  - transforming objects, 365

files
- book, synchronizing attributes across, 276–281
- Flash
  - creating, 353–356
  - editing, 356
  - viewing, 354–355

imported, that use transparency
- applying alpha channel selection, 263–265
- applying path selection, 265–267
- overview, 262–263

lesson, loading, 4

multimedia, 144

multiple, creating books from
- document order, 273–276
- overview, 272
- pagination, 273–276

PDF
- creating, 291, 303–306
- interactive, 351–353

Photoshop, importing layered, 167–169

unlocking, 4

XHTML
- CSS formatting, 310
- generating, 306–308
- versus HTML, 307

Fill Frame Proportionally option, 148, 151

Fill icon, 215

fills
- applying effects to, 245
- opacity, 229
- tables, 185–186

Fills tab, 185

Find/Change
- applying object styles using, 252–253
- dialog box, 25–27, 81, 83, 94–95

Find Font dialog box, 115

finding
- missing fonts, 114–115
- missing images, 140–141
- text to change, 80–84

Fit Content Proportionally option, 148

Fit Content to Frame option, 148

Fit Frame to Content option, 148

fitting images within existing frame, 148–150

Fitting options, 148, 344

fixed row height, 199–201

fixing missing fonts, 114–115

Flash CS4 Pro (XFL) format, 353

Flash documents, 342

Flash files (.swf)
- creating, 353–356
- editing, 356
- viewing, 354–355

Flash Player, 5–6

flow, text
- manual, 98–99
- overview, 21–23

indent, hanging, 75
InDesign CS5
   graphics. *see* graphics
   help resources, 39
   navigating documents
      changing magnification, 16–18
      overview, 15
      Pages panel, 15–16
   new features and improvements
      animation, 349, 367
      answers, review, 369
      Buzzword documents, 368
      Content Grabber, 364
      Content Indicator, 31, 33, 147
      Document Fonts, 367–368
      drawing multiple frames in a grid, 361
      file distribution, 367–368
      Gap tool, 8, 363–364
      GREP. *see* GREP
      interactive elements, 367
      Live Corner Effects, 217–218, 362
      metadata captions, 360
      Mini Bridge. *see* Mini Bridge
      multiple page sizes, 362
      overview, 357–358
      Page tool, 363
      previewing your interactive document, 348
      review, 369
      self-study, 368
      spanning and splitting paragraphs, 366
      transforming objects, 365
   overview, 7
   panels. *see* panels
   resetting workspace and preferences, 3
   review, 40
   self study, 40
   starting
      Macintosh OS, 3
      Windows OS, 2
   styles. *see* styles
   system requirements
      Macintosh OS, 2
      overview, 1
      Windows OS, 2
   tools. *see* tools
   type. *see* type
   workspace. *see* workspace
InDesign CS5 Digital Classroom, Adobe
   book series, 6
   fonts used in book, 3
   lesson files, loading, 4

   overview, 1
   resources for educators, 6
   video tutorials
      setting up for viewing, 5
      viewing with Adobe Flash Player, 5–6
indexes
   cross-references, adding, 288–289
   generating, 290–291
   overview, 286
   topics, adding, 286–289
Index panel, 286–287
initial caps, 79–80
Ink Manager, 311
inline objects, 163
In Port, 22, 99–100
in-product help, 39
Insert Pages dialog box, 57–58
Insert Table dialog box, 175
inset, text, 96–97, 188–189
interactive documents
   animation, 349, 367
   design considerations, 342
   Flash files
      creating, 353–356
      editing, 356
      viewing, 354–355
   interactive PDF files
      creating, 351–352
      viewing, 352–353
   multimedia content
      creating buttons to control, 344–347
      importing, 343–344
   overview, 341–342
   page transitions, 350–351
   previewing, 348
   review, 356
   self study, 356
inventory, package, 296–298

J

jump, story, 104–105

K

kerning, 71–72
keyboard shortcuts
   cutting, 203
   guides, showing and hiding, 10–11
   layout pages, adding, 57
   magnification, increasing and decreasing, 17, 157

N

Numbering & Section Options dialog box, 59–60

O

objects
    anchored, 163–166
    applying blending modes to, 259–262
    applying opacity to, 243–244
    colors, applying to multiple, 233
    creative effects, adjusting for, 248–249
    transforming, 365
object styles
    applying, 27–28, 134
    changing, 134–135
    defining, 131–133
    with effects, 251–253
    Find/Change used to apply, 252–253
    overview, 118
    using for images, 155–157
Object Styles button, 156
Object Styles Options dialog box, 134
Object Styles panel, 252
one-click color edits
    applying to multiple objects, 233
    Eyedropper tool, 232
    updating, 234–235
on-line help, 39
online layouts, 342
opacity
    applying to objects, 243–244
    fill, 229
Open a File dialog box, 52
operating systems
    Mac
        Flash Player on, 5
        starting InDesign CS5, 3
        system requirements, 2
        unlocking files on, 4
    Windows
        starting Adobe InDesign CS5, 2–3
        system requirements, 2
options
    Allow Master Item Overrides, 56
    Bleed, 11
    Create Outlines, 256
    Fill Frame Proportionally, 148, 151
    Fit Content Proportionally, 148
    Fit Content to Frame, 148
    Fit Frame to Content, 148
    Fitting, 344
    page numbering, 58–60

Place, 258
    section, 58–60
    Update Links, 141
    Use Typographer's Quotes, 113
order, document, 273–276
organizing
    styles into groups, 130–131
    XML tag structure, 327–328
Out Port, 22, 99–101
overrides, 53–56, 108, 187–188
overset text, 89–90, 285

P

Package Inventory, 296–298
Package Inventory dialog box, 297–298
Package Publication Folder dialog box, 302
packaging documents, 301–303
padlock icon, 37
pages
    footers, 50–51
    guides, 10
    layout
        applying to multiple pages, 65–66
        creating classified page, 62–63
        images, adding, 63–65
        numbering options, 58–60
        overview, 57–58
        section options, 58–60
        text, adding, 63–65
        text, placing formatted, 60–62
    master
        automatic page numbering, 46–48
        basing on other master pages, 52–53
        creating, 44–45
        custom page sizes, 42–44
        formatting, 45
        overriding items, 53–56
        overview, 41–42
        planning documents, 42
        review, 66
        self study, 66
        text variables, 48–51
    numbering
        automatic, 46–48
        setting options, 58–60
    rulers, 46
    size
        custom, 42–44
        multiple, 362–363
    transitions, 350–351
Pages button, 13

Preserve Styles and Formatting from Text and Tables radio button, 113
preview
    interactive documents, 348
    separation, 310–312
Preview panel, 348
Preview viewing mode, 39
Print dialog box, 292, 313–314
printing from Book panel, 292
printing proofs, 312–314
Process Color Simulator guide, 310
proofs, printing, 312–314

Q

questions, review
    advanced document features, 293
    color, 239
    document delivery, 315
    effects, 267
    graphics, 171
    interactive documents, 356
    master pages, 66
    styles, 138
    tables, 212
    text, 116
    XML, 340
Quick Apply feature, 128–130

R

Rectangle Frame tool, 54
Redefine Style command, 159
redefining styles, 107–109
Reject Change button, 91
Relative to Spine checkbox, 165
Relink button, 142
Remove Styles and Formatting from Text and Tables radio button, 113
removing image background, 161–163
resolution, actual versus effective, 298
resources
    for educators, 6
    help, 39
reviews
    advanced document features, 293
    color, 239
    document delivery, 315
    effects, 267
    graphics, 171
    interactive documents, 356

master pages, 66
new features and improvements, 369
styles, 138
tables, 212
text, 116
XML, 340
Right-Justified Tab button, 75
Roman Numeral style, 59
root element, 319, 321
rows
    dimensions of, 199–202
    formatting, 183–185
rulers, page, 46
rules, 76–78

S

Sample Buttons panel, 348
Save Preset button, 314
Save Style button, 284
saving
    gradients, 228–229
    new color swatches, 219–222
    paragraph styles, 189–192
    spot colors, 236–238
    workspace, 14–15
scaling images, 30
Screen blending mode, 259–260
scrolling, 16
section options, 58–60
Select Data Source dialog box, 337
Selection tool, 13, 22, 53–54, 364
self study sections
    advanced document features, 292
    color, 238
    document delivery, 315
    effects, 267
    graphics, 170
    interactive documents, 356
    master pages, 66
    new features and improvements, 368
    styles, 138
    tables, 212
    text, 115
    XML, 339
semi-autoflow, 101
seminars, 39
separation preview, 310–312
Separations Preview panel, 311–312
shift, baseline, 72
shortcuts, keyboard

cutting, 203
guides, showing and hiding, 10–11
layout pages, adding, 57
magnification, increasing and decreasing, 17,
157
Pages panel, opening, 45
pasting graphics in tables, 203
selecting all type, 121
Text Frame Options dialog box, opening, 97
toggling between modes, 11, 39
viewing, 8
sizing
images, 30, 148–150
pages, 42–44, 71
slug area, 270–271
snippets
InDesign, 339
XML, 336, 339
soft returns, 20
spacing
character, 71–72
line, 71
paragraph, 73
Span Columns drop-down menu, 366
spanning and splitting paragraphs, 366
special characters, 47, 93–96
Special Characters menu, 47
Specify Attributes to Change button, 26
spelling
automatically correcting, 88–89
checking
overview, 84–85
while typing, 86–87
dictionary
adding words to, 85–86
centralized, creating, 86
drag-and-drop text editing, 92–93
finding and changing, 80–81
overview, 80
Story Editor, 89–92
Spine button, 47
spot color
colorizing grayscale images, 237–238
saving, 236–238
separation preview, 310
starting InDesign CS5
Mac OS, 3
Windows OS, 2–3
Step and Repeat dialog box, 55
stops
color, 226, 231

tab, 74–76
Story Editor
editing text, 89–92
formatting tables, 194
Track Changes, 90–92
story jump, 104–105
Stroke icon, 215
Stroke panel, 156, 222, 224–225
strokes
applying creative effects to, 245
color
applying to text, 221–222
dashed, 224–226
structure, XML tag, 327–328
Structure panel, 325–329
Style Mapping dialog box, 113
styles
cell
applying, 207–208
creating, 205–208
overview, 118
resetting, 187–188
character
applying, 25–27, 123
defining, 121–122
overview, 118
globally updating, 125–126
GREP, 118, 136–138
loading from another document, 126–128
mapping XML tag to, 334–335
object
applying, 134
changing, 134–135
defining, 131–133
with effects, 251–253
Find/Change used to apply, 252–253
overview, 27–28, 118
using for images, 155–157
organizing into groups, 130–131
overview, 117–118
paragraph
applying, 23–24, 121
defining, 119–120
overview, 118
saving, 189–192
Quick Apply, 128–130
self study, 138
table
applying, 209–211
creating, 208–209
overview, 205
type, changing, 69–70

baseline grid, 103–105
character attributes
    baseline shifts, 72
    character spacing, 71–72
    font styles, 69–70
    line spacing, 71
    overview, 69
    size adjustment, 71
color, applying to, 214–217
converting
    to paths, 256–259
    to tables, 178–179
    tables to, 178–179
entering, 18–20
flow
    manual, 98–99
    overview, 21–23
    semi-autoflow, 101
formatting, 18–20
    within cells, 189–192
    by column, 193
    headlines, 105–106
    overview, 18–21, 105
    placing, 20–21, 60–62
    styles, applying, 105–106
    styles, importing from other documents, 107, 126–128
    styles, redefining, 107–109
importing
    columns, changing number of, 102
    flowing text manually, 98–99
    from Microsoft Word, 112–113
    overview, 98
    semi-autoflow, 101
    threading between frames, 99–101
inset, 188–189
missing fonts
    finding and fixing, 114–115
    overview, 114
    warning, 3
overview, 18, 67–68
on paths, 109–114
review, 116
self study, 115
special characters and glyphs, 47, 93–96
strokes, applying to, 221–222
wrapping
    alpha channels, 159–161
    anchored objects, 163–166
    applying, 34
    bounding boxes, 158–159
    clipping paths, 159–161
    removing image background, 161–163

setting, 56
Type Preferences dialog box, 92
Type tool, 19, 23–24, 47, 50, 68, 82, 196
typing, checking spelling while, 86–87

U
unlocking files, 4
Update Links option, 141
updating
    color, 234–235
    style, globally, 125–126
Use Global Light effect, 248
Use Typographer's Quotes option, 113

V
Validate Structure Using Current DTD button, 328
variable, text
    adding, 270–272
    defining, 48–49
    page footers, 50–51
vertical text alignment, 97–98
video tutorials
    setting up for viewing, 5
    viewing with Adobe Flash Player, 5–6
    viewing
    DVD video tutorials
        with Adobe Flash Player, 5–6
        setting up for, 5
    Flash files, 354–355
    keyboard shortcuts, 8
    XML attributes, 328–330
    XML tag structure, 327–328
viewing mode, 11
visibility icon, 35–36, 177
volume, video tutorial, 6

W
width, column, 201–202
Windows OS
    starting Adobe InDesign CS5, 2–3
    system requirements, 2
Word application, importing text from, 112–113
workspace
    document window, 9–10
    guides, 10–11
    modes, 11
    resetting, 3